Glimpses of God's LOVE

Glimpses
of God's
LOVE

James A. Tucker and Priscilla Tucker

This book is published in collaboration
with the Youth Department as an enrichment of
the Morning Watch devotional plan.

Review and Herald Publishing Association
Washington, DC 20039-0555
Hagerstown, MD 21740

Copyright © 1983 by
Review and Herald Publishing Association

Editor: Raymond H. Woolsey
Cover Design: Lou Skidmore

Library of Congress Cataloging in Publication Data

Tucker, James A.
   Glimpses of God's love, by James A. Tucker
and Priscilla Tucker.

   1. Devotional calendars—Juniors. 2. Natural
history. I. Tucker, Priscilla.   II. Title.
            242.2

Library of Congress Catalog Card Number: 83-61683

ISBN 0-8280-0216-9

Printed in U.S.A.

DEDICATION

To Burton Floyd Tucker, born in 1883—one-hundred years ago! In many ways he gave us the thinking that has resulted in our belief in a close relationship between God's two books. B. F. Tucker's earliest memories are of a dedicated Christian home on the Kansas prairie—a humble sod house, where he listened to the wolves at night and watched herds of buffalo by day. His parents taught him to listen to the word of God. When he became a parent, those lessons were passed on, and they have now been passed to the third and fourth generations.

In this, his 100th year, B. F. Tucker watches the seasons change from his home in the South Carolina hills. He still arises before dawn to commune with the Creator—to read God's word in the Bible and in the messages that the Master Painter has etched on the ever-changing countryside.

We are thankful for those who have gone before and who walked the trail of faith, ever instructing and inspiring those of us who follow, in the belief that the way is never so dark that Jesus cannot light it for us. Burton Floyd Tucker has been one of those.

THE AUTHORS

The authors, James A. Tucker and Priscilla Tucker, live with their family on a farm near Austin, Texas. Dr. Tucker is an educational psychologist and works with school systems throughout the United States, helping to develop educational programs for students with learning difficulties. All his hobbies center around nature study and the out-of-doors, but his primary focus is on birds and gardening. Priscilla Tucker is a journalist. She is currently the managing editor for the American Birding Association. Her hobbies are reading and sewing—quilting, in particular. Together, Dr. and Mrs. Tucker publish *Outdoor Ministry,* a monthly newsletter designed to help Christians use the study of nature and the outdoors as a means of getting better acquainted with Jesus.

PREFACE

God is the author of two books—the Bible and the book of nature. God's first book was the book of nature, spoken by His words into existence (Psalm 33:6-9) during the six days of Creation. The Creator's second Book, the Bible, was written over a period of hundreds of years by His servants the prophets as they were impressed by Him to write (2 Peter 1:21). Both books bear the signature of the Creator and both books are worthy of our thoughtful and prayerful study.

The only text that Adam and Eve had in the beginning was the book of nature, and they were taught by the Master Himself to read on its pages the marvelous illustrations of the eternal character of God. They learned of His matchless love, His eternal justice, and His unswerving nature. They needed no other text—their school was perfect, and it was a joy to attend.

When Adam and Eve sinned they lost the privilege of studying the original version of God's book of nature. For many years the altered, though still beautiful, lesson book was handed down from generation to generation, but since the pages of the original became so drastically marred and since the devil began to perfect his own version of how the book should be interpreted, it was necessary for God to provide a supplement to it. Beginning with Moses, God used faithful servants to record His truth in writings that were collected into the Bible.

Only by studying the Bible can we understand what God originally wrote on the pages of nature. And only by asking for the guidance of the Holy Spirit, promised by the Creator when He walked among men, can we understand the complete message of salvation that God has provided in His two books.

It has been said that the book of nature contains the pictures of God's word, while the Bible contains the captions. What a beautiful illustration of the way in which these two books go hand in hand. Children and youth especially need the motivating force of God's word as revealed in nature.

The messages presented in this volume are intended to illustrate a few of the lessons that God has provided in His two books. They are only examples of the many lessons that could be drawn from the experiences and facts presented. As a reader, you may see other lessons. Let the Holy Spirit guide your thoughts as you learn of God through His created works.

THE SUN SURVIVES BY GIVING

Then shall the righteous shine forth as the sun in the kingdom of their Father. Matthew 13:43.

Jesus has just finished explaining the parable of the tares and is comparing the righteous people to the brightness of the sun. Do you know how bright that is?

Let's think of the sun as a tremendously large light bulb. Usually we don't buy light bulbs with an output of more than 300 watts. But in order to think of the sun as a giant light bulb, you really have to stretch your imagination. The sun shines with the power of 380 septillion watts. That's 380 with 24 zeros after it—or 380 million million million million! That's a very bright light indeed!

The light streams forth from deep within the sun, where hydrogen atoms are bumping into each other so hard that they combine into helium atoms. This causes energy to be released in immense quantities. The energy streams out as light from deep within the sun and shines in every direction, illuminating all the planets, their moons, and every other object in the solar system. The sun's light also streams to the farthest points of the universe, being visible there as a distant star. Thus the earth receives only a tiny portion of the sun's light energy—but how important that portion is to life on our planet!

Scientists tell us that if the sun didn't give forth its energy it would just get hotter and hotter—and then would explode. Giving warmth and light is the sun's way to keep on shining and producing more warmth and light. It survives by giving.

That is exactly the way the followers of Jesus can be described. He said, "It is more blessed to give than to receive" (Acts 20:35). By giving we continue to be able to give. When we stop giving, our "temperature" begins to rise, and we may even explode (not really, but selfish people do have a way of being very impatient and blowing up over little things).

The sun, shining in the sky, is a daily reminder of how important it is to give!

CLANCY

That they should seek the Lord, if haply they might feel after him, and find him, though he be not far from every one of us. Acts 17:27.

There are many stories of dogs that have returned home over long distances, but the best such story that I have ever heard is found in the book *The Strange World of Animals and Pets,* by Vincent and Margaret Gaddis. The story is about Clancy, a collie. (I wonder why such stories are so often about collies?)

From new puppy until he was 6 months old, Clancy had lived with a family in Buffalo, New York. Buffalo was home—the only home he had ever known—and the members of that family were the only people he knew as friends. They were part of his home, too.

But Clancy's family decided to move to Michigan City, Indiana. They decided that they couldn't take Clancy and that, since he was so young, he would adapt to another family in the neighborhood. So the only family Clancy had known moved away, leaving him with a neighbor in Buffalo. The neighborhood was right, but somehow it didn't seem like home without his family.

So, without warning, Clancy left the new family, and he even left his home neighborhood. He went in search of his own family. Of course, he couldn't know where to look, but that is the touching part of the story.

Six months later he scratched at the door of *his* family in Michigan City, Indiana—a place far from anywhere that he had ever been before. He was very thin, and his paws were badly worn, but when he was let into the house by an incredulous family, he spied the familiar throw rug that had served as his bed. He immediately went over to it, curled up, and, with a great sigh, dozed off. Michigan City or Buffalo, it made no difference. This was home!

As Christians we are like Clancy. The only place that feels like home is where Jesus is, and we will go to any lengths to find Him.

10

BLUE BLOOD AND ARMOR

Then said David to the Philistine, Thou comest to me with a sword, and with a spear, and with a shield: but I come to thee in the name of the Lord of hosts. 1 Samuel 17:45.

Goliath with all of his armor was not able to stand up to young David and his sling. Goliath loved to taunt his enemies. No doubt even his own fellow Philistines gave him wide berth lest he become angry at them. An animal that lives in the sea has a similar disposition.

The lobster is covered with armor and has a very bad disposition. It has been referred to as one of the meanest-tempered animals on earth. A lobster doesn't even get along with other lobsters!

The largest lobster on record weighed more than forty pounds and is said to have been 50 years old. But most lobsters don't live nearly that long these days, mainly because of the pollution that is increasing so rapidly. A very small amount of crude oil or harmful chemicals dumped into the ocean where a lobster lives will be enough to do away with him in spite of his armor and meanness.

A mother lobster may lay fifteen thousand eggs, but the babies aren't protected by armor, and they are very tiny; so, of that number, only about fifteen will survive to grow up.

The American lobster uses its legs to breathe, its antennae to taste, has its teeth in its stomach, has no ears of any kind, and has blue blood. You could say that anybody with all these problems has a reason for being so mean, but, of course, these are normal conditions for the lobster.

When God created the lobster's ancestors, I am sure that they weren't so mean, any more than was Goliath's ancestor Adam. But through many generations of living in a world of sin, people and lobsters and their personalities have degenerated. Even armor cannot protect us in this world. It takes only a little thing—a small stone, in the case of Goliath, or a very small bit of pollution, in the case of the lobster—to do away with the organisms of this world. Only the Lord of hosts can protect us, and only He can make us delightful to be around.

11

NO ANT KNOWS THE DAY
OR THE HOUR

And at midnight there was a cry made, Behold, the bridegroom cometh; go ye out to meet him. Matthew 25:6.

As we all know, this is a parable concerning the coming of Jesus and how we should be getting ready to meet Him so that we can be ready at any time. In the Bible the second coming of Jesus has been likened to a marriage, where the Groom arrives at the wedding and receives His bride—the church. The fact that no one knows when this will take place is illustrated in a unique manner by the marriage flight of the ants.

There is only one time in the lives of both the male and the female ants when they have wings—when the winged brides and grooms leave their respective nests and fly off into the day or night to begin a new colony in another realm. The interesting thing about the flight is that the males and females are ready long before the flight takes place and they are eagerly awaiting the day. But the workers won't let them go until the time is right.

It is the ant workers that decide when the bridal parties will depart. No one knows why they wait. They may be waiting for some particular type of weather, or they may have an inner clock that tells them the best time for ant marriage. But whatever the signal is, when the doors finally open, the ants swarm out by the millions. Either there is some form of communication between ant colonies or the signal to fly comes from some external source that affects all colonies the same, because the day and the hour of flight will be the same for all colonies in an area—even those that are widely separated from one another.

In the book of Revelation we are told of four angels who are holding the four winds of the earth until God's people—His church, the bride—are ready. Like the worker ants, the angels are waiting for a command to release the doors and let the action take place. But until everything is ready the flight cannot take place. Are we ready?

12

FLYING HIGH

Who is like unto the Lord our God, who dwelleth on high.
Psalm 113:5.

Until 1973 the highest that any bird had ever been known to fly was 26,902 feet above sea level. Back in 1953 a small flock of alpine choughs (pronounced chuffs) followed a climbing expedition on Mount Everest up to that altitude, but they were still at ground level, even though high on the mountain. In 1962 a mallard collided with a plane over Nevada at twenty-one thousand feet above sea level, but much, much higher above the ground than the choughs. That was before 1973.

On Thursday, November 29, 1973, a commercial airline pilot was flying high over Abidjan, a city in the Ivory Coast of Western Africa. He felt a jolt; the aircraft apparently had hit something. Checking the altimeter, he noted that the plane was flying at thirty-seven thousand feet. What could possibly be up that high? That is more than seven miles above sea level, much higher than any bird had ever been known to fly. Whatever it was, one of the plane's engines had been damaged enough so that it had to be turned off, and the plane limped on into the next airport.

On the ground the maintenance crews began taking apart the damaged engine, looking for clues. All they found were a few feathers: five complete feathers and fifteen pieces of feathers from the wings of a bird. The feathers were sent to the United States National Museum of Natural History in Washington, D.C., and were identified as belonging to a vulture called Ruppell's griffon. This large bird lives in the arid regions of Central Africa from Ethiopia to the Atlantic Ocean.

What was that vulture doing up so high? Why was it there? How did it breathe at that altitude? Just how high does Ruppell's griffon usually fly? Can it fly even higher than thirty-seven thousand feet? These are questions that scientists are asking. At this time only "the Lord our God, who dwelleth on high," knows the answers.

THE PARADOX FROG

Wherefore let him that thinketh he standeth take heed lest he fall. 1 Corinthians 10:12.

It is easy to become puffed up about something that we have done well, and we *should* do work that we can be proud of. But when we become proud of *ourselves* as the result of work well done, and begin to think that we are somehow better than others because of what we can do or have done, then it is time to beware. If you find yourself in that condition, then you need to listen to Paul's words to the Corinthians.

The paradox frog is a good example of getting all puffed up about nothing. To begin with, the paradox frog hatches from eggs like any normal frog. But as the paradox tadpole grows to junior age it begins to be obvious that this is no ordinary tadpole—it reaches the enormous length of ten inches!

You would think that a ten-inch tadpole would become quite a frog. The large bullfrogs of the United States emerge from tadpoles that aren't that long, so what sort of monster frog would grow from a ten-inch tadpole? Well, prepare yourself for a shock, because if you wait for large frogs to come from these monster tadpoles, you will be waiting forever. It doesn't happen. When the paradox tadpole finally turns into a paradox frog and hops out onto land, where it will spend much of its adult life, it is less than two inches long! What a letdown!

The paradox frog lives in northern South America, where the people refuse to believe that such a small frog can come from such a giant tadpole. They turn the story around and believe that the large tadpole comes from the little frog. Humans are steeped in the belief that as you get older you get bigger, and the bigger you are, the better you are—right?

Bigness, smartness, prettiness, or any other similar "ness" has nothing whatsoever to do with how important you are or how good you are. We are all equally important because God loves us and because Jesus died for us. To believe otherwise will lead to a certain fall.

THE CRISLERS' CHOICE

The Spirit of the Lord is upon me, because he hath anointed me to preach the gospel to the poor; he hath sent me to heal the brokenhearted, to preach deliverance to the captives, and recovering of sight to the blind, to set at liberty them that are bruised. Luke 4:18.

Chris and Lois Crisler were camping in the Brooks Range of northern Alaska, studying caribou. One day five wolf puppies were brought to the Crislers to raise. The little wolves had lost their home in the wilderness and now, separated from their natural parents, had to depend on the Crislers for their future. Chris and Lois welcomed the little bundles of fur with mixed feelings. They had raised several wolf puppies and seen them return to the wild, but this time things were different. They were scheduled to leave the Arctic in just a few months. There would not be time to raise the wolves, train them to hunt, and get them accepted by one of the packs in the region.

The five little wolves soon controlled things around the Crisler camp. First, they were named: Miss Alatna, Mr. Arctic, Mr. Barrow, Miss Killik, and Miss Tundra. That was in June. In October the plane would touch down on the frozen lake to take the Crislers away, and they agonized over what to do with the five little wolves. The wolves were wild and free in the Arctic. To take them with them back to Washington would mean caging them for the rest of their lives—a fate worse than death, the Crislers thought. It was finally decided that the young wolves would have to be shot; that would be the merciful thing to do, they thought, under the circumstances. The wolf pups could never survive the coming winter on their own and they would never be happy in cages.

The fateful day came, but the wolves, with tails wagging, looked expectantly into the Crislers' eyes. "Here, you shoot the first one," choked Chris, handing the gun to Lois. Neither of them could bear the thought of ending the lives of these bounding bundles. The wolves went to Washington, where the Crislers made a haven of happiness for these lovable creatures.

15

"IS ANYBODY OUT THERE?"

Then shall ye call upon me, and ye shall go and pray unto me, and I will hearken unto you. And ye shall seek me, and find me, when ye shall search for me with all your heart. Jeremiah 29:12, 13.

In a natural hollow in the mountains of Puerto Rico is the Arecibo radio telescope. Unlike most telescopes, which you look through, this is a telescope that you *listen* through. Arecibo is a reflector a thousand feet in diameter set to receive radio transmissions from outer space, and—believe it or not—to send radio transmissions into space.

Astronomers who operate Arecibo aren't sure that there is any intelligent life in space, but they are hoping that their receiver will pick up a message that will allow them to talk to any beings that *may* be out there. It cost millions of dollars to build this telescope, which is made of about a thousand tons of aluminum and steel, not to mention the thirteen thousand cubic yards of concrete.

The telescope is connected to a very expensive system of computers watched over day and night by scientists who are listening for some word—any word—from space. Is anybody out there? If you ask these astronomers that question, they reply that they don't know.

In 1974 the scientists decided to speak to space, so they prepared a message and beamed it into space. The message lasted 2 minutes 49 seconds, and it consisted of scientific equations, a description of human beings, the population of the earth, a map of our solar system, and a description of the Arecibo telescope. This exercise probably seems very worthwhile to scientists who don't believe in God. They hope that somebody out there hears the message, figures it out, and sends back a reply that they will hear and understand as well.

For those of us who believe in the Bible and what it says, we know by faith that God is out there and that He hears and answers our simplest prayers—without the aid of a multimillion-dollar piece of equipment.

LARKY AND CHARLIE

I will not leave you comfortless: I will come to you. John 14:18.

An almost unbelievable story of feathered devotion is told by the eminent poet George Abbe. One January morning when the temperature was below zero and powdered snow whirled in the wind, Mr. Abbe was driving up his ranch road. A flock of horned larks flew up from their feeding, but one bird remained, wing drooping, trying to run fast enough to escape. Mr. Abbe slammed on the brakes and with his wife's help was able to catch the bird. It appeared to have a broken wing, and they decided to see whether they could nurse it back to health.

They called the lark, a female, Larky. Thus begins a fantastic story of care and keeping that has seldom been equaled. There isn't space here to share all the wonder of that story, but one aspect of it is perhaps the most wonderful of all.

Mr. Abbe made a cage for Larky and put her in the field; there she fed and exercised each day. One brightly colored male from the lark flock came boldly near the cage and began to sing the sweet song for which the larks are so famous. This was incredible, since horned larks rarely if ever sing in the winter—and certainly not in the snow. The Abbes called the male Charlie.

Charlie was Larky's mate. He never left her. Every day when she was brought out to her pen, he would be there and begin his serenade. Several months elapsed before Larky was strong enough to begin exercising her wings. But Charlie was always there. He showed little fear of the Abbes, approaching them to within four feet. His only concern seemed to be for Larky.

The day finally came when Larky could be released. She made a short flight, and do you know where she flew? She went to Charlie, who hopped over her and all around her in his best lark greeting. That pair of larks stayed and eventually built a nest and raised a flock of their own.

THE CLUMSY BABY

Even a child is known by his doings, whether his work be pure, and whether it be right. Proverbs 20:11.

Being a child has its problems. Children have so much to learn. Of course, adults don't know everything, but they are supposed to have had enough experience to enable them to provide for themselves. Children, on the other hand, need much training. Some things simply can't be learned until the brain and body develop enough, but other things can be learned very early.

There is a rule in zoology that says the longer a youngster of a species stays with its parents and learns, the smarter that species is. There is no animal that comes anywhere close to human beings in the length of time that the young remain in childhood, learning. Some animals are born or hatch out and are adults almost immediately; from the start they can fend for themselves, and never even see their parents. The mound birds of the South Pacific are such creatures.

The young of other animals remain with their parents for years. Take the elephant, for example. A baby elephant is born with a brain only one third the size of an adult elephant's brain. There is only enough development in the baby elephant's brain to operate its vital organs, but there isn't enough to keep him from tripping over his trunk! A baby elephant is a very clumsy baby. It takes many months of patient training on the part of the mother elephant before the baby learns how to live with that long nose. Until then, if it wants to drink, the elephant calf must kneel and put its face under water. Young elephants spend at least the first ten years of their lives being trained by the mature members of the group. And, as do smart people, they probably never stop learning from their elders.

When we are born we aren't even developed to a point where we can be clumsy—that comes later. We need so much help in growing up. That's why Jesus made moms and dads!

TREASURES OF THE SNOW

Hast thou entered into the treasures of the snow? Job 38:22.

In this chapter, God is challenging Job to explain some of the secrets of nature that were familiar sights but that were mysteries in many respects. You have heard that no two snowflakes are alike. That is true, of course, but there is more to snowflakes than that.

The shape and structure of a snowflake are determined by the temperature of the air where they form, by the winds that they meet as they are forming, and by the composition of the air vapors from which they form. The reason snow crystals are always six-sided is that they are formed of water, which occurs only as a six-sided crystal in its solid form (which is ice, of course). The reason all of the six sides look alike, a condition called symmetry, is that the atmospheric conditions surrounding the forming snowflake are identical on all sides.

It takes about fifteen minutes for one snowflake to form. Every snowflake starts as a microscopic dust particle to which water molecules begin to stick. It continues forming outward in all directions until it is a full-grown snowflake, but it never grows larger than three or four millimeters across; the larger fluffy flakes that you see in gentle snowfalls are actually clumps of many snowflakes.

To grow a snowflake, the cloud must be between 4 and 14 degrees Fahrenheit, and it must be thick with water vapor. The thicker the cloud, the more detailed and intricate will be the snowflake.

In the absence of winds, snowflakes fall to the ground at a speed of about two miles per hour. If the air at ground level is above 32 degrees Fahrenheit, the snow will melt and fall as rain. If the air is below 32, then it will fall as snow. There is much more to learn about snow; for example, at different temperatures the crystals freeze into different shapes—but scientists don't know why. Only God knows all of the treasures of the snow.

THE MOST ABUNDANT MAMMAL

Yea, though I walk through the valley of the shadow of death, I will fear no evil: for thou art with me; thy rod and thy staff they comfort me. Psalm 23:4.

What do you think is the most abundant mammal in the world? Is it the dog or the cat? There are certainly a lot of them. Or is it the mouse? Mice are everywhere! Well, it isn't the dog, or the cat, or the mouse, or even rats. Let's give you some hints.

The most abundant mammal in the world prefers darkness, but doesn't mind coming out in the daytime—especially in the evening before dark. There are many varieties of this animal, ranging in size from about three inches long up to several feet in length, and their diet primarily consists of insects (although they also eat small mammals, fruit, and even the nectar from flowers). Have you figured out what the animal is yet?

Here is the best and final clue: This mammal flies. That's right—it's a bat. It is estimated that one out of every ten mammals in the world is a bat. Can you imagine how many millions and millions of them there must be?

You've heard the saying "Blind as a bat." No statement could be more true and false at the same time. Although it is true that bats don't see very well, if at all, sight as we know it is not so important, because they can fly through the darkness just as successfully as you and I can walk in the dark with a flashlight. Experiments have shown that, in the dark, bats can recognize and avoid wires that are only two thousandths of an inch in diameter.

Bats illustrate perfectly how to live by faith. By relying on powers of perception given to them by the Creator, they can avoid all danger and live quite safely in a situation that we find difficult. When Jesus is in our heart He gives us the power to avoid the dangers of this world of sin in just as sure a manner. We never need fear the darkness of this world when Jesus is our friend—and He *is* our friend.

HOW DARK IS DARK?

Let your light so shine before men, that they may see your good works, and glorify your Father which is in heaven. Matthew 5:16.

Have you ever been down deep in a cave when someone turned off all the lights? How do you describe that darkness? Sometimes we hear people say, "It was so dark that I couldn't see my hands in front of my face." That is really dark. But how dark is dark? Darkness is measured by the amount of light that is *not* there. We say it is dark at night, but there is always a little light, either from the moon, the stars, the streetlights, or from somewhere.

In order to have complete darkness you have to shut out all light. Every little pinpoint of light has to be eliminated. When there is absolutely no light whatsoever, there is total darkness. Under such conditions you cannot see anything at all, no matter how close an object is.

What if *suddenly* all the light in the world went out? There would be no sun, no moon, and no stars. There would be no electric lights, no candles, no lamps, no fires, no matches, no northern lights, no lightning bugs, and no worms that glow. There would be no lightning, no sparks from striking flint, no flashlights, no glow from radioactive materials. There would be nothing but complete darkness. And suppose there would be no hope of ever seeing any light again. How would you feel?

If there was no light of any kind you would not be able to see your mother's face, or your dog, or the sunset; you wouldn't ever glimpse a butterfly flitting over the meadow or the flowers growing there. You would see nothing. It would be a dark world indeed.

Can you believe that that is how dark the world is in the hearts of most of the people? Jesus is the light of the world (John 8:12), and He is the *only* source of light. Can't you imagine how wonderful it would be, if the world were as dark as we described it, to have someone turn on the light? That is the way it is when Jesus comes into our lives and into the lives of others through us.

WHY IS THE CARDINAL RED?

Wherefore art thou red in thine apparel, and thy garments like him that treadeth in the winefat? Isaiah 63:2.

In olden times when it came time to make grapes into wine it was usually done by a person getting into a large tublike container full of grapes and stomping them with his bare feet to squeeze out the juice. In the process the person would be covered with the red grape juice. In today's text Isaiah is writing about Jesus, who died for our sins and was therefore stained with the blood of that sacrifice.

Throughout the Bible red and scarlet seem to be identified with blood—either with the sacrifices pointing to Jesus and with the sacrifice that He made on the cross or with the shedding of blood as the result of the evil deeds of the followers of Satan.

Why should Jesus be characterized as a person wearing a blood-red garment? Perhaps the northern cardinal can help us understand. Red has the interesting property of being highly visible in the light of the sun but very hard to see in the deep shade of trees and underbrush. So, when the male cardinal wants prominently to advertise his territory to attract a mate, he perches in the sun and sings amid all the splendor of his brilliance. However, when it comes time to feed, to build the nest, or to care for young in the nest (which is nearly always built in a shady location), the bright-red cardinal is no longer easily spotted by would-be predators.

I think that it is interesting that Jesus, the King of the universe, who could shine as the sun in all its glory, could also quietly slip away unseen by the crowd around Him when He came to the darkness of this earth.

When Jesus is standing as King of kings and waiting for His bride, the church triumphant, He will show forth in the dazzling brightness that befits Him. But He will also undoubtedly show, at least in the scars, if not stains, in His hands and feet, that His blood was shed for us.

Precisely correct
exactly right as
the result of ever

a very hard mineral
Composed of silica.
agate, amethyst, and many other stones are

ACCURATE AS QUARTZ

Every good gift and every perfect gift is from above, and cometh down from the Father of lights, with whom is no variableness, neither shadow of turning. James 1:17.

You know what an electric shock is. Perhaps you have touched a live electric wire and gotten a real jolt, or maybe you have experienced the tiny shock that happens when you walk on certain kinds of rugs and then touch a metal object, such as a doorknob. Shocks have interesting effects on other things besides you. For example, if you shock a quartz crystal, it vibrates. You can't see it vibrate, but it vibrates nonetheless.

Someone took the time to measure the vibration of quartz and found that it vibrates at exactly 32,768 times a second—another reason why you can't see it. That one discovery made a dramatic change in our timekeeping. You have heard of quartz watches; you may even have one. Because quartz vibrates at exactly 32,768 times per second when it is shocked, even an inexpensive quartz watch is the most accurate timepiece ever invented; it is accurate to within one minute per year!

It works like this: If you were a mathematician you would know that there is something special about the number 32,768. If you take the number one and double it, you get 2; if you double that you get 4, and so on. Well, if you double your answer 15 times you will get exactly 32,768. Knowing that, the watch producers then knew that if they could find a way to cut the number of quartz vibrations in half 15 times they would have exactly one second. And that is exactly what they did. Your quartz watch has a tiny bit of quartz, a battery, and a series of tiny electrical circuits that cut the electrical pulses in half 15 times so that there is a burst of electrical energy every second. That little burst operates your quartz watch.

Our God, who made the quartz, keeps exact time also; He knows exactly when He is coming to pick us up and take us to heaven. There is no doubt about it, and we must be ready.

23

PECKING DEATHS

O Jerusalem, Jerusalem, thou that killest the prophets, and stonest them which are sent unto thee, how often would I have gathered thy children together, even as a hen gathereth her chickens under her wings, and ye would not! Matthew 23:37.

Have you ever watched a mother hen with her chicks? If a hawk or cat or some other harmful creature appears the hen gives her clucking orders to the chicks, and they scurry for the safety of her wings. When there is a big clutch of chicks they often have to struggle to get under her wings; the last ones in jump and push and poke around, trying to find an opening, but they usually manage to get under there, and there they stay until the danger is past.

Jesus had bestowed His special blessings upon the house of Israel and upon Jerusalem, the fair city wherein the great Temple to His name had stood for centuries. Now as He was about to be slain by the very people whom He had sought to protect, His heart was filled with indescribable grief, and He uttered the words of this text.

Poultry farmers call the loss of chickens killed by other chickens "pecking deaths." In every pen of chickens there is a chicken that is lowest in status. All the other chickens may pick on this one, until often it is pecked to death. This same mob-type behavior occurs in humans; a person is suddenly turned on for one reason or another, and everyone attacks that person as if he or she were a mortal enemy.

This is what happened to Jesus, isn't it? He had been the people's friend. Many of those in the crowd who were yelling, "Crucify him," were those who just a few days before were hailing Him with hosannas as their king. Many of them had been healed by Him of incurable and dread diseases, and many of them had been fed by Him when they were hungry. Now they wanted to kill Him. Jesus was like the chicken that was lowest in the pecking order; but even then, Jesus, like that hen with babies to protect, was yearning to protect His people.

24

HORSESHOE CRAB EYES

For I tell you, that many prophets and kings have desired to see those things which ye see, and have not seen them; and to hear those things which ye hear, and have not heard them. Luke 10:24.

Wouldn't it have been wonderful to be one of Jesus' disciples? They knew Him as a personal friend. They saw things that no other humans before or since have seen. Did they have special eyes? Can we see the Lord as the disciples saw Him?

Well, there are different kinds of eyes. Take the horseshoe crab, for instance. One pair of eyes is not enough for this creature—it has *three* different kinds of eyes!

First, it has the large compound eyes that you see on top of its shell. These eyes are sensitive to extremely slight changes in visible light, ultraviolet light, and even polarized light. Each compound eye is composed of about eight hundred separate facets, each of which is, in turn, connected by special receptors to the brain. Therefore, the brain of the lowly horseshoe crab has a complex data-processing center in each eye. Extensive studies are being made of these eyes to determine how they operate. It is believed that the findings will help prevent and treat blindness in humans.

Second, there are two tiny eyes in the center of the top of the horseshoe crab's shell. They appear to be sensitive to ultraviolet light only and may aid the crab by warning it of overexposure to these dangerous rays and causing it to burrow into the sand and wait for night or high tide.

Finally, there is a single eye on the underside of the crab, just in front of the mouth. This eye is sensitive to visible light, but no one knows the purpose of the eye.

You may think that you have only one kind of eyes—the two on the front of your face. But have you forgotten your "mind's eye"? Even though we weren't there when Jesus walked among men, we can see Him with our imagination and feel His smile as we look into His face.

THE JAPANESE MACAQUES

And he took bread, and gave thanks, and brake it, and gave unto them, saying, This is my body which is given for you: This do in remembrance of me. Luke 22:19.

On an island off the coast of Japan there lives a colony of monkeys. They are macaques (pronounced ma-KAKS) and they originally lived in the forest, rarely, if ever, venturing onto the beach or into the seawater. Then came the scientists who wished to study the monkeys. The scientists placed food on the beach for the monkeys. Eventually the macaques learned to live on the beach, as well as in the woods. But there was a problem.

Naturally there was sand on the beach, and it would stick to the food, and the macaques didn't like eating sand any more than we do. They tried eating around the sand and they tried spitting out the sand, but they could not avoid getting sand in their mouths.

A particularly bright young macaque discovered how to wash sweet potatoes. Eventually other young monkeys followed the example of the first monkey. And when the young macaques grew up and had babies of their own, they taught the youngsters how to wash the sand from their sweet potatoes.

Strangely, however, none of the older macaques ever learned how to wash their food—only the young ones did. This was some years ago, and today most of the monkeys on that island are descended from the generation that discovered that washing sandy food made it easier to eat. So now all of the new generation wash their sweet potatoes. They all learned by example.

We all struggle with little problems in life that are like sand on our food. We try to get around them; we try to spit them out, so to speak. But nothing we do seems to work very well, and we are still left with the problems. Jesus came to live and to die so that our sins could be washed away. He is our example. By following His actions and by living as He lived, with His help, we will be happy Christians. Let us not be so set in our ways that we fail to learn to follow Jesus' example in all things.

WE ARE ALL RELATED

These are the families of the sons of Noah, after their generations, in their nations: and by these were the nations divided in the earth after the flood. Genesis 10:32.

We have all said at one time or another that we are all related—through Noah (or through Adam). But have you ever bothered to figure out what that means? A man once claimed to have figured out mathematically how closely related we are to everyone else in the world. If his figures are correct, we cannot be more than thirtieth cousins of anyone on earth. And that would be the upper limit of how *unrelated* we can be. Actually we are probably more closely related than that to everyone in the world. Guess what—you have 5 billion cousins! Now don't forget their birthdays, and be sure to send presents to every one of them this Christmas. Don't play favorites by remembering only 2 billion or 3 billion. It is all or none!

Perhaps we are being a bit silly, but this is to make the point that we are really quite closely related to every human on earth. You might think that this doesn't include the people of other races and colors and nationalities, but it does! If you are Swedish you would be no more than thirtieth cousin to the Peruvian Indian girl born yesterday in the Amazon headwaters at the base of the Andes Mountains. Did you send her parents a congratulations card?

The average person would have about a million "relatives" from just the past five hundred years, so don't get too carried away with your family tree. And all of your ancestors had descendants other than you and your immediate family, so things become complicated very quickly when we try to prove that we have pure blood lines.

Actually, in the sight of God we are all brothers and sisters if we belong to His huge family. Jesus came down as God, became our brother, and died for us. Now stop and think a minute. Remember that you are closely related to every human being who ever lived. Jesus was and is a human being, in addition to His being divine.

27

BONSAI

And that from a child thou hast known the holy scriptures, which are able to make thee wise unto salvation through faith which is in Christ Jesus. 2 Timothy 3:15.

Bonsai (pronounced BAHN-sigh) is an Oriental hobby that is centuries old. The word means "potted tree," and it is exactly that—a growing or full-grown tree that will fit in a flowerpot on your desk. Growing bonsai goes back at least one thousand years to China. Originally the collectors of bonsai simply went out into nature and looked for naturally dwarfed trees that they could transplant into a pot for their homes. But about three hundred or four hundred years ago there were not enough dwarfed trees occurring naturally to supply the demand. As a result the culture of dwarf trees from seedlings developed.

In this day and age, when we want everything to happen in a hurry, it is hard to imagine that it takes decades to grow a potted bonsai tree, but the best specimens are just as old as an old, gnarled tree in the forest.

It is quite out of the ordinary to see a grove of seven or eight full-grown juniper trees growing in a flat dish on a table. You see the gnarled roots and even the dead stubs of limbs that look as if they were broken by the weather over the years. Actually all of these effects are produced with painstaking effort on the part of the person growing the grove or the individual bonsai tree. The main ingredient that it takes to be successful as a bonsai grower is *patience.* Some of the Japanese growers study their trees for ten years before deciding which way to train a limb to grow. The wisdom of being patient is summed up in the old proverb "As the twig is bent, so grows the tree."

Just as great care is taken in training a young bonsai tree, so the Lord has given parents particular responsibilities to take care of the young, growing Christians entrusted to them. The Word of God, carefully nurtured in the heart as we grow, will pay rich dividends in a life of peace and happiness in Jesus.

THE SPARROW MURDER

And fear not them which kill the body, but are not able to kill the soul: but rather fear him which is able to destroy both soul and body in hell. Are not two sparrows sold for a farthing? and one of them shall not fall on the ground without your Father. Matthew 10:28, 29.

As I write this I am stunned by the realization that just yesterday a woman who lived next door was brutally murdered. We live in a terrible world where a human life has little value. The fact that one person can strike down another for any reason is bad enough, but when it appears that there is no reason at all, then fear begins to take hold in the hearts of those still living—that is, unless we know Jesus and trust in Him. Then we need have no fear of death.

When we think of people who do such cruel actions, we sometimes liken them to ferocious beasts that prowl and stalk their prey; but sin has made its mark on even the seemingly gentle sparrow. On a January morning in 1976 a woman in Louisiana watched as one female house sparrow viciously attacked another female house sparrow. The attacker dived like a hawk on the other, grabbing the sparrow by the neck and holding her until she went limp. Then, perching on top of the apparently lifeless form, the attacker delivered hammering blows to the victim's head. Several other sparrows flew in as if to watch, and then they all flew off together, leaving the dead sparrow on the ground. Some minutes later a sparrow (perhaps the same attacking female) returned, jumped on the dead sparrow, and delivered several more blows to its head before flying away.

No one will ever know what caused the incident, but this morning, as I ponder the human tragedy so nearby, my thoughts are turned to Jesus, who might have seen just such a sparrow fight, leading Him to give the comforting words of our text to a people who feared for their lives.

"Fear ye not therefore, ye are of more value than many sparrows" (Matt. 10:31).

WHAT'S THE MATTER?

When I consider thy heavens, the work of thy fingers, the moon and the stars, which thou hast ordained; what is man, that thou art mindful of him? and the son of man, that thou visitest him? Psalm 8:3, 4.

Wallace Tucker, a professor of astrophysics at the University of California, writes that there is a problem with our ideas of the universe. And the problem is a very big one. In fact, the problem is just about as big as the universe.

When all of man's ideas about everything are put together and when all of the theories are laid out in man's best understanding of how everything in the universe is built, from the tiniest atom to the largest galaxy, there is something missing. And what's missing is most of what it would take to explain why the universe stays put and doesn't fly to pieces.

So what's the matter? The answer is simple, according to Dr. Tucker. Matter is what's the matter—missing matter in the universe. In simple terms the problem is this: If you take all the stars, planets, moons, asteroids, celestial dust, and everything else that is in the universe and wad it all together in a lump, it would represent only one tenth of what is out there. As much as 90 percent of the matter that it would take to explain the universe has never been found. Scientists believe that the missing matter is out there, but they don't know where to look for it.

Where do you think it is?

Wallace Tucker writes that, according to old theories, the universe should have blown apart billions of years ago—yet something is holding it together. New theories say that there must be a vast amount of something out there that keeps the universe in order. But astronomers and physicists with all their tools have not been able to find out what that is.

What do you think it is?

LIMOUSINE

Behold, I stand at the door, and knock: if any man hear my voice, and open the door, I will come in to him, and will sup with him, and he with me. Revelation 3:20.

We have a cat. His name is Limousine. He is fairly big and all black. He used to belong to the neighbor, but when she got a new dog, a big black Labrador retriever, Limousine moved in with us. Well, he didn't really move in; he came in for food and occasional petting.

Over the years Limousine has developed a way of letting us know when he wants to be fed. At first we tried feeding him outside, but that didn't work, because the food attracted all the cats in the neighborhood, as well as an opossum and a couple of raccoons. Now that wasn't bad either except that we couldn't afford the cat-food bill, so we had to adopt a different approach. We moved the food inside and made sure that we let Limousine in often enough to eat. But our schedule and his weren't always the same, and he would become impatient. He would climb the screen door and meow.

We soon had a problem, because the cat was destroying the screen on the door. We took off the spring that closes the door, and that did the trick, because when Limousine tries to climb the screen now, the door swings open, and he doesn't like that one little bit. So he's quit climbing the screen.

Now that the door swings, he's discovered the best of all answers—the one he still uses today, and one that we can live with and even appreciate for its cleverness. He knocks! That's right, when Limousine wants in, he just pulls the screen door enough to let it swing back of its own weight; it bangs shut several times, letting us know that he is there and needs to come in. We never neglect to let Limousine in, because his knocking gets very persistent.

Are we as responsive to Jesus, who is knocking at our heart's door?

BIRDBANDING

But the very hairs of your head are all numbered." Matthew 10:30.

People are identified by numbers. There are telephone numbers, house numbers, credit card numbers, driver's license numbers, and Social Security numbers, to name a few. Numbers are used because keeping track of everyone would be impossible if we used names only.

Just after the turn of this century, scientists began placing numbers on leg bands for birds. Birdbanding, or bird-ringing, as it is also called, was started as a way to learn such things as where birds go, what routes they take, and how long they live. But when the idea was conceived no one knew exactly what to put on the bands. In 1903 a gull was banded in Germany; it was later found in France, where there was quite a debate as to what the band meant. Some thought it was a message from a shipwrecked sailor, and some thought it a token sent from a maiden to her lover.

Eventually scientists agreed on what should be stamped on the bands, but there was one humorous mistake. At one time the U.S. agency in charge of birdbanding was the Biological Survey in Washington, D.C. Once when they ordered bands, they instructed the factory to abbreviate the address as Biol. Surv. Wash. When the bands were received they read, "Wash, Boil, and Surv"! Hunters might think the banded bird would make a tasty dish!

Millions of birds have been banded, and when one is found we know where the bird came from, how far it may have traveled, how long it has lived since banding, and more.

I wonder how Jesus keeps track of the birds. He knows each sparrow and notes when it falls. Jesus knows the number of hairs on our head, and He doesn't need numbers to remember who each of us is—He knows us by name. When Jesus comes, all of our earthly numbers will be meaningless. I can hardly wait to hear Jesus call my *name!*

FREEZING TO DEATH

Ye have sown much, and bring in little; ye eat, but ye have not enough; ye drink, but ye are not filled with drink; ye clothe you, but there is none warm; and he that earneth wages earneth wages to put it into a bag with holes. Haggai 1:6.

"Brrr-r-r! I'm freezing to death!" Perhaps you have said it, but you didn't really mean it. People who are freezing to death usually don't know it.

If you aren't dressed for extreme cold or if you are plunged into very cold water and the temperature of your body surface drops to a point where your body can no longer keep your system operating at 98.6 degrees Fahrenheit, the body will shut off the supply of blood to the skin and extremities in order to keep your vital organs alive. If your body temperature falls below the normal range, you have hypothermia. The first symptom is violent shivering, which is the body's attempt to generate heat by exercise. If that doesn't work, you may become forgetful, confused, and unable to make decisions. You will probably not feel the cold. At this point, if the cold continues and help is not provided in the form of warmth, you will lose coordination, and the shivering will change to muscle spasms and then muscle rigidity. You appear drunk, drugged, or even unconscious. Death follows.

You can freeze to death even in the summer. If you happen to be in an area—as in the mountains—where the temperature changes rapidly and you aren't prepared, you can experience hypothermia just as surely as if it were the dead of winter. It pays to be prepared at all times. First-aid manuals usually provide instruction on staying warm.

Of course, there is also such a thing as spiritual hypothermia. The vast majority of people in the world are spiritually freezing to death and don't know it. When Peter was warming himself by the fire at Jesus' trial he was not even aware that his relationship with his Lord had grown cold. But the warmth of Jesus' love found Peter, and saved him.

A WALKING WHALE?

I have more understanding than all my teachers: for thy testimonies are my meditation. Psalm 119:99.

Not long ago a professor from The University of Michigan was exploring for fossils in the Hindu Kush Mountains of Pakistan, not far from the famous Khyber Pass, when he chanced upon the fossil skull and several teeth of a previously unknown animal. That's all he had—the skull and a few teeth. By deduction he reasoned that the animal had been a 500-pound, 6- to 8-foot-long walking whale that lived at the edge of the sea that he believed had been in that area 50 million years ago.

The professor reasons that because the skull was found in sand that had been either a seashore or a riverbank, and because the teeth were very similar to those of another fossil believed to be a whale, which was found on the west coast of India, the animal must have been a whale. But what about the legs? Well, apparently the presence of legs is just a long-shot guess. Since most whale experts believe that whales evolved on land and moved into the sea, there had to be a time when they had legs. So the professor believes that the skull that he found in the sand that had once been at the edge of water could be very likely one of the whale's early ancestors and therefore might have had legs. He will return to the place where he found the skull and teeth to look for the leg bones, but he admits that they would be a very lucky find. Lucky, indeed!

Not only does the professor believe that the animal was a walking whale but he also believes that its immediate ancestor was a land-bound wolflike creature with hoofs!

We know that strange creatures lived, and we believe that they were destroyed by the Flood. And even though we may not understand all the details, it seems much easier to believe the Word of God. The Bible tells a straightforward Flood story that can account for all of these strange locations of fossils. Why try to make up extensive theories about what *might* have happened?

34

TALKING FLEAS

He giveth to the beast his food, and to the young ravens which cry. Psalm 147:9.

Perhaps it is a stretch of the word to call a flea a *beast,* but when it bites it can be quite a monster. It would also be a stretch of the truth to say that fleas talk, but, believe it or not, fleas do communicate. All tiny beasts communicate with one another. In most instances we don't know how they do it, but we do know that they send messages to one another, either by sound or by scent.

Recently an entomologist at West Virginia University found evidence that fleas communicate by using very high-frequency sound waves—sounds that are much too high for us to hear. A group of tiny hairs is located in a certain area on every flea's abdomen. The area is called the sensillum and is constructed very much as is an antenna. In the presence of high-frequency sounds the hairs on the sensillum vibrate very rapidly, leading entomologists to believe that the hairs are receivers of sound.

In addition, fleas are also able to produce the same sounds that make the sensillum hairs vibrate. They produce their ultrahigh-frequency sounds through tiny openings, like portholes, along their abdomen. It appears, then, that fleas have all the necessary equipment to communicate with one another. What do you suppose they say? The entomologist thinks that fleas have little else to talk about other than food, so he feels that when a flea finds a juicy dog or cat or other animal, it begins to telegraph the message to all other fleas in the neighborhood.

Of course, fleas aren't very popular with people, or even with dogs and cats, for that matter. We don't know what changes fleas have undergone since their ancestors were created, but the Creator has provided even fleas with a marvelous method of survival.

SEQUOYAH'S TALKING LEAVES

In the beginning was the Word, and the Word was with God, and the Word was God. . . . All things were made by him; and without him was not any thing made that was made. John 1:1-3.

Sequoyah was a half-Cherokee Indian who lived in the early 1800s in Tennessee. When Sequoyah saw a book for the first time, he was told by a friend that white men had cast a spell on the pages, a spell that enabled them to read thoughts. Sequoyah called pages of paper with words on them "talking leaves." He and his ancestors had known only the book of nature, and the printed page was a form of knowledge that he had never even imagined. He was so impressed by the written word that he learned to read and then invented an alphabet for the Cherokee people, which they used.

Jesus, our Creator, wrote two books. He wrote the first book with His own hand—the book of nature as it appeared in Eden. Then God moved upon holy men and inspired them to write another Book, which we have as the Holy Bible—talking leaves. These two books, along with other forms of inspiration, such as special visions to prophets and the impressions of the Holy Spirit, represent God's way of telling us what He is like and how much He loves each one of us. It is important that we study both of God's books.

We know that we should study the Bible. But to realize that we should study God's message as portrayed in the book of nature is sometimes not so clear. Throughout the Bible the men and women of God were students of nature, ever listening to the word of God as spoken through the many things written therein. Sin made the pages of nature blurry, so we can't read them right without the help of the Bible's talking leaves. Under the direction of the Holy Spirit we can prayerfully study all of God's words.

When we are first introduced to the book of nature and have not yet learned to read its pages, we may be skeptical. Perhaps we need to ask the Creator to teach us the alphabet of the book of nature so that we can read the rest of His words.

THEY HAD 64 DOGS!

And he shall lay his hand upon the head of the sin offering, and slay it for a sin offering in the place where they kill the burnt offering. Leviticus 4:33.

Mr. and Mrs. Snyder, of Pennsylvania, had sixty-four dogs! All the dogs were pets, but the neighbors complained, and the case went to court. The judge ordered the Snyders to get rid of all but five of their dogs. To the Snyders the dogs were like a very large family. They loved their dogs. You may think it strange that they had so many, and it was a bit out of the ordinary, but the Snyders were grief-stricken at having to lose their dogs. What were they to do?

Apparently they tried to give the dogs away but could not find homes soon enough to satisfy the court, so they were ordered to turn the dogs over to the authorities. They couldn't bear the thought of what would happen to their pets at the Humane Society, so they decided to have them put to sleep one at a time by injection while they held them.

After forty of the dogs had quietly gone to sleep they came to Champ, their Saint Bernard. After three attempts to put Champ to sleep had failed, Mr. Snyder, a 55-year-old steelworker, with tears rolling down his cheeks, gave up. He said, "Champ fought so hard to live, I just couldn't kill any more. I held every dog and I cried for every one."

The Snyders decided to board the rest of the dogs until they could find suitable homes for them, and the authorities allowed them to carry out this plan. Champ had made the difference. His desire to live had saved the rest of the dogs. Animals can teach us so much.

When I read the story I cried too. It is so sad to see our loved pets die. But, you know, our dearest Friend in all the world, even a closer friend than any pet, is Jesus. After sin entered the world, God gave man a way to learn about what sin does. A lamb was to be slain by its master. Sin kills. Jesus saves, but He had to die. He was the Lamb of God that was slain for you and for me. Don't you love Him?

37

PLAYING DEAD

*For we which live are alway delivered unto death for Jesus'
sake, that the life also of Jesus might be made manifest in our
mortal flesh. 2 Corinthians 4:11.*

One January morning Mr. McNair was walking his dog on
the beach near Wellfleet, Massachusetts, when the dog found a
common eider duck that was unable to fly and was stranded
some distance from the water. As the dog approached the duck
Mr. McNair noticed that the eider seemed to drop dead of
fright—not a rare thing among wild birds. The duck's body had
slumped forward, its neck was twisted, and its eyes were glassy
and rolled back, exposing much white. There was no sign of life.
Mr. McNair, assuming the duck was dead, lifted its neck to
inspect the head and then released it, whereupon it dropped to
the ice. He tugged at the feathers on the bird's back and wings,
but there was still no sign of life. He turned the duck over, and
suddenly both of the duck's feet started to paddle in an apparent
attempt to turn right side up! So the bird was not dead after all.

Mr. McNair gently turned the duck right side up. It was
apparently lifeless again. He picked it up and carried it to the
water's edge and set it down on the ice. He then withdrew to
watch. There was absolutely no movement of any kind for
nearly a minute. Then all of a sudden the eider's head and neck
popped up; it looked toward Mr. McNair and the dog. Upon
seeing the duck move, the dog was interested again and went
after it. But this time the bird quickly escaped into the
water. Once in the water, the eider preened vigorously, as if
nothing had happened.

That eider was instinctively aware that a dog isn't interested
in a dead duck. And since there was no other possible escape
anyway, the duck played dead—and it worked! You and I are up
against a pretty wily foe going about seeking whom he may
devour. Although we can't play dead, we can claim the death of
Jesus, and His real death will deliver us from that old dog the
devil.

DOX, THE DETECTIVE DOG

But if ye will not do so, behold, ye have sinned against the Lord: and be sure your sin will find you out. Numbers 32:23.

There are some really incredible stories about the detecting abilities of man's best friend. We won't go into the stories of how dogs are used to sniff out drugs, foodstuffs, and other plant materials that are being illegally transported, but we will concentrate on one story of a dog that was assigned to a homicide squad in Italy. Dox held the rank of corporal, which meant that all lower-ranked officers had to salute whenever they passed him. There are numerous stories of the extraordinary feats that Dox performed in the line of duty, but here is perhaps one of the best.

A man had been murdered in the storeroom of a jewelry store. Dox came on the scene. He sniffed around and then led the officers on a scent trail that ended in the cellar hideout of the man whom they assumed had committed the crime. So the officers extensively questioned the man, only to be convinced, instead, that the man had not done the dastardly deed. They could not arrest the man without any evidence, so they had to leave without taking him. But Dox had other ideas.

Back at the jewelry store, the squad wanted to try for another trail. But Dox was not interested in another trail. He nosed around the storeroom until he came up with a button. He then led the officers back to the same cellar hideout where the suspect was living. While the policemen apologized for the intrusion and the man again asserted his innocence, Dox went to the closet door, nosed it open, and pulled a raincoat off its hanger. You can guess the rest of the story—the raincoat was missing a button, and it was the one found in the storeroom of the jewelry store. With this evidence before him the suspect admitted his guilt, and Dox's reputation remained intact.

It is quite possible that not-so-dumb animals are more sensitive to the sins of man than we are.

FEVER

And not only so, but we glory in tribulations also: knowing that tribulation worketh patience. Romans 5:3.

Since we spend so much effort trying to bring a sick person's temperature back down to normal, we might tend to think that fever is a bad thing. On the contrary, if it weren't for fever, the body's defense system wouldn't work nearly so well. Sometimes fever is just what the doctor ordered. At other times it is dangerous—especially if it goes too high.

In the seventeenth century Dr. Thomas Sydenham stated that fever is "Nature's engine which she brings into the field to remove her enemy." The enemy, of course, is infection.

When body temperature goes above normal, things begin to happen: The flow of blood speeds up, racing new supplies of disease-fighting white blood cells to the point of infection; antibody production is increased; and the protein interferon works more effectively.

Research with lizards has shown that those that are ill will seek heat if given the chance. Those that were kept in a cool place died at a higher rate. Since lizards are coldblooded animals, they cannot generate a fever from within, so they make one by basking in the heat of the sun.

In our relationships with others and with Jesus, things sometimes begin to heat up. There is a problem of one sort or another. At times we are the cause of the heat, maybe because we don't know how to act or because our behavior makes others unhappy.

There are also times when because of our following Jesus other people become angry. Jesus in our lives might cause them to see the sin in their own lives, and because they do not want to change, they make things a bit uncomfortable for us. Our little world may have a fever under those conditions, but we are told to rejoice in such tribulations, because dealing with them increases our patience. It is quite possible that our continuous life of peace in Jesus will be the very thing that will win the hardhearted person to Him.

SUPER ROACH

Not by might, nor by power, but by my spirit, saith the Lord of hosts. Zechariah 4:6.

In the southern part of the United States, where we live, one of the most persistent insect invaders is the cockroach. For people who move to this part of the world from areas farther north, it is especially hard to get used to seeing cockroaches around the house. In spite of very careful pest-control measures, the roaches continue to arrive by one means or another. There seems to be no way to win the war against them.

And now we learn that the use of pesticides has fostered the development of a super roach that is quite immune to the standard insecticides. In order to rid the premises of these unwanted guests, people have used stronger and stronger chemicals. The poison dosage has had to become so strong that it now threatens the very lives of babies and small children who live in the homes.

Recently an 8-month-old baby suffered a heart attack from the quantity of insect-killing chemicals that it had ingested around the house. The child had to be revived by artificial respiration.

Professional exterminators used to have no trouble getting rid of our unwanted bugs. Thirty or forty years ago DDT was the most popular insect-killing agent. At that time minimal contact with such a substance would eliminate all of the pests. Now, however, you could spray DDT directly on the insects—with almost no effect whatsoever. The generations of insects that have been produced in the intervening years have become more and more immune to poisons, until there is hardly anything left that will eliminate them yet is also safe to use. It appears that the great war between man and cockroach is going to be over soon, and man will have lost. You would think that with all our knowledge we could do something about this problem, but we are apparently helpless against the mighty roach.

We are just as helpless against Satan, but we have a remedy that will work without fail—Jesus.

41

THE REAL LIONS

Be sober, be vigilant; because your adversary the devil, as a roaring lion, walketh about, seeking whom he may devour. 1 Peter 5:8.

You will probably not like what I am about to tell you. Sometimes we don't like to hear the truth when we have been led to enjoy the belief that things are different. Lions provide a perfect example. Almost the entire world believes them to be noble beasts with great hunting skill and majestic grassland leadership—the king of beasts. If that is so, then why did Peter in his letter compare the devil to a roaring lion? The answer is the part that you perhaps won't enjoy hearing, because the real lions in Africa *are* perfect examples of the devil. The lions of myth and legend never existed!

The most extensive study of lions ever undertaken was done by George Schaller, a biologist with the New York Zoological Society. Schaller spent 2,900 hours observing hundreds of lions in the wild in Africa and published his findings in a book entitled *The Serengeti Lion* (1972). Schaller's description of real lions doesn't sound like anything I ever heard about the king of beasts.

The real lions prefer to steal their food rather than get it for themselves. Rather than killing their prey and letting the hyenas feast after they leave, lions more often let the hyenas do the killing, and they steal the kill.

When food is scarce the real lions feed themselves first and let their own cubs starve to death—from one quarter to one third of all lion cubs suffer such an end. The same number of cubs die because their mothers abandon them. And, worst of all, it is not uncommon for both male and female lions to kill and eat cubs—even their own.

Do those traits sound as if they belong to an animal that really is the king of beasts? They certainly do not, but they *do* represent exactly the type of being that the devil is. Satan would like nothing better than to have us believe that he is a wonderful king while he is going around being his real self.

HUMMINGBIRD ENERGY

Withhold not thou thy tender mercies from me, O Lord: let thy lovingkindness and thy truth continually preserve me. Psalm 40:11.

What would you say if you saw a person sit down one day and eat 370 pounds of potatoes? Such a feat is probably impossible, but that is how much you would have to eat to match a hummingbird's daily energy requirements!

A hovering hummingbird is putting out ten times the energy of a man running at nine miles per hour. Furthermore, a person can't run even that fast for more than a few minutes, but the hummingbird generates ten times that energy level and keeps it up off and on all day—even increasing it to fly in some direction, to speed up, to turn, to fly backward, and to stop again. It is said that a hummingbird, with an initial burst of energy, can accelerate from zero to sixty miles per hour within a distance of three feet!

A hummingbird actually produces about the same amount of energy, for its size, as a modern helicopter. If a person could generate the same amount of energy he would evaporate about a hundred pounds of his body's water content in an hour. When the water ran out, his body temperature would rise past the melting point of lead, and he would probably burst into flames. But the hummingbird's system can easily handle the output of that much energy.

To maintain its level of energy output, a hummingbird has to feed all day, constantly taking high-energy nectar from flowers as it makes a circuit, visiting all the blossoms that it can find. Some people try to act like the hummingbird and eat all day, but our system is not at all like that of the hummingbird, and it is just as unhealthful for us to eat like that as it is healthful for the hummingbird to do so.

God sustains the hummingbird, with its great energy requirements, just as He has promised to sustain us in our physical needs. Perhaps even more important is the promise of God to sustain our spiritual health when we feed daily on His Word.

FROM DRUGS TO THE WOODS

And Lot went out, and spake unto his sons in law, which married his daughters, and said, Up, get you out of this place; for the Lord will destroy this city. But he seemed as one that mocked unto his sons in law. And when the morning arose, then the angels hastened Lot, saying, Arise, take thy wife, and thy two daughters, which are here; lest thou be consumed in the iniquity of the city. Genesis 19:14, 15.

What a terrible decision that must have been for Lot. Everything he owned, all of his friends, and most of his relatives were there in Sodom, and he had to decide whether to stay or to go. He tried to get his loved ones to go with him, but they believed that he was crazy. At the urging of the angels, at the very last possible minute Lot left with his wife, who didn't want to go, and his two daughters.

Peter Beach was a very successful businessman in Chicago a few years ago. But the Beach family had a problem. At first it was not so bad: They simply had a house full of teen-age boys who were experiencing normal adolescent problems. As often happens in such a setting, the boys had friends who gave them advice. That advice was primarily based on the use of drugs to make them feel better.

Mr. and Mrs. Beach just happened to be two of those rare parents who, when they recognize that they have a severe problem, are willing to take strong measures to solve it. The strong measure in this case meant selling most of their worldly wealth, leaving a prominent and successful career, and moving to a cabin in the woods of northern Wisconsin.

If you ask Mr. Beach why he made the move, he says, "I saw my family disintegrating around me. It was a matter of life and death."

Today all five boys have made dramatic changes in their lives and thank their parents for having had the courage to make such a sacrifice.

MINKY AND SIMBA

The Lord openeth the eyes of the blind: the Lord raiseth them that are bowed down: the Lord loveth the righteous. Psalm 146:8.

We have all heard stories of hero dogs, such as dogs that led their owners or masters and mistresses to safety from a burning building. There are also stories of dogs that saved other dogs or saved property from damage. Then there are the stories of dogs as heroes in a different way. They don't do anything spectacular, but they are heroes nonetheless. Their heroism is a gentle sort in which they live a life of dedicated service over a long time. The story of Minky and Simba is just such a gentle-hero story.

Minky and Simba were two dogs that lived in England some years ago. Minky was an elderly cocker spaniel that had lost her eyesight. Simba was a 3-year-old German shepherd. Without being trained or told to do so, Simba decided to be Minky's Seeing Eye dog.

Whenever Minky wanted to go out, Simba would grip her companion's long, floppy ear gently in her mouth and lead her down the stairs to the front door. There Simba would let go of Minky's ear and open the door with her paws. Grabbing the ear again, Simba would lead the spaniel out and help her to go wherever she wanted to go. Every day Simba took Minky by the ear to the feeding bowl and sat beside her while she ate, and then led her back again. Whenever the two dogs went out for a walk Simba would hold onto her old friend's ear for dear life. When they reached an intersection Simba would stop just as a good Seeing Eye dog would, wait for the traffic to clear, and then lead Minky safely across to the other side.

The two dogs were inseparable. Simba lived a life of completely dedicated service to Minky. By sharing her eyes with Minky, Simba made Minky's final days peaceful and pleasant. We can compare their love to the kind of love that Jesus has for each of us and to how close He stays to our needs.

TREES OF RIGHTEOUSNESS

To appoint unto them that mourn in Zion, to give unto them beauty for ashes . . . ; that they might be called trees of righteousness, the planting of the Lord, that he might be glorified. Isaiah 61:3.

Trees are beautiful. When you are driving through the countryside the various kinds of trees scattered here and there, each with its own hue of color, make the vista both relaxing and stimulating at the same time. The Creator knew just the right mix of things when, on the third day, He said, "Let the earth bring forth grass, the herb yielding seed, and the fruit tree . . ." (Gen. 1:11).

Have you ever noticed that a natural woodland is usually filled with trees of different kinds? Only man plants extensive groves of trees that are all alike, and in the process I think some of the beauty is lost. But there is another reason, besides having an eye-pleasing assortment, for having different kinds of trees growing together in the woods: Different kinds of trees complement one another's healthy growth, as well.

Robert Rodale, editor of *Organic Gardening,* described his attempt to establish a pure stand of walnuts on his land. He planted them the right distance apart and did all the right things to make them grow vigorously, but they have never done well. He now knows that trees do better when there are other types of trees around. Mr. Rodale said it like this: "Trees like to look at strange leaves and branches and to touch toes underground with strange roots."

When the trees are all alike the scenery is monotonous; when they are different the variety is pleasant. Tree experts tell us that trees in mixed stands work together to take care of one another by protecting one another from pests and disease.

Trees are something like people. Wouldn't it be boring if every person looked and acted just like all others? God's church on earth is like a mixed stand of beautiful trees showing the beauty of the Creator and providing help for one another.

CHITA AND GORAB

And he taught, saying unto them, Is it not written, My house shall be called of all nations the house of prayer? but ye have made it a den of thieves. Mark 11:17.

Jesus loved to tell nature stories to help His hearers understand His messages. How I would love to have been one of those hearers and listened to His stories! If Jesus had known about Chita and Gorab, perhaps He would have told a story about them. Actually, they would have made great Pharisees.

Chita was a baboon. Gorab was a pied crow. The two became acquainted in Africa, where they are native. Chita had the run of the compound and amused herself by stealing the cook's bread and other delicacies, so the cook and Chita did not get along at all—much to Chita's apparent delight. Chita was a born thief. She had plenty to eat but spent most of her time stealing food anyway.

Baboons and crows aren't natural friends, and Gorab's arrival was not to Chita's immediate liking. Chita would rush at Gorab, hiss, and make all sorts of intimidating threats. But Gorab soon learned that Chita was all bluff, and the next time that Chita came rushing up to him Gorab pecked her on the nose. That changed things immediately. Chita suddenly had respect for Gorab, and before long they were inseparable friends.

Gorab would even spread his wings and let Chita pick the insects from between his feathers—a gesture of true baboon affection. Gorab also became Chita's partner in crime. One of them would distract the cook by pretending to be after something. While the cook was chasing him or her away the other partner would sneak in and steal a different item. But when one of the two managed to steal some food it would not be shared with the other. You have probably heard the expression "thick as thieves"; well, that saying fit Chita and Gorab.

Yes, I think Chita and Gorab would have made fine Pharisees. God's church is not the place for Chitas and Gorabs, but they are often there nonetheless.

47

A POCKETFUL OF DIAMONDS

Again, the kingdom of heaven is like unto treasure hid in a field; the which when a man hath found, he hideth, and for joy thereof goeth and selleth all that he hath, and buyeth that field. Matthew 13:44.

A pocketful of the best diamonds is worth about $5 million. There is probably nothing else on earth that one could easily carry in his pocket that is worth that much.

But what would I do with such a treasure? I don't wear them; I can't eat them; they won't keep me warm in winter; they won't save me from dying in this world; they won't make me well, as some of the ancient peoples thought; they don't make me strong—the finest diamonds aren't really much good for anything (who would think of using perfect specimens for cutting tools, abrasives, and other useful purposes?) except that they are pretty to look at. They sparkle like the stars at night and like the sun on new snow. The way diamonds take sunlight and make it dance like a thousand sparklers makes them worth looking at. It is almost as if there were a little piece of the sun inside each diamond.

But if I kept a pocketful of diamonds just to look at I'd always be taking them out to look at, and soon people would know that I had this treasure in my pocket. Then I'd never be safe, because there would always be someone after me to get my diamonds for himself. And, besides, I wouldn't need a pocketful of them to enjoy their beauty—just one would do!

I would want the one that was the prettiest. The diamonds that are worth the most are the clear, flawless crystals with no cracks visible, even under a magnifying glass. These stones reflect the most light and sparkle the brightest, showing every color of the rainbow.

Yes, it would be wonderful to have a beautiful, clear diamond, but on this earth such a treasure will never be in *my* pocket. But wait, there is a wonderful thought here. Even though I may not have diamonds, I can be like a diamond, reflecting the light of Jesus, who was without blemish. And He is worth everything to me.

WATCH, FOR THE COMET IS COMING!

And great earthquakes shall be in divers places, and famines, and pestilences; and fearful sights and great signs shall there be from heaven. Luke 21:11.

"Watch," Jesus said, "for ye know not what hour your Lord doth come" (Matthew 24:42). We are to look for the signs and be ready to meet Jesus when He comes.

There is another event that is coming in the heavens, and it will be visible to all who can see the stars. Halley's comet is coming back! It will happen in 1986; the best date for viewing will be March 26 of that year—don't miss it, because it won't be back for 76 years. The last time Halley's comet paid us a visit was in 1910. Ask your grandfather and grandmother to tell you about it.

Halley's comet is named for Edmund Halley, an Englishman who first proved that comets move in orbits around the sun, as do the planets. According to the history books, the most dazzling occurrence of Halley's comet was in the year A.D. 837, when it was brighter than any star in the night sky and its tail streamed halfway across the sky. The 1986 visit by Halley's comet will not be nearly so spectacular. In fact, this visit is predicted to be the least spectacular in the recorded history of the comet. But even then it will appear as bright as a star of the third magnitude, which is about as bright as any average star in the sky, so most of you will be able to see it.

Professional and amateur astronomers around the world are getting ready for Halley's comet. They are studying about it, making sure that their telescopes are in the best possible working order, and arranging their schedules so that they will not have other things interfering with this once-in-a-lifetime event. And sometime that year it will finally be visible. Everyone wants to be first to see the comet.

Are we as anxiously awaiting the return of Jesus? Are we watching for the signs?

THE ELEPHANTS OF ADDO

Keeping mercy for thousands, forgiving iniquity and trans-
gression and sin, and that will by no means clear the guilty;
visiting the iniquity of the fathers upon the children, and upon
the children's children, unto the third and to the fourth
generation. Exodus 34:7.

In 1919 the forest that now comprises the Addo Elephant
National Park in South Africa contained more than one
hundred elephants. These elephants, although wild, were not
particularly dangerous. They kept to themselves, and no one
feared them. But the elephants would emerge from the forest
quite often to partake of the fruit in the surrounding citrus
plantations. They didn't know the difference between a wild
forest and a farm. You can imagine how the plantation owners
felt about losing their prized and valuable fruit to a herd of
ponderous pachyderms. The farmers determined to end the
pillage at once, so they hired a hunter.

Now, any modern elephant hunter knows that in order to
eliminate a herd of elephants you have to kill them all at once, or
you may never get them all; even if you eventually do find and
shoot all of them it will be at great expense and take much
longer. Why is this? Because the elephants are so smart: They
somehow teach not only one another but their young about what
to watch out for.

The hired elephant killer found it easy to shoot the
elephants, one at a time. At first the elephants didn't know what
to do. However, it didn't take them long to figure out what was
going on, and they became wary of the hunter and aggressive
toward other people. Within a year, even though there were only
twenty or thirty elephants left in the Addo forest, the hunter
could not find even one! He eventually gave up—but the
elephants did not.

Today, more than sixty years later, the elephants of Addo are
the most dangerous elephants in all of Africa. All of the original
elephants are long since dead, but they somehow passed on their
experience with man to their young. It takes a long time to
overcome the effects of hurting someone.

THE LEVIATHAN

Canst thou draw out leviathan with an hook? or his tongue with a cord which thou lettest down? Canst thou put an hook into his nose? or bore his jaw through with a thorn? Job 41:1, 2.

There is little question that Job is referring here to the crocodile. All of the figures of speech that he uses in Job 41 are easily recognizable as being characteristic of this large reptile. You might not be aware of just how large a monster this creature once was. Today all the large ones have been exterminated and the larger ones are taken for their skins, so it is rare to find a crocodile anywhere in Africa that is more than six or eight feet long. Long ago, however—certainly when the book of Job was written—the crocodile commonly attained a length of fifteen to twenty feet and weighed up to at least a ton.

If you have ever had the idea that the crocodile is little more than a large, sluggish reptile that spends most of its time sunning itself, think again. When the crocodile decides to hunt there is nothing in the water that is safe, and few things on land near the water are any safer. A crocodile feeds both in the water and on land. According to two crocodile experts, when the leviathan wants to catch something on land and the crocodile is in the water, it can, with a few powerful strokes of its legs, attain enough momentum to rocket straight out of the water onto the land. Then if it must pursue its prey on land it can raise itself up on all four legs and run as fast as any man. You don't tease a crocodile! It is quite probable that legends of dragons and dungeons had their start with the reports and drawings made of the crocodiles that inhabited the watercourses of the warmer parts of the whole world.

In the forty-first chapter of Job, God is reminding Job of the power of the well-known dragon of the deep. Job was asked whether man's power is anything compared with what God has given to even such a lowly creature as the crocodile.

BIG BIRD

Whereby the world that then was, being overflowed with water, perished. 2 Peter 3:6.

Can you imagine a flying bird with a wingspread of 25 feet! That is the size of a small airplane, and it is more than twice the wingspread of any flying bird existing today. Yet a recent discovery in Argentina uncovered the fossil skeleton of such a bird. It is supposed to have weighed 160 to 170 pounds and have measured 11 feet from the tip of its beak to the end of its tail.

It is hard to imagine a bird of that size soaring overhead, yet the bones were found, and scientists tell us that the bird was capable of flight. While it is true that there have been larger birds, they are or were usually flightless, such as the ostrich and the prehistoric elephant bird.

We don't know why this bird was so big, and there may have been birds that were even bigger than that. We do know that before the Flood, and certainly at the time of Creation, man was much larger than he is today; some of the birds and animals were very large also. This bird, like other very large prehistoric animals, was not able to survive. Most of them were probably destroyed by the Flood. The only record we have of life before the Flood is that given to us in the Word of God, in the Spirit of Prophecy, and in the record of the fossils that remain.

The world was so very wicked that God in His mercy had to destroy it. But God loved mankind so much that He made a way to escape the destruction. The world is again becoming that bad, and again the Lord will have to destroy it. But we have a way of escape, as did Noah. This time Jesus is our ark of safety. Of another big bird, the eagle, Jesus says, "Ye have seen . . . how I bare you on eagles' wings, and brought you unto myself" (Ex. 19:4).

AVALANCHE!

Before the mountains were brought forth, or ever thou hadst formed the earth and the world, even from everlasting to everlasting, thou art God. Psalm 90:2.

One of the most terrifying and devastating forces in all of nature is an avalanche. People who dwell at the foot of steep, snow-covered slopes in the high mountain areas of the world are living dangerously indeed. As the ground begins to rumble, the people below turn pale with fear, knowing that tons of snow are hurtling down the slope at speeds up to two hundred miles per hour. Someone screams, "Avalanche!"—but there is almost no time for escape.

Today advanced engineering techniques have made many of the danger spots in the mountains virtually free of destructive avalanches. However, it takes constant watching and frequent cannon fire to loosen the snow, letting it slide down the mountain in tolerable amounts.

The world's worst known avalanche occurred in Peru in 1970, when 18,000 people died. In the United States the worst avalanche took the lives of 96 persons in 1910, when two trains near Stevens Pass in the State of Washington were buried. Then, two days later, another avalanche buried 62 of the railroad workers who were trying to clear the tracks. In 1916, during World War I, the Italian and Austrian armies were battling it out in a valley when both sides got the idea of using the snow above. Directing their cannon at the ridges, both sides caused multiple avalanches that wiped out an estimated 18,000 soldiers.

The Creator of the mountains certainly doesn't want to see the death and destruction that are caused by avalanches. Such natural disasters always remind us that life on this earth is only temporary. This world is not our home. Jesus is coming soon and will put an end to all such disasters. He will make a new earth, where no one will utter the terrified scream—

"Avalanche!"

A LIVING FOSSIL

The grass withereth, the flower fadeth: but the word of our God shall stand for ever. Isaiah 40:8.

If there ever was a tree to represent the endurance of God's Word, this is it. What we know today as the ginkgo was, many centuries ago in China, called the duck's foot tree, because of the shape of its leaves. The tree has also been called silver apricot tree and silver fruit tree, because of the color of the fruit.

The most remarkable thing about the ginkgo tree is its ability to withstand disease, pests, and pollution. From all that we can tell, the tree has no natural enemies, and it thrives even in an industrial situation where the air is choked with chemical wastes. This is the reason why I like to think of this tree as a good representative for the Word of God: It can endure in even the worst settings.

The ginkgo tree flourished even before the Flood. Its leaves are found in fossils around the world. And the fossil leaves are identical to the leaves of the ginkgo trees living today, leading Charles Darwin to call the tree a living fossil.

Today the ginkgo grows around the world where man has introduced it. It grows in the wild only in a small area of mainland China, about seventy miles west of Hangchow. There the trees are so common that the local folk cut them for firewood. Elsewhere the tree is prized as an ornamental plant. The first one in the Western world was planted in the Netherlands in 1754. The ginkgo was taken to England in 1771, and the first one to reach America was planted in Philadelphia, in the Woodlawn Cemetery, in 1784. Today it is a common ornamental tree throughout America.

Perhaps it is fitting that healing powers have been attributed to the ginkgo. While I don't believe in such powers, the tree is certainly an example of the continuing strength of the healing Word of God, who spoke the trees into existence and created at least one tree—the tree of life—that has leaves that are "for the healing of the nations." Could the ginkgo have been an Edenic tree also?

YOU CAN COUNT ON IT!

The law of the Lord is perfect, converting the soul: the testimony of the Lord is sure, making wise the simple. Psalm 19:7.

This is one of my favorite texts. We don't usually think of the law of the Lord as anything but the Ten Commandments, and they are indeed one expression of the complete law of God. But His law is as big as the universe. Everything you see, everything you hear, everything you feel, and even everything you think about is controlled in some way by the perfect law of God. I believe that the same laws that govern our lives govern the stars in their courses; the Bible tells us so in other verses of Psalm 19.

Think about the perfect law of God for a minute. Do you have any doubt that the sun will come up tomorrow? The day may be cloudy, but the sun will rise and there will be daylight. You can count on it!

Is there any question whatsoever in your mind that if you throw a ball up in the air it is going to come back down instead of heading off into space on its own? The law of gravity is absolute. You can count on it!

If you put a pan of water on a stove at sea level and heat it to 212 degrees, is there any doubt in your mind that the water will boil? There is no question about it!

If a mother duck lays a nest full of eggs and those eggs hatch, can you imagine their being anything other than ducklings? Ducks produce ducks. You can count on it!

Does an oak tree have acorns? Do most roses smell good? Is the sky blue? Does a rabbit hop? Is pure water clear? Is lead heavy? Does a bird have feathers? Is the world round? Do you need oxygen to live? Can a fish swim? Is ice cold? You can count on it!

Does sin bring pain, disappointment, and death? Yes, that's the law. There is no question about it. Did Jesus overcome sin and give us life if we follow Him? You can count on it!

GORILLA MYTHS

Jesus saith unto him, Have I been so long time with you, and yet hast thou not known me, Philip? he that hath seen me hath seen the Father; and how sayest thou then, Shew us the Father? John 14:9.

When Jesus came to earth to live among men, people had become so confused about the character of God that they did not recognize Jesus as having much similarity to the great God Jehovah, whom they believed that they knew. Myths and legends had so permeated religion that it was very hard for Jesus to convince even His own disciples that God the Father was as gentle, as loving, and as merciful as was Jesus.

A good illustration of how popular myths can shape the opinions of man is the usual way that people regard gorillas. Because of movies, television programs, and many stories about the monstrous gorilla, we tend to have a mental picture of an aggressive and very dangerous creature of immense size, swinging from tree to tree or standing on its hind legs, beating on its chest, and charging toward you through the jungle. Nothing could be further from the truth.

Those who study gorillas rarely, if ever, take weapons with them; they simply hang around the gorilla band until accepted. Then they literally move in with the gorillas—they sit with them, lean up against them, hug them, scratch their fleas, sleep with them, and romp with them on the forest floor. Gorillas almost never walk on their hind legs, and they spend almost all of their time on the ground, rarely going up into trees, and then usually to sleep. They occasionally fight one another, but they do not attack humans. They sometimes roar, bellow, and make loud noises, but they do so usually to see what effect it will have on another gorilla or on a human. If the sound has no effect, the noise-making gorilla loses interest and does something else.

See how far from the truth we can be led when we listen to all the legends of the storytellers instead of taking the truth from its source?

THE CHRISTIAN ROADRUNNER

Wherefore seeing we also are compassed about with so great a cloud of witnesses, let us lay aside every weight, and the sin which doth so easily beset us, and let us run with patience the race that is set before us. Hebrews 12:1.

Perhaps the most interesting bird that we see in our neighborhood is the roadrunner—named that because it prefers running to flying. It will fly if you corner it and if it has no place left to escape by running, but as soon as possible it will be on the ground again, running down the trail as fast as its long legs will carry it.

The roadrunner is perhaps the most well-known runner of all. Cartoons have featured the bird, and cars have been named after it. Actually, cartoon pictures of the roadrunner look quite like it. When it is running at full speed the roadrunner's beak is straight out in front, and its long tail is held straight out behind. It looks, and it is, streamlined. But its speed is deceptive; actually it travels only ten to fifteen miles per hour.

You should know one thing, however, if you have seen cartoons about the roadrunner: It *doesn't* say *beep-beep*. It has a low dovelike call, but it also has a vibrating call that is more like a rattle.

Roadrunners are among the most beneficial birds, for they eat snakes (even rattlesnakes!), lizards, grasshoppers, crickets, scorpions, centipedes, snails, mice, and the like. So, you can see, the roadrunner is a grand bird to have around the farm or ranch. Roadrunners live throughout the Southwestern United States and south into central Mexico.

There are many legends about the roadrunner, but one is perhaps the most interesting to me: It is said that this bird is a wonderful Christian bird because wherever it runs it leaves the sign of the cross for a footprint. Also the roadrunner is called *paisano,* which means "fellow countryman" and "friend." What better witness could there be?

MAGNETIZED MICROBES

I have stuck unto thy testimonies: O Lord, put me not to shame.... Teach me, O Lord, the way of thy statutes; and I shall keep it unto the end. Psalm 119:31-33.

In 1975 a microbiologist at the University of New Hampshire was looking at some mud samples that he had collected from ponds in the vicinity of Woods Hole, Massachusetts. He noticed a certain kind of bacteria that he had not seen before. That in itself was not unusual, for there are many different kinds of bacteria everywhere. But what made these bacteria unusual to the scientist was the fact that they were all moving north. Even in the very small space under the microscope, the tiny microbes were all wiggling in a northerly direction. Why?

Wondering whether the polarized bacteria were responding to the earth's magnetic field in the same way that a magnet does, the scientist brought an iron magnet close to the swimming microbes; they changed direction immediately and began swimming toward the magnet. In fact, with the use of sophisticated electromagnets, the scientist was able to completely reverse the magnetic field within which the tiny creatures were moving, and they immediately started moving in the opposite direction—south! The idea of such magnetic orientation had never been observed in a creature before.

Seeking an answer to what was causing the microbes to act in such a magnetic fashion, the scientist, with the help of others, analyzed the biochemical makeup of these microscopic magnets, and within the bacteria they found iron—magnetized iron! Every one of those bacteria had incredibly small iron magnets inside to keep it pointed north.

The Christian also has an ability to orient toward the truth. When we are under the guidance of Jesus we have built-in "magnets" that keep us aimed in the right way, just as surely as do the microscopic magnetized microbes. Throughout Psalm 119 the psalmist tells us that the laws of God work (as built-in magnets) to keep us headed right.

LITTLE FISH

There is a lad here, which hath five barley loaves, and two small fishes: but what are they among so many? John 6:9.

We have no way of knowing how big those little fish were, but we do know that Jesus performed one of His greatest miracles by causing those two little fish and those five barley loaves to be enough to feed thousands of people. Of course, Jesus is the Creator, and He was simply doing what He does every day as He sustains and multiplies all living things in order to provide food for not just thousands, but billions of people on earth. Not only does Jesus provide food for the people of this world, He sustains all the creatures and plants of the world—quite a task, when you think about it.

Sometimes we think of God's power in big ways, but He is also powerful in very small ways. He takes just as great care of the small fish, for instance, as He does the large ones. The largest fish in the world is the whale shark, which can be sixty feet long and weigh fifteen tons. That is an impressive fish! But do you know how small the smallest fish in the world is? We are not talking about baby fish (they can be very tiny when they first hatch or are first born). But how large do you think the smallest fish in the world gets when it is full-grown?

The world's smallest fish lives in the Philippines. It doesn't have a common name, but it is only one third of an inch long. It is also the smallest vertebrate animal on earth. There is another tiny fish in New Guinea that is a bit longer—one-half inch—but it is lighter in weight, because it is thinner in body. It would take more than one thousand of these tiny fish to weigh as much as a dime. Since they are completely transparent except for their eyes and their swim bladders, they are very difficult to see.

The Creator, who fed the thousands on the hillside of Galilee, also feeds the millions of these midgets in the world of fish. He sustains all of His creatures.

AN INCREDIBLE CATERPILLAR

Lift up your eyes on high, and behold who hath created these things, that bringeth out their host by number: he calleth them all by names by the greatness of his might, for that he is strong in power; not one faileth. Isaiah 40:26.

There are some things in the natural world that almost defy belief. There are also things that we simply take for granted but that are equally amazing. First, let me tell you about an incredible caterpillar from South America.

This caterpillar, as does any normal caterpillar, eats green leaves. Now, that isn't so incredible, is it? But wait—there's more! The caterpillar is often green, the same color as the leaves on which it feeds—and neither is this very strange.

Here is the incredible part: since the caterpillar is often preyed upon by birds, the Creator has given this humble creature the ability to foil the efforts of its would-be attackers. Before beginning a meal of green leaves, this green caterpillar uses its sharp jaws to clip out three to five silhouettes of itself; these bits of leaf make a close match to the caterpillar in size, shape, and color. Then, with threads that it produces, the caterpillar attaches all the decoys to the opposite end of the leaf where it intends to feed. Birds seeing several facsimiles of juicy green caterpillars will be immediately attracted to the opposite end of the leaf from the place where the real caterpillar is feeding, and after being disappointed by the fake caterpillars, the birds will move on, leaving the real caterpillar in peace and safety.

Now, I think that you will agree that this caterpillar demonstrates an extraordinary ability. And we certainly praise God for providing such ingenious ways for a lowly caterpillar to survive. The greatest miracle of all, however, is how we can be saved from Satan, the predator of all predators. God provided not a fake, but His real Son to die for our salvation.

LANA THE CHIMPANZEE

Make me to understand the way of thy precepts: so shall I talk of thy wondrous works. Psalm 119:27.

Lana is a chimpanzee working at the Yerkes Primate Center in Atlanta, Georgia. I say she is working; what I mean is that she has chores to do in a study of ape language ability. Lana has a computer keyboard that she operates. Each key represents a different word, and Lana has learned to string these words together in various phrases and sentences to request what she wants, such as food, or to respond to coded instructions presented to her on a lighted panel above the keyboard.

Lana once asked for a drink in twenty-three different ways. Her trainer put cabbage into her food container but falsely told her that he had put monkey chow into the feed drawer. She checked the container and responded by pushing the buttons that said, "You move cabbage out of machine."

Lana seems to enjoy her work very much. She sometimes pushes the buttons to request her favorite "hit record." She uses correct grammar in asking for such food as bananas and M&M's. In "her laboratory" Lana talks to the computer by pushing the buttons at any hour of the day or night. A closed-circuit video camera records her activities through the night, when she is often found seated in front of the keyboard, communicating with the machine.

It would be relatively simple to teach Lana to recite Bible passages, such as the Lord's Prayer and the twenty-third psalm. But would such verses mean the same thing to her as they do to us? Don't answer too quickly, because if all we do is memorize these verses with no thought for their meaning, then they don't mean any more to us than they would to the chimp.

But if the texts in God's Word are taken by us as valuable passages to be stored in our memories and to be drawn upon in our fight against sin, as Jesus drew upon them, then we have something much more valuable than the button-pushing ape can ever attain from memorizing.

CONTACT LENSES FOR CHICKENS

But if we walk in the light, as he is in the light, we have fellowship one with another, and the blood of Jesus Christ his Son cleanseth us from all sin. 1 John 1:7.

A California egg farmer began to notice that his chickens were getting along better: he wasn't losing so many from the pecking that goes on constantly in the cages where the chickens live. The farmer asked a chicken specialist why they seemed so peaceful. The specialist found that the reason was simple: many of the farmer's chickens had developed cataracts. They couldn't see well and for some reason had stopped pecking one another so often.

To make a long story short, the specialist had an idea. He would make contact lenses for chickens and see whether the wearing of them would produce the same effect as cataracts. And for no reason in particular, some of the contact lenses happened to be tinted red. To his amazement and delight he discovered that the chickens wearing the red-tinted contacts lost the urge to peck others. It seems that chickens like to look at the world through rose-colored glasses.

In the beginning there were problems getting the contact lenses to stay in, but at last word the problem has been solved. Soon chickens on chicken farms around the world may be wearing red contacts, and it is possible that as a result your eggs and mine may cost less.

Now, why do you suppose the red contacts work the way they do? Another chicken doctor, A. T. Leighton, professor of poultry science at Virginia Polytechnic Institute, says that the pecking instinct is intensified by the sight of blood. By wearing the red lenses, chickens don't see the blood. The blood is there, but the chickens can't see it.

You know, humans are a lot like chickens. There is an increasing amount of bloodshed around the world except where Jesus lives in the hearts of people. When we accept Him our lives are changed; His blood, like the red contact lenses on the chickens, causes us to have a wonderful fellowship one with another.

IS THE CENTER OF THE MILKY WAY A BLACK HOLE?

And thou sayest, How doth God know? can he judge through the dark cloud? Thick clouds are a covering to him, that he seeth not; and he walketh in the circuit of heaven. Job 22:13, 14.

The center of our galaxy, the Milky Way, has always been obscured from telescope-viewing astronomers by massive clouds of interstellar dust. So until the radio telescope was invented there was no hint at what might be located at the center of our own island universe.

Galactic dust does not stop the electromagnetic radiation that is produced by the stars of the universe. By carefully receiving the impulses that would seem like nothing but static to most of us and by analyzing the radio waves that come our way, astronomers now have a picture of the very center of our galaxy for the first time.

When radio waves from the center of the Milky Way are translated into photographs, what is seen is the image of an immense gaseous cloud perhaps hundreds of light years across but containing in the center core what may be, as it is called, a black hole. Spiraling out from the center are jets of superhot gas, which are often characteristic of black holes.

You should know that a black hole is not really a hole in space, but is, rather, a compacted star that has condensed to a point where its gravity is so strong it will not even let light rays escape into space. Other forms of radiation do escape, however, especially from around the edges, and there are patterns of the surrounding material being pulled to the black hole in a spiraling fashion. This leads astronomers to feel certain that there is actually a star in the center that looks like empty space. To give you some idea of how dense and, therefore, how heavy a black hole is, consider this: If the earth were compressed into a black hole it would be less than three quarters of an inch in diameter!

What do you suppose a black hole is from the Creator's point of view?

HOW BIG IS A WOLF?

The wolf also shall dwell with the lamb, and the leopard shall lie down with the kid; and the calf and the young lion and the fatling together; and a little child shall lead them. Isaiah 11:6.

Can you imagine having a group of pets consisting of a wolf, a lamb, a leopard, a goat, a calf, and a lion? That is the picture that Isaiah presents for us of the new earth. But on this earth wolves are rarely kept as pets.

Wolves vary in size, depending on the race. They range in size from the small Arabian wolf, which weighs about 45 pounds, up to the North American timber wolf, which averages about 100 pounds. The largest wolf ever known weighed 175 pounds. The races of wolves that inhabited Bible lands were relatively small: they were hardly larger than medium-sized dogs. But their behavior was certainly different from that of dogs!

One thing that is enormous on a wolf is its feet. An Alaskan timber wolf may have a foot pad more than five inches across. You might think that such big feet would cause the wolf to lose a lot of heat on the ice and snow. But the wolf has a special heat-regulating system that allows its feet to maintain a temperature just above freezing, while the rest of its body is toasty warm.

Wolves have special fur, too. They can curl up and lie right out in the open with their backs to the wind and sleep warmly in temperatures down to 40 degrees below zero. And the wolf is one of only two animals designed so that the moisture condensing from their warm breath will not collect and freeze on their fur. The other animal is the wolverine.

Wolves have incredible endurance. Two wolves in British Columbia were followed for 22 miles as they broke trail, without stopping, through 5 feet of snow! Wolves travel an average of about 30 miles a day in winter, and 50 miles a day is not unusual. Those who study wolves tell us that the wolf is also one of the most gentle of all animals when handled properly—but I think I will wait until the earth is made new to have such a pet. Won't it be grand!

BUILDING A BRAIN

And I will put my spirit within you, and cause you to walk in my statutes, and ye shall keep my judgments, and do them. Ezekiel 36:27.

This text is one of the most reassuring in the Bible. Jesus has promised to actually take over in my life and cause me to do what He requires. His leadership is a good thing because I could never do right on my own.

When we do anything we engage a part of our brain called the cerebellum, which is responsible for all voluntary movement. A group of Stanford University scientists are building a computer model of the cerebellum. To do so they have put together 2 million computerized "brain cells"; this makes the model only about as complex as a frog's cerebellum, but they have to begin somewhere. They are a long way from simulating any part of the human brain, but they feel that if this project works they can expand it.

The first thing that the scientists discovered is that when some body movement is ordered, thus engaging the cerebellum, an electrical charge passes from brain cells to brain cells along many channels, but rarely, if ever, along the same paths. The action that was ordered will take place, but there are billions and billions of ways to get that order translated into action. This is just one more bit of evidence that we are "fearfully and wonderfully made" (Ps. 139:14).

Of course, your cerebellum, located in the back part of your skull, is also connected to the foreward parts of your brain, and inside that entire organ called your brain there is a whole universe of possible combinations for thinking, imagining, acting, seeing, smelling, hearing, and feeling. Man has only begun to understand what God has made in your head.

But the thing that thrills me most is that Jesus is able to program my brain so that the cerebellum will rightly control those things that I should do. And the programming is very simple: I look to Jesus and become changed.

WARMED BY ICE

My brethren, count it all joy when ye fall into divers temptations; knowing this, that the trying of your faith worketh patience. But let patience have her perfect work, that ye may be perfect and entire, wanting nothing. James 1:2-4.

Would you believe me if I told you that dousing plants with water that will freeze into an icy coat on the plants will make the plants warmer? It's true!

In order for water to freeze into ice it must lose heat. Let's say that the temperature is dropping outside and what farmers call a hard freeze is expected. Plant juices could freeze, killing precious crops. The farmer springs into action. The sprinkler system is turned on, and all of the plants are soaked when the temperature of the air is at about 32 degrees Fahrenheit. Since this is the freezing point of water, the water on the plants begins freezing, giving up its heat. Where does the heat go? Within the forming ice, next to the plants, the warmth is absorbed by the plants, keeping them at safe temperature levels.

Of course, this procedure won't help much if the temperature drops so low that the amount of heat taken by the plants is overcome by the added cold outside. It also doesn't work well when there is a wind. But it is such a useful method that some Southern farms are equipped with giant sprinkler systems.

Scientists are working on a computer that will constantly monitor the weather conditions and turn the sprinklers on at precisely the times when they will do the most good.

James tells us to rejoice when temptations come, because they give us a chance to depend upon Jesus for help to meet the temptations. We should not go looking for temptations, any more than the plants would want a freeze. But just as there is warmth in freezing water, so Jesus has promised that with every temptation He will provide a way of escape (1 Cor. 10:13) at precisely the right time.

THE GOSPEL MANGROVE

But ye shall receive power, after that the Holy Ghost is come upon you: and ye shall be witnesses unto me both in Jerusalem, and in all Judaea, and in Samaria, and unto the uttermost part of the earth. Acts 1:8.

Mangrove trees teach, by example, that the method specified by Jesus in this text for spreading the gospel is a good one. Mangroves have been called "mothers of islands" because they are often responsible for building islands where none existed before and for enlarging existing islands, expanding them in every direction. There are three primary ways that the mangrove spreads its life.

First, mangroves have roots that grow from the trunks of the main plants. These roots arch outward in all directions, and where they penetrate the water and reach the bottom, new trunks spring up, expanding and strengthening the trees.

Second, the seeds that are produced by the mangrove fruit do not fall immediately, but remain on the tree and begin germination, producing a long preliminary root right from the seed. This root is spear-shaped; when the seed falls the root acts like a dart, imbedding itself in the mud where it lands. This process takes the mangrove's growth a bit farther than the special roots do, starting new trees.

Third, if the dartlike sprouted seeds fall into water that is too deep for them to penetrate the mud and become established, they float and are carried away by the current. The sprouted seed is specially designed, though, so that the center of gravity gradually shifts until the pointed end—the dartlike root—hangs downward. This arrangement is now a floating plant ready to grow as soon as the point touches bottom in a shallow place—maybe a thousand miles away.

We spread the gospel the same way—first, at home; then, nearby; and finally, to the uttermost parts of the world.

HARMLESS GRASSHOPPER— RAIDING LOCUST

The locusts have no king, yet go they forth all of them by bands. Proverbs 30:27.

There is perhaps no plague on earth more devastating than the locusts of Africa and the Near East. The strange thing about them is that the black-red-yellow grasshopper that does the damage is the same insect that is usually a harmless green grasshopper living quietly in the sparse grass and brush of the African desert. But when conditions are right these insects change completely. It rarely rains where the natural locusts live, but when it does, green plants grow in profusion, millions more locust eggs than normal hatch, and the tiny hoppers have plenty of food. Under such conditions they grow up to be plague locusts, no longer harmless by any means.

It is hard to imagine the size of a swarm of locusts. The insects are so thick as they fly over that they can blot out the sun; the cloud of locusts can be 5,000 feet high. When they decide to come down, woe to the land below. Trees fall under their weight. The swarm literally covers the ground with a crawling, chomping carpet of destruction. Each square mile of locusts will eat from 200 to 600 tons of grain and vegetation a day; that's equivalent to the daily food of 200,000 people. In 1958 one swarm in Somalia consumed from 40,000 to 80,000 *tons* of grain a day! Can you imagine such a thing?

After the locusts leave, the people starve. About all the people can hope for is good rains to grow more crops soon—but if it rains too much, more millions of locusts will hatch and start another swarm! The inhabitants of more than fifty countries fight an almost-constant battle with the locust, which, having no leader, nevertheless goes forth as organized destruction.

Satan has caused so much tragedy in the world. Here he has taken harmless ordinary grasshoppers and turned them into an awesome army of destruction, with himself giving the orders. How it hurts Jesus to see the things He has made used in this way to harm the very people for whom He died.

68

A BIONIC BEE

Thou art the God that doest wonders: thou has declared thy strength among the people. Psalm 77:14.

Sometimes one of the greatest indications of wisdom and strength is the way someone deals with little things. God's ability to create a bee is a wonderful illustration.

Let's say that you want to build a bionic bee—a $6-million honey hunter. What would you need to build into the system? Well, we don't even know all of the things that you would need, but to start with, you would have to have a built-in clock, a polarized-light sensor, an instrument to measure true vertical, dead-reckoning equipment, a sun-angle-azimuth computer, a wind-speed-and-direction indicator, air- and ground-speed indicators, trigonometric calculators, an extremely sensitive scent-sensing-and-selecting computer, weather-detecting instruments, and a computer to process all of the input from this equipment and translate it into useful data for making decisions relative to hunting flowers, checking the quality of the nectar in the blossoms found, calculating the number of such flowers, returning to the hive, and informing the rest of the bees of the precise location, distance, quality, and quantity of the nectar-bearing flowers.

Now, believe it or not, you could probably put together such machinery from available modern equipment, but you would then be faced with a real challenge: you would have to fit all of it into a flying machine one-half-inch long! Don't forget to allow room for the engine and fuel, as well as a cooling system. You will also need landing gear and a baggage compartment for transporting nectar and pollen. Since there is no ground crew, you will have to build in a self-cleaning system. Finally, you would need an effective defense mechanism to protect your bionic bee from enemies.

Are you ready to become a bionic bee builder, or are you ready to leave the job to God?

THE CASSOWARY KILLER

And take heed to yourselves, lest at any time your hearts be overcharged with surfeiting, and drunkenness, and cares of this life, and so that day come upon you unawares. Luke 21:34.

You had better be wary of a cassowary! It is a large bird—six feet tall and weighing up to 180 pounds. It cannot fly, but there is no need for it to do so, because there is no enemy that would attempt to take on a cassowary in a battle. The bird is well armed, with its large bony helmet and its daggerlike center claw on powerful legs.

There are three species of cassowaries, and all three live on the large island of New Guinea. They inhabit the dense jungle undergrowth on the island. They are rarely seen but often heard as they crash through the brush, bellowing as they go. The bird runs at full speed on powerful legs, with head stretched out in front, much as a roadrunner. The cassowary has a bony, hornlike helmet that parts the brush ahead and protects it from collisions with trees and other objects.

Any human moving through the jungle where the cassowaries live had better beware. When startled the bird acts first and looks later. The action consists of jumping straight up and sending a vicious kick forward with one of its legs. At the end of that powerful leg are three claws, the middle of which is razor-sharp and capable of ripping a man's stomach open with a single slash. The cassowary is said to be the most dangerous bird in the world, as far as humans are concerned.

You would not want to come upon a cassowary unawares. It would very likely be the end for you. Similarly you would not want to come upon the end of time or the end of your life unawares—that is, without being ready to meet Jesus. The only way to plan for an event that might come at any time is to be ready at all times. Are you ready for Jesus to come? What if He were to come today?

ANIMALS THAT SENSE EARTHQUAKES

And great earthquakes shall be in divers places, and famines, and pestilences; and fearful sights and great signs shall there be from heaven. Luke 21:11.

It is reported that late in the afternoon of May 6, 1976, the animals in the Friuli area of northeastern Italy went berserk. According to the *Time* magazine report, "Dogs began barking and howling, cats ran into the streets, and hens refused to roost. Mice and rats scurried out of their hiding places and ran in circles. Horses and cows fidgeted in their stalls. Pet birds flapped their wings and emitted agonizing calls." At nine o'clock that evening the Friuli region was rocked by a major earthquake.

Scientists used to scoff at such reports of animal behavior, but research has now proved that animals do indeed have such a sensitivity to imminent earthquakes. Scientists have put forth a theory to explain how the animals know in advance that an earthquake will occur. As pressure builds up along the cracks (called fault lines) in the earth's crust, gigantic masses of charged atomic particles are released into the atmosphere. Thus the air near where the quake will occur is alive with electricity. Apparently people are not sensitive to these charges, but animals can sense them; as the time for the quake comes closer, the amount of charged particles in the air becomes so great that the animals are very uncomfortable.

Humans may also be sensitive to the charges, but the effects, such as headaches, irritability, and even nausea, are so common as routine ailments that people don't recognize the signs as indicating anything unusual. Scientists are studying the effects that such charges have on animals in the hopes that perhaps these warnings can be used to help people prepare for earthquakes.

Jesus is coming soon, and one of the signs is an increase in earthquake activity. We have been told in the Bible that this will happen. Are we sensitive to the world's condition? Are we preparing for the return of our Lord?

STALACTITES AND STALAGMITES

And he said unto them, Ye are from beneath; I am from above: ye are of this world; I am not of this world. John 8:23.

If you have ever been inside a fair-sized cave or seen pictures of some of the beautiful caves that people visit, you will remember seeing columns and pillars of mineral material hanging from the ceiling of the cave and standing on the floor of the cave. These mineral deposits come in all sizes and shapes, and, depending on the associated minerals, they can be many different colors. Essentially, the mineral growths of a cave can be divided into two forms: stalactites and stalagmites.

Stalactites are deposits of calcium carbonate that hang from the ceiling, like icicles. They are formed from the slow drip of mineral-containing water that runs down the stalactite and hangs at the tip, waiting to fall. As the drop of water hangs there, some of the minerals in the water attach themselves to the tip of the stalactite, making it a little bit longer with each drip. Obviously it takes a very long time to make a long stalactite.

Stalagmites are deposits of calcium carbonate that grow up from the floor of a cave as the result of mineral-containing water dripping from above. As in stalactites, some of the minerals in the drops of water that fall stick to the stalagmite, causing it to grow ever so slowly upward. Stalagmites cannot grow of themselves; they are dependent on the water from above. If the water stops they stop growing.

The beautiful columns that you see in caves are often the result of stalactites that have come so low and stalagmites that have grown so high that they fuse into one long pillar in the cave. It continues to grow larger as the mineral-rich water runs downward over its surface.

We can think of ourselves as stalagmites waiting here below for Jesus. He, like the stalactite, provides us with the water of life, and also comes down to meet us, until we become one.

BRAIN TRANSPLANTS

Let this mind be in you, which was also in Christ Jesus.
Philippians 2:5.

How would you like to get an injection of brain cells that would automatically make you smart? You could get a shot of math brain cells or a shot of science brain cells. Whatever you needed to know would be available at a special school—a school where you could get an information injection instead of book learning. The idea of transplanting brain cells has been studied for some time, but only in small animals, such as rats.

One scientist took brain cells from a healthy rat and planted them in the brain of a rat that had a brain disease. The diseased rat immediately began to improve, and it eventually overcame most of the effects of the disease. This is an example of what scientists believe is possible by the transplanting of healthy brain tissue into unhealthy brains.

One of the questions that scientists specializing in brain transplants will be studying next is whether or not memory can be transplanted in brain cells. Based on studies of trained worms, it appears that transplanting memory cells may be possible, but no one knows for sure yet. The process will be tested by first training a rat to run through a maze. Then some brain tissue from this rat will be transplanted into the brain of a rat that has not been taught to run the maze. If the memory transplant works, the rat that has not learned to run the maze will be able either to run the maze or to learn to run the maze more quickly.

Some doctors hope that someday such maladies as Parkinson's disease can be cured by transferring brain cells from a person who does not have the disease into one who does. (There is a problem, though, about whether such tampering with the brain is a good thing to do.)

In the meantime there is a promise that God has made to each of us: He will transplant into our mind the very thoughts and abilities that Jesus had, to overcome evil and live for God. What a promise!

73

CLEVER HANS

But God hath chosen the foolish things of the world to confound the wise; and God hath chosen the weak things of the world to confound the things which are mighty. 1 Corinthians 1:27

At the turn of this century an extremely clever horse by the name of Hans lived in Germany. Hans was owned and trained by Wilhelm von Osten, who claimed that the horse could solve complex arithmetic problems by tapping out the answers with his hoof. Many observers claimed that Hans could even read the instructions of a mathematics problem written on the blackboard—and then tap out the right answer! He was never wrong. How would you like to have an ability like that which Hans was supposed to have?

Scientists came and performed all kinds of tests. They would get total strangers to present the math problems. Nothing made any difference: Hans always came up with the right answer. For a number of years the scientists studied Hans and finally concluded that he must have a brain that was at least as bright as that of a human—perhaps the horse was even smarter than a human!

But, as often happens with such seeming wonders, along came a scientist who refused to be convinced. His name was Oksar Pfungst. Dr. Pfungst proved beyond any doubt that Hans was not solving the arithmetic problems at all: he was only exceptionally good at observing the people who presented him with the problems, and he would simply tap his foot until he saw some slight flicker of behavior, on the part of the person, that told him that it was time to stop tapping his foot. But was that any less amazing?

Hans was better at reading people than people are at reading the behavior of horses. He was so gifted that he could recognize the slightest change in the facial expression of any number of different persons. When I think of the abilities of God's simple creatures, I am moved to acknowledge humbly that I have nothing to brag about.

74

STINGING NETTLES

The best of them is as a brier: the most upright is sharper than a thorn hedge: the day of thy watchmen and thy visitation cometh; now shall be their perplexity. Micah 7:4.

Can you imagine a situation so bad that the very best person is like a brier or a thorn hedge? Those folks must have been difficult to live around. Perhaps they also had sharp tongues, such as the one described by the apostle James: "But the tongue can no man tame; it is an unruly evil, full of deadly poison" (James 3:8). If you put together the two ideas of a thorn and poison you get a good description of the stinging nettle.

The leaves of stinging nettles are covered with hundreds of thousands of brittle spines. And each one of those spines is a hollow tube with a cap on the end. At the base of each spine, in the main part of the leaf, is a tiny bulb filled with poison.

When your leg brushes against the stinging nettle the extremely brittle tip breaks off, exposing the equivalent of a sharp hypodermic needle. Your leg creates just enough pressure against the leaf to put pressure on the bulb full of poison, and up comes the poison through the needle spine and into your leg. You immediately feel the burning fire of the poison.

If you are fortunate the pain will go away in a matter of hours, but in some cases the doctor is needed. There is a species of stinging nettle in the East Indies, called devil's leaf nettle, that injects a venom so powerful that its victims can feel the pain for periods up to a year from the time they encountered the leaf.

Probably no one likes stinging nettles. They are a curse wherever they grow and they hardly have any redeeming features. Have you ever known a person like a stinging nettle? He hurts other people with his poison, and the pain may take years to overcome. Pray that your actions will never be like the stinging nettle's.

DISAPPEARING GOLDFISH

If we say that we have no sin, we deceive ourselves, and the truth is not in us. 1 John 1:8.

Sometimes when we are having problems, we fail to recognize the cause of our worries—even when it is obvious. This is especially true when we break the rules of good health. We feel tired and sluggish, or we have headaches and stomachaches. We may also have been staying up all hours of the night, eating sweets, and not exercising. To ask a doctor what is wrong with us when our life style is to blame is somewhat like the following story.

An engineering professor at a major State university decided to build a lily pond in his back yard. When the pond was finished the professor planted cattails at one end, floating waterlilies in the middle, and other lovely plants all around. The pond was beautiful, and the goldfish swimming peacefully in the pool set off the loveliness even more.

About a year went by, but the professor had a recurring problem with his pool. He needed some assistance in figuring out what was happening to his goldfish. They kept disappearing. So the engineering professor invited a biology professor to visit his home, look at his pool, and help him figure out what might be happening.

The biologist arrived and looked at the pool. It was as beautiful as he had heard it described. He asked all kinds of questions about what and how the professor fed the fish, how many he had released in the pond, and so forth. He checked all of the plants as best he could, and they seemed healthy enough. There just didn't seem to be anything wrong that would explain why the goldfish continued to disappear, even the recent replacements the professor had put into the pond. Finally the biologist told the professor that there was just no reason that he could see why the fish were disappearing.

"Well," said the professor, "it certainly is a mystery, especially since the little alligator I put into the pool is doing very well."

VENUS BRIMSTONE

The same shall drink of the wine of the wrath of God, which is poured out without mixture into the cup of his indignation; and he shall be tormented with fire and brimstone in the presence of the holy angels, and in the presence of the Lamb. Revelation 14:10.

Brimstone is sulfur, and the Bible talks about brimstone and fire being "rained" down (as in the destruction of Sodom). Conditions on Venus provide an example of such an environment.

The *Pioneer* spacecraft missions that explored the planet Venus revealed that the surface of that planet is the most hostile of all the planets in our solar system. This is significant in view of the fact that Venus is considered the sister planet to Earth. Surrounding Venus are four different layers of clouds made up of a constant, searing rain of hot sulfuric acid. On the planet Venus it is literally raining fire and brimstone.

Even some scientists who don't necessarily believe in the Bible do believe that the ultimate fate of the Earth will be similar to that of Venus. Let me quote from an article that appeared in *Science Digest* in 1982: "As our sun begins to run out of nuclear fuel, . . . it will start to swell to many times its present size. As it does, temperatures on Earth will increase by several hundred degrees. The oceans will boil away, filling the atmosphere with an oppressive water-vapor cloud cover. A runaway greenhouse effect will ensue, and as the temperatures on Earth climb to about 1,000 degrees Fahrenheit, all the carbon dioxide in the limestone and marble will be baked out, adding still more gases to an already hellish atmosphere. Thus, in exploring the origin of Venus we may be seeing the terrible fate of our own planet."

Please don't make the mistake of thinking that we can use heaven as a fire escape. The only motivation for going to heaven should be to be with Jesus. All of the other benefits will be added unto us because He loves us so much.

ELEPHANT SLUMS

And Jesus went forth, and saw a great multitude, and was moved with compassion toward them, and he healed their sick. Matthew 14:14.

Today there are hundreds of millions of people in this world who live in the ghettos and slums of vast cities. These people need to know Jesus because hope in Him is the only answer for the hurt and poverty that exist. How do you feel when you see the extensive poverty that exists all around? Is your heart moved to help? You may not have much in the way of money, but you can love, and that is what people need most.

The world is growing old; it is close to death. A new world is coming, where Jesus will wipe away all sorrow and poverty. We can help it come sooner. But sometimes we don't want to. Why do you suppose that is? Let me tell you about the Tsavo elephants, and perhaps your heart will be touched.

The Tsavo National Park was established in Kenya. It provided a refuge for the wildlife that was being hunted without mercy in the surrounding country. Somehow the word spread through the elephant herds, and they began to arrive. It takes a lot of land for elephants, and there are 8,000 square miles in Tsavo. But no one realized the need. When the elephants stopped coming the park was more like an elephant refugee camp. Today there are between 20,000 and 30,000 elephants crowded into this space.

Tsavo, once a lush tropical paradise for wildlife, has been stripped of its vegetation by hungry elephants and drought. The park holds the largest concentration of elephants in the world. But the food is almost gone, and there is no place for the poor beasts to go. Eventually Tsavo will be a desert, and the elephants will be gone. Philip Glover, director of the Tsavo Research Project, said, "It takes a lot of patience to stand by and do nothing."

Before long the whole world will be a wreck worse than a desert. The people will be gone. There is something you can do—tell others about Jesus!

ZEBRA FINCHES

O sing unto the Lord a new song: sing unto the Lord, all the earth. Psalm 96:1.

You have probably seen zebra finches in pet stores. They are cute little birds. The males sing soft, sweet little warbling notes; the females do not sing. In fact, research on the brains of zebra finches shows that there is a well-developed set of brain nerves in male zebra finches that is responsible for the singing. This area in the brains of female zebra finches is not developed. Therefore, it has been assumed that the females were physically incapable of song—that is until Dr. Julie Miller began her studies of zebra finch song.

Dr. Miller wondered whether the singing ability could be explained by chemicals, or hormones; for males and females have different types of hormone. To find out, tiny pellets of hormone-releasing material were placed in the zebra finch females as soon as they hatched. Then additional hormones were implanted in the females when they reached adulthood. The birds were placed into soundproof chambers so that there could be no chance that they might accidentally overhear sounds and copy them.

After five days of the hormone treatment the adult zebra finch females began to warble, and within a month they were singing the full-fledged zebra finch song that had never before been heard from a female zebra finch. Dr. Miller had proved that lady zebra finches have the physical ability to sing if they are given the right "songbook."

I feel certain that in the Garden of Eden all the birds sang—females as well as males. In the world there are many bird types in which both the males and the females sing, but since song has become associated with the establishment of territory—a job usually performed by the male—most birdsong is uttered by males.

In the new earth, when Eden is restored, I believe that we will hear songs from the birds, as well as from one another, that will be so beautiful that we cannot now even imagine them.

DEEP-SEA REFINERY

He maketh the deep to boil like a pot: he maketh the sea like a pot of ointment. Job 41:31.

While this text describes God's power as exhibited in the mighty leviathan, it is also a fitting introduction to a condition that exists at the bottom of the sea. Until recently, petroleum products were thought to be available only from refineries that made them by very extensive and expensive processes. But in studying the activities of newly discovered volcanic vents on the ocean's floor, scientists have learned that there are natural refineries there that are producing petroleum products similar to gasoline and other refined petrochemicals.

Volcanic vents are located at points where the sea floor is being ripped open by the movement of the earth's surface. The action opens up channels for superhot volcanic material to emerge and have an effect on the sea water and the decaying material that is lying on the bottom of the ocean.

At one of these vents, scientists found that the heat from the vents is literally cooking the thick layer of organic material on the sea floor and turning it into petroleum. Then as the petroleum rushes to the surface it undergoes the same treatment that petroleum products receive at a refinery in the fractionating towers, the tall tanks that you see at a refinery. At various levels on a fractionating tower different petrochemicals are drawn off while the basic petroleum continues to rise, creating other petrochemicals. The petroleum from the ocean floor is doing the same thing, but there is no way to capture it, because it is in the form of tiny bubbles and is constantly changing form as it rises.

The interesting point for us about this process is that scientists are now seeing oil produced at the bottom of the sea in a matter of *only* thousands of years, while they believe that it took millions of years to produce the world's vast petroleum reserves.

EUPHORBIA: THE POISON TREES

But of the fruit of the tree which is in the midst of the garden, God hath said, Ye shall not eat of it, neither shall ye touch it, lest ye die. Genesis 3:3.

You are probably aware of such poisonous plants as poison ivy, poison oak, and poison sumac, but these vines, shrubs, and trees may cause only uncomfortable skin irritation. You may also know about the oleander shrub, which is deadly poisonous.

There are several trees in Africa, all of which are members of the *Euphorbia* (pronounced u-FOUR-bee-uh) group, that not only are deadly poisonous but can cause excruciating pain, as well. The local people use the sap of the euphorbia trees to make fish poison and poison for the tips of their hunting arrows.

One plant-and-animal collector in Africa found out just how painful and dangerous the poison tree is when he attempted to get some cuttings for his yard. Now, I have no idea why he wanted to plant poison trees in his yard, but he did. At any rate he was about five minutes from home, cutting tree limbs for his project.

A tiny drop or two of sap from the poison tree happened to splash into his right eye. As soon as he felt the splash he headed for home. By the time he arrived his eye was in great pain, and before long it was throbbing with extreme pain, his nose was running, and his temperature rose to 100 degrees Fahrenheit. He washed the eye in water, in boric acid, and then in salt water, but felt little relief. After two hours his temperature went down to normal, but it was nearly a week before the man could see normally out of that eye again.

When Eve encountered Eden's "poison" tree she suffered no immediate pain. In fact, at first she felt that she had discovered the secret of the gods. Then the poison of sin began to be evident. If Jesus had not stepped in immediately and begun using the plan of salvation we would not be here.

AND THERE WAS LIGHT

And the earth was without form, and void; and darkness was upon the face of the deep. And the Spirit of God moved upon the face of the waters. And God said, Let there be light: and there was light. Genesis 1:2, 3.

For a long time I was curious about the light that God created on the first day. What do you suppose that light was? You can't say it was the sun, because the sun didn't shine on the earth until the fourth day of Creation. You can't say it was the light of candles because wax is made of vegetable products or is produced by bees; and plants weren't created until the third day, and bees didn't come into being until the sixth day. So where did the light come from on the first day, and what was it?

Well, I don't know exactly what that light looked like or just how God did it, but I think I do know where it came from and why it was there. The Bible tells us that Jesus is "the light of the world" (John 8:12). We are also told that the Word of God is a light unto our path (Ps. 119:105) and that "the Word was made flesh, and dwelt among us" (John 1:14) in the person of Jesus. John also tells us that that Word, who was Jesus, was the Creator of all things (verse 3). Now, if Jesus is the light of the world and if Jesus was the Creator of the world, then when He arrived on the scene on the first day of Creation you can be sure that there was light.

That same Jesus, who by His Spirit brought light to a dark world in the beginning, can bring light to our hearts. "For God, who commanded the light to shine out of darkness, hath shined in our hearts, to give the light of the knowledge of the glory of God in the face of Jesus Christ" (2 Cor. 4:6).

Are you ever afraid of the dark? Since Jesus is the Light of the world, we can always ask Him to come into our hearts and keep us safe in this world of darkness. It is far safer to be with Jesus in the dark than to be without Him in broad daylight.

DO CATS AND DOGS REALLY DREAM?

As a dream when one awaketh; so, O Lord, when thou awakest, thou shalt despise their image. Psalm 73:20.

In this text the psalmist talks of the fantasies of dreams and the return to reality when you wake up. We have all experienced the relief in waking up after a bad dream. Dreams can seem very real, and it sometimes takes quite a while to calm down from a particularly frightening one. The Bible writers were not silent on the subject of nightmares. Job, in the early part of his experience with boils, blamed God for scaring him with dreams (Job 7:14). There is a difference, of course, between the natural dreams that we experience and those dreams and visions that God has used to inform His messengers of important messages.

Common dreams are experienced under a form of sleep that scientists call REM sleep. REM stands for "rapid eye movement," which occurs when you are experiencing the sleep that accompanies dreams. You don't always dream. In fact, it is normal to go through a period of REM sleep on your way into and as you come out of deep sleep. As far as we know, you don't dream in deep sleep.

All mammals, from shrews to whales, exhibit REM sleep, and it is assumed that these animals also dream. Cats that have had damage to certain portions of their brains will go into REM sleep and begin acting out what appears to be a dream, as if they were awake. These cats play with imaginary toys and pounce on imaginary foes. One such cat bit its own tail. All the while, these cats are being monitored with wires connected to their scalp, and they give all the appropriate readings for REM sleep. Scientists feel that they know enough about dream characteristics in humans to assume that these cats, and therefore other mammals, are dreaming real dreams, just as you and I do.

Normal dreams are nothing to fear; they are not special messages from God or from the devil. But I suspect that Satan can use dreams to scare us—unless our trust has been placed in Jesus.

LIFE IN THE COUNTRY

Let the sea roar, and the fulness thereof: let the fields rejoice, and all that is therein. 1 Chronicles 16:32.

It is nice to live in the country. There is always something happening. For example, as I was sitting here at the typewriter just a few minutes ago our son Michael's friend Shannon came running in to tell me that the coyotes were calling. I dashed outside with her, and we heard them in the field across the road. They were yelping, barking, and carrying on as if it were the middle of a moonlit night, but the sun had scarcely set, and it was still as light as day. The coyotes were out early tonight. I wondered what this meant? There are so many secrets yet to be discovered.

During the almost four years of Michael's life before we moved to the country, he had not experienced the wildlife that occurs naturally, but he had seen wild animals on television and pictured in books. So he was prepared, in a way, for the move. Take cats, for example. Michael knew about cats because we have had our pet cat, Limousine, ever since Michael was born. But one day, just after we had moved to the country, I noticed a gray tabby walking through the grass in our field. It was a domestic cat that had probably taken to the wild and was obviously doing quite well. I pointed to the animal and said, "Michael, look! What's that?"

Michael looked at the cat, and then looked at me quizzically. "Is it a jaguar?" he asked.

He was not afraid, nor was he surprised that such an animal might be there. For him the country was the same as the wild places he had seen in pictures, and as far as he was concerned a jaguar would be perfectly normal there.

I thought about Michael's answer and decided that it would be wonderful if we always had the sense of wonder and adventure that comes from seeing something in the wild for the first time. The animals in our field are rejoicing tonight. I'm thankful that Jesus gives us adventures.

THE ORIGINAL SUBMARINE

When my soul fainted within me I remembered the Lord.
Jonah 2:7.

Imagine that you are watching a modern submarine. First it submerges. It travels some distance underwater and then it resurfaces. There is nothing surprising about that. But let's imagine some more. The submarine heads for land, beaches itself, and, finding a road, chugs down the highway, going some distance away from any water. Then, wonder of wonders, the submarine begins to pick up speed, wings emerge from the ship, and it takes off! The submarine now gains altitude and is soon out of sight in the clouds.

Do you think that my imagination ran away with me? Not at all! I was simply describing the ordinary behavior of any one of a number of water birds—loons, grebes, cormorants, and most ducks, for example. All of these birds are perfect submarines, but they can also move on land and they can fly.

Bird submarines have special air compartments in their bodies. If they fill these with air they can float high in the water. If they squeeze the air out of these compartments they begin to sink. They can control how low in the water they want to be by how much air they keep in their air compartments. A grebe can submerge all but its head, which, like a submarine's periscope, can turn in all directions to see what's around.

Jonah took a ride in another one of God's submarines. He was swallowed by a great fish and then he had to make camp in there for three days. For Jonah it must have been like getting down in a modern sub and not knowing how to bring her up again. He was not only down in the sea, he was down in spirit. God had to introduce Jonah to a situation where he was "like a fish out of water."

God's original subs depend on the Creator in the water, on land, and in the air. When we get into trouble over our heads and don't feel right at all, the Creator will care for us as completely as He does the water birds and just as surely as He took care of Jonah.

THE FLYING AIR HAMMER

And when he was come nigh, even now at the descent of the mount of Olives, the whole multitude of the disciples began to rejoice and praise God with a loud voice for all the mighty works that they had seen. Luke 19:37.

You probably know what an air hammer is—that deafeningly loud, rattling tool that construction workers use to break up concrete. The worker who uses an air hammer often has to wear earplugs to keep from damaging his ears.

There is a mammal whose voice, while it is a similar rattle, is up to sixty times louder than an air hammer! Maybe I had better repeat that: This animal's call is a series of sounds up to sixty times louder than an air hammer! Before you begin arguing with me, let me add that this animal is common and that you may well have seen it many times. The animal calls almost constantly, and you probably have heard it, but there is something I haven't told you.

The mammal with the loud voice is the bat. That's right—the bat! The reason you haven't noticed the volume of its call, however, is that the pitch is higher than most human ears can hear. Though the volume is exceedingly great, we hear only faint squeaks.

The bat uses its vocal sounds to find its way around and to locate food. The bat utters its sounds in rapid succession; these sounds, like machine-gun bullets, stream forth from the bat's mouth to strike whatever is in its path and then return to the bat's large ears. By this process, called echolocation, the bat is able to determine the exact location of its prey, the direction in which the prey (usually an insect) is traveling, and the speed at which it is moving. With this data the bat may be able to intercept the insect in less than one half of a second.

With sounds sixty times louder than an air hammer, the bat proclaims its presence. The people in our text today proclaimed their praises to Jesus in a loud voice. Maybe we don't have to shout as loud as an air hammer, but let's let the world know about our Jesus and His wonderful works.

MICROSCOPIC PERFECTION

Be ye therefore perfect, even as your Father which is in heaven is perfect. Matthew 5:48.

In looking at some photographs of insects taken with an electron microscope, I was struck by the perfection and the beauty of design that the unaided human eye has never beheld. Sometimes we get so used to seeing beauty in nature that we cease to be amazed by it, but here was something that defied imagination.

For example, there was a photograph of an antenna of an insect called a springtail; it was magnified two thousand times! On the surface of each section of the antenna is a design that looks like an endless interlocking mesh of chainlike patterns, each composed of a circle of six perfectly formed and precisely placed spots. And the microscopic hairs on the springtail's antennae, or feelers, each have many even tinier hairs on them. All of this detail is on the antennae of an insect that is itself so small that it takes a magnifying glass to see it!

Another example was the photograph of the leg of a common ground beetle, magnified eight hundred times. The leg has numerous spines that are perfectly formed and look like the spines on the back of some prehistoric dinosaur. Some are slender; some are long and curved, with scalelike covering; and some are short, curved, and mounted in perfectly shaped depressions along the beetle's leg. But most startling of all is the fact that sitting right on top of the leg, surrounded by all these spines, is a mite—another creature whose home is the leg of the ground beetle. The mite looks much like a horseshoe crab, with a smooth two-piece shell designed with precisely spaced tiny bumps.

When I view the perfection with which the Creator has put together living things, I am astounded at His power. Then I look at the imperfections that abound in my own life and in the lives of people everywhere. Only such a great God could make me perfect again, and I praise His name that He loves me enough to make me perfect, too.

KUDZU

For if after they have escaped the pollutions of the world through the knowledge of the Lord and Saviour Jesus Christ, they are again entangled therein, and overcome, the latter end is worse with them than the beginning. 2 Peter 2:20.

At the United States Centennial celebration in Philadelphia in 1876, the Japanese pavilion was decorated with a vine never before seen in the United States. It was a beautiful vine with large, soft green leaves, and in summer it produced clusters of reddish-purple flowers that smelled like crushed grapes. The Japanese called the vine *kuzu*.

The kudzu vine was an instant hit in the United States. At first it was used to decorate yards and became known as porch vine. Then, during the great depression, the vine was used to cover eroded gullies and hillsides in the South. Soon kudzu was a hero, as it turned all the barren ground into living green—and it did so with amazing speed.

It is now more than one hundred years since that Centennial celebration. Somewhere along the way the kudzu vine got out of hand. The vine didn't stop when it had covered the bare spots. It now covers vast stretches of former forest, where it has suffocated the trees under its overwhelming growth. The vine covers more than 7 million acres from Maryland to Texas and from Missouri to Florida. In case you don't know how much land that is, it is more than the total area of the State of Maryland or almost as much land as the country of Belgium.

Kudzu is one of the fastest-growing plants on earth—a kudzu vine can grow up to 12 inches per day. Kudzu has a taproot, like a giant turnip, that weighs 300 to 400 pounds, from which 40 to 50 vines grow. In the South during winter the vines don't die; they lose their leaves, only to pick up in spring where they left off.

The plant that was thought to be the savior of the land has turned out to be a creeping curse. Some people take the wonderful truth of salvation and turn it into a curse by attempting to take on themselves the job of covering their sins—a job that only Jesus can do.

WHERE WOULD YOU START?

Praise ye him, sun and moon: praise him, all ye stars of light. Praise him, ye heavens of heavens, and ye waters that be above the heavens. Let them praise the name of the Lord: for he commanded, and they were created. Psalm 148:3-5.

If you were asked to name the one thing in all of creation that you are most thankful for, what would it be?

Would it be the stars in the heavens—the untold billions of heavenly bodies that are spread out over billions and billions of light years of space? Or would it be the basic materials from which all creation appears to have been built—the atoms, molecules, protons, electrons, neutrinos, quarks, photons, X-rays, and the many more that we don't even know about yet?

Perhaps you are most thankful for the furry animals that you can pet or for the birds that sing. Or maybe you would name the green grass or the shade trees in the summertime or the flowers that flood the fields and meadows with color. Tell me, what would you choose?

How about the love of your mother and your father? Or how about the love that you feel for them and others? How about the smiles of those you love? All of those things were created too. God created everything good, so you can choose anything you like—anything at all! What will it be? Could you choose one thing above all of the others?

Let's not play this game anymore. I couldn't choose even ten things. The list is endless because everything is related to something else, which is, in turn, related to yet another set of things. Everything throughout nature and the universe is completely interrelated. And it is all an expression of the character of God—except where sin has done its damage.

If I had asked you to name the one *being* in the universe for whom you are the most thankful, you wouldn't have had any trouble answering at all. It is Jesus, of course. Without Him there is nothing else, and everything else without Him is also nothing.

PINEY

For the Son of man is come to seek and to save that which was lost. Luke 19:10.

Piney introduced himself to a Vermont family by slapping the family dog in the nose with his quills. The tiny orphaned porcupine was promptly adopted, provided with a cardboard-carton home, and given lettuce and wild plants that porcupines love to eat.

But the half-starved little pincushion refused to eat or sleep. He didn't even look at his food; his only response to his new family was to turn his back to them, bristle, and just dare anyone to touch him. The baby prickle-pig was so busy defending himself that he wouldn't eat, so he was force-fed a mixture of milk, honey, and a speck of salt. This ordeal required his adopted parents to wear leather jackets and heavy ski gloves to handle him without getting quilled, and most of the milk mixture ended up all over the porcupine and the person feeding him.

After several days of dealing with this stubborn baby, the daughter in the family had an idea. It seemed to the girl that this porcupine simply missed his mother and the security of a warm log. So she made a "hollow log" out of another cardboard box and gently lowered it over the baby. Then she slipped a heating pad under him. But it was her final touch that really worked—she gave him a teddy bear.

After a while the family peeked into the hollow log, and there was Piney, snuggled up to the teddy bear, sleeping—his first sleep in a week. Soon Piney began eating voluntarily, and he even became an affectionate pet, often riding around on the shoulders of family members. Piney lived with this family for about a year and then returned to the wild to enjoy the natural life of a porcupine in the woods.

I am so glad that our heavenly Father loved us so much that He sent Jesus, who came looking for us and found us when we were lost, and has provided us with such a warm and safe place with Him—aren't you?

ALEX THE PARROT GENIUS

In all labour there is profit: but the talk of the lips tendeth only to penury. Proverbs 14:23.

The old saying "Talk is cheap" means much the same thing as the proverb. Almost everyone talks. Just having the ability to talk is not the mark of intelligence, but if what you say makes sense and is marked by wisdom, then your talk is *not* cheap.

Now here is a question for you: Does a parrot know what it is talking about? Before answering, consider the case of Alex, the African gray parrot that was the subject of research by a pair of scientists studying animal communication. Alex has learned to do more than simply to repeat words at random.

The scientists wanted to find out whether the parrot could learn to recognize objects and colors and to name them. The two trainers would name various items and hand them to each other while Alex watched. When Alex would accidently repeat the name of one of the objects that he had heard the trainers mention, he was given the object to play with. Alex caught on quickly, and when the trainers tested him later, he could name all the items when they were presented to him, in any order. Alex could also tell them what color each item was.

Alex also learned to use the word *no.* If an object was offered to him that he did not want, instead of naming the object, which he could do, Alex would say No. He also said No when a stranger tried to handle him. He learned to say other things also, such as "Wanna go back." He was a smart parrot, much smarter than anyone thought that parrots were, and now no one is quite sure just how much birds can learn or how much they understand.

Remember, there is a difference between simply repeating what you have heard others say and learning to use what you say for the good of those around you. Remember, too, that we are held accountable for what we say, "for by thy words thou shalt be justified, and by thy words thou shalt be condemned" (Matt. 12:37).

PLASTIC TREES

The trees of the Lord are full of sap; the cedars of Lebanon, which he hath planted; where the birds make their nests. Psalm 104:16, 17.

Woodpeckers love dying, dead, and decaying trees. The woodpeckers are part of nature's natural janitorial crew. They feed on insects that harm trees. They literally tear apart dead limbs and trees, which hastens their decay and elimination. Woodpeckers also use dead trees and limbs for their homes. Woodpeckers need the woods, and the woods need them. But with more and more people taking the space where woods used to be, there aren't as many woodpeckers as there used to be. And when the forestry crews weed out the dead wood in the forest, woodpeckers don't have nest sites.

So a group of scientists at the Ohio State University decided to help the woodpeckers. The scientists made artificial trees— fifty-foot-tall cylinders of brown-painted soft plastic—and "planted" them among natural trees. Apparently the woodpeckers didn't know the difference between the false and real trees, or didn't care, for they pecked out roosting cavities in nearly all of the plastic ones.

But a problem arose when the woodpeckers tried to drum out their mating call on what they thought was dead wood. Normally the drumming sound of a woodpecker, which can be heard a great distance away, is used to attract a mate and to post a bird's territorial boundaries. The drumming sound made by pecking the soft plastic trees didn't ring true; the woodpeckers forsook the plastic trees and returned to real wood.

The researchers are planning to try again, this time covering the plastic trees with plywood shells that will sound off when the woodpeckers peck. It will be interesting to see whether the woodpeckers will use the fake trees. It is also interesting to note that the scientists decided to use real wood to make the woodpeckers happy. The woodpeckers like the easy digging that the soft plastic provides, but when it comes to communicating, they need solid wood. It is impossible to improve on the Creator's plan, even though it may seem that we can do so for a time.

PINK PIGEONS AND ECHO PARAKEETS

Lift up your eyes to the heavens, and look upon the earth beneath: for the heavens shall vanish away like smoke, and the earth shall wax old like a garment, and they that dwell therein shall die in like manner: but my salvation shall be for ever, and my righteousness shall not be abolished. Isaiah 51:6.

What is the rarest bird in the world? One could name any one of several birds as possible candidates, but maybe the answer should be a species with so few remaining individuals that it will probably be extinct in the not-too-distant future. The echo parakeet of the island of Mauritius fits this qualification. Only five echo parakeets were alive on the island in 1981, two females and three males, and they have not nested successfully since 1975. It is only a matter of time before these five become old and die, and then the echo parakeet will join such birds as the dodo, another native bird of the same island, which became extinct three hundred years ago, in the 1680s.

Today there are only eleven kinds of native bird left on Mauritius, and eight of them are in danger of extinction, including the echo parakeet. Another one of the endangered birds is the lovely pink pigeon; there are less than fifty of them left on the island. Young birds are being bred, with the hope that they can be released on the island and make a comeback. But the future is dim, for pink pigeons need native forest in which to live, and less than one percent of the original forest is left. What little forest there is left is overrun by black rats and marauding monkeys brought by sailors several hundred years ago. What this island needs is a savior.

Mauritius provides a good illustration of our world, a world that is falling prey to Satan and his helpers, who, like the rats and monkeys on Mauritius, would like nothing better than to eliminate every beautiful Christian on earth. But we do have a Saviour!

BREATHE EASY!

And the Lord God formed man of the dust of the ground, and breathed into his nostrils the breath of life; and man became a living soul. Genesis 2:7.

When God breathed the breath of life into Adam and Eve, He started something absolutely wonderful! Just in the breathing process alone, man has a marvelous miracle at work all the time. Without thinking about it we breathe all day and all night, every day of our lives.

Just resting, a man breathes an average of 17,300 times every day. When you realize that that averages out to more than 6 million breaths a year and about 500 million breaths in a lifetime, that is a lot of breathing. A woman, on the other hand, breathes about 28,800 times per day, or more than 10 million times per year; she will breathe almost a billion times if she lives to a good old age.

Even though men and women breathe at different rates, the amount of air that is inhaled and released is about the same—an average of 23,000 gallons of air per day. That is more than 8 million gallons per year and about 700 million gallons per long lifetime. It makes me tired just thinking about it, but my body is well equipped to handle that amount of air and that many breaths. In fact, when we are working or excited about something, the number of breaths and the amount of air increases, so the numbers given above are only low estimates. Do you see what Jesus started when He gave Adam that first breath?

The motor that does the work of breathing for us, however, is not our lungs; it is the diaphragm, which is that big muscle between the chest and the stomach. The lungs are simply very efficient and wonderful air sacs. The diaphragm is the force that fills the lungs with fresh air and expels the stale air.

We also must breathe in our Christian life. Prayer has been called the "breath of the soul." How many times a day do you pray? How much of the life-giving love and light of Jesus do you take in each time you pray?

BARK, WHINE, AND GROWL

But as he which hath called you is holy, so be ye holy in all manner of conversation. 1 Peter 1:15.

According to one scientist, all of the vocal sounds that animals make can be divided into three types: barks, whines, and growls. He based his theory on the language that dogs and their relatives use when communicating with one another.

A growl is any sound made in a threatening way by an animal that wants to appear bigger than it really is. The growl is usually a low-pitched sound that seems to be an attempt to get something by intimidation—"I'm bigger than you are and I want you to give me what I want." Sometimes, of course, it simply means, "You'd better leave me alone."

A whine, on the other hand, is the sound made by an animal wanting to seem smaller than it really is. It is usually a high-pitched sound and is often accompanied by hanging the head and tail. In effect it says, "Poor me, I'm so small. Please don't hurt me. I'm miserable. Help!"

All the sounds that aren't growls and whines are called barking. Barking is simply communicating anything from "Hi, I'm glad to see you" to "How is the hunting?" According to the theory, a wolf's or coyote's howl would be considered a bark, since it is not a growl or a whine.

Also according to the theory, these rules hold not only for mammals like dogs but for all the other mammals and birds, as well. The scolding call of a wren is its growl, the frightened peep of a baby bird is a whine, and a robin's song is its bark. Now, if none of this makes any sense to you, remember that it is just an idea that a scientist had, and it may not prove to be exactly correct. He was simply trying to make sense out of all the different sounds that animals make.

The theory could certainly apply to humans, couldn't it? You know people who growl and you know folks who whine, don't you? As Christians there is seldom a time when we need to growl or whine; simple straightforward talking—or barking, if you prefer—is sufficient.

DIRT

But the wicked are like the troubled sea, when it cannot rest, whose waters cast up mire and dirt. Isaiah 57:20.

As far as we can tell, there are no more than three references to the word *dirt* in the King James Version of the Bible, and all three of them refer to a substance that is extremely unclean. The word is not used to denote the soil in which we plant seeds, but rather to describe some detestable product of wickedness or decay. Today we use *dirt* as a synonym for *soil,* but that was not its meaning at all when the Bible was translated.

In the text above, *dirt* is used to describe the murky waters that occur in stormy seas. There are some beaches where swimming is not very good when the winds of a storm have stirred up the water to the point where it brings up the mud and mire from the bottom. The water becomes brown or black, and swimmers are loathe to go into it. The turbulance can also make the water dangerous where such predators as barracuda hunt for food; even though they don't normally bother humans, they may see only the flash of a foot in the murky water and think that it is a small fish—just the right size to eat!

Such filth is the way of the wicked. It seems that their lives are always in the midst of a storm and that they are forever churning up life's dirt—the uncleanness and filth that one should not be talking or even thinking about.

One comparison often used to describe the difference between dirt and soil is the difference between the soil in your garden and the soil on your floor, tracked in there by your muddy boots from the garden, perhaps. In the garden it is useful, but on the floor in your house it is something unwanted that you get rid of as quickly as possible.

As we come closer to Jesus we are more able to tell the difference between good soil and dirt. When we see dirt in our life we ask Jesus to clean our heart, and He does.

ALPHA AND OMEGA WOLVES

I am Alpha and Omega, the beginning and the ending, saith the Lord, which is, and which was, and which is to come, the Almighty. Revelation 1:8.

There are two extremes of importance in a wolf pack: the alpha and the omega. The alpha is the head wolf, the top dog, which is usually a male but can be a female. Whether male or female, the alpha wolf leads the pack and makes most of the really important decisions, such as where the hunt will take place and where this year's den will be located.

Omega wolves are individuals that have been cast out of the pack but are allowed to trail along behind to feed on the leftovers. If it is needed to fight off a common enemy, the omega wolf will be accepted back into the pack just long enough to help deal with the emergency; then it's back to the "caboose" for the omega.

The alpha wolf has to defend his or her position against any other wolf that would like to have top ranking. Not all alpha wolves are good leaders, any more than are all human leaders. When a particularly abusive wolf becomes top dog, its alphaship is resented by all of its subjects. You can bet that when overthrown by a wolf that is larger, faster, and stronger, the mean alpha immediately will be relegated to the omega position, where it will receive the same unmerciful mistreatment that it once doled out.

Jesus is the Alpha and Omega. He is the Alpha, King of kings and Lord of lords; at the same time, He is the Omega, despised and rejected of men. He was rejected, not because He abused anyone, but because the devil—the real outcast—wanted to be the Alpha. For a while the devil managed to appear to be in charge of the world pack, but his abusing ways will finally be found out by everyone, and all those whom he has led astray will turn on him, just as the wolves turn on mean alpha wolves. Our true Alpha will be victorious.

THE GREEN HERON'S LURE

And he saith unto them, Follow me, and I will make you fishers of men. Matthew 4:19.

Fishermen use various kinds of lures, and one of the most common—and best—types of material used to make fishing lures is feathers. To a fish there seems to be something irresistible about a feather that falls lightly onto the water.

Not long ago a bird photographer came upon a young green heron that was apparently fishing along a ditch. The strange thing about this otherwise common sight was what the small heron had in its bill. Grasped tightly between the tips of the bird's mandibles was a conspicuous white feather. The photographer became very still and set up his camera slowly, hoping that the bird would drop the feather and pose for its picture to be taken. But the photographer was completely unprepared for what was about to happen.

The heron walked slowly along the edge of the water, holding the feather and peering into the shallow water. After a few steps more the bird froze, then slowly stretched its neck out over the water and deliberately dropped the feather onto the water. The bird again froze in a typical heron pose prior to striking. Suddenly the green heron's beak shot forth into the water under the feather and came up with a small fish that had apparently been attracted to the feather. The heron then retrieved its feather lure and continued fishing along the bank in the same manner. The photographer took pictures to prove that he had not imagined the whole thing.

Just as fish are fooled by what appears to be tempting bait, people are lured into all kinds of situations. The devil, of course, has many lures. But Jesus also is calling His own to come unto Him, and when we work for Him our Christian ways become lures that attract people to Jesus. It is thus that we become "fishers of men." What kind of lure are you?

SPIDER HEAVEN

Let your conversation be without covetousness; and be content with such things as ye have: for he hath said, I will never leave thee, nor forsake thee. Hebrews 13:5.

One morning as I was fixing breakfast I looked out the kitchen window and noticed something. Between the window and the screen was a large house spider. The spider's web was fairly extensive, and it had several packages of instant food wrapped up for the future.

I wondered how that spider got in there. I checked all around the screen, and there was no crack wide enough for a spider of that size to have crawled through. The kitchen window had not been opened for months, so the spider could not have gotten in that way. The more I thought about it, the more I was puzzled. Then it occurred to me that probably that spider had crawled right through the screen when still a tiny spiderling, smaller than a pinhead.

The spider couldn't know that once it grew larger than the mesh in the screen wire it would be forever trapped between the window and the screen. I began to feel sorry for the spider, for it could never get out. Actually, I was thinking about how I would not like to be caged up like that, and I was not thinking about the situation from the point of view of the spider.

As I considered opening either the window or the screen and letting the spider out a question came to mind: How had that spider managed to live in there all this time? Maybe it wasn't in such a bad place after all. The tiny insects that the spider ate could come and go through the screen, so there was an unending supply of food. All of the spider's enemies—birds, lizards, snakes, frogs, and the like—couldn't get into that space for the same reason that the spider couldn't get out. So the spider didn't have any spider worries. That space was just about as close to heaven as a spider could hope for.

Then I thought some more, this time about my own life. I decided that even if I were imprisoned I could be content, knowing that Jesus is with me and will not leave me.

BIRDS ARE SUPER NAVIGATORS

And Elisha prayed, and said, Lord, I pray thee, open his eyes, that he may see. And the Lord opened the eyes of the young man and he saw . . . horses and chariots of fire round about Elisha. 2 Kings 6:17.

Elisha and the young man seemed to be trapped, and the youth was afraid. Elisha wasn't worried at all. Not only did he have faith in the guiding hand of God, but he was also able, with expanded powers of sight granted to him by God, to see the Lord's forces always ready to protect and deliver. He asked that the young man experience this special sight.

That God is able to grant such powers of perception should be no surprise in light of recent discoveries of the birds' ability to pick their way through darkness to exact locations year after year, traveling across trackless oceans, through fog and storms.

It has been known for some time that birds navigate by the stars. Without compass, watch, or map, they know exactly where to go by using the stars to guide them. More recently it was discovered that birds are also sensitive to air-pressure changes that are so slight that weathermen have to use special instruments to detect them. By using this sensitivity, birds can avoid storms in their path.

Also, birds are able to hear infrasound (sound so low in pitch that our ears cannot hear it) that is made by storms, waves, and earthquakes more than a thousand miles away. That means that they can hear the waves on a beach hundreds of miles away! And now we have learned that birds can see polarized light, which allows them to pinpoint the location of the sun even when the sun is behind the clouds. They know where they are going even on cloudy days.

So birds possess at least four perceptual abilities that we don't have. Just as Elisha and the youth were able to escape openly through the blinded enemies, so the birds thread their way easily through what seem to us to be impossible barriers. That is only a glimpse of the powers of perception that God, in His love, wants to open for us.

AN EMERALD RAINBOW

And he that sat was to look upon like a jasper and a sardine stone: and there was a rainbow round about the throne, in sight like unto an emerald. Revelation 4:3.

During Bible times the emerald is said to have symbolized kindness. This is certainly fitting in light of a special quality that the emerald possesses. It is one of the very few gems that appears the same color in sunlight and in artificial light. This should also be the quality of a kind person; there should be no difference between such a person's kindness in one situation and in another.

Emeralds seem to have a special value that is not affected by time. As far back as we can know from recorded history, emeralds were treasured gems. In ancient Babylon this gem was a favorite at the market. Cleopatra, queen of Egypt, had her own emerald mine from which she brought stones for her own decoration.

But just in case you should be tempted to think that the stone itself had some special power of producing kindness, you should know that Nero, the wicked ruler of Rome, had a large emerald through which he would view the fights of the gladiators.

Today the most precious emeralds come from the mines of Colombia. The other major source of emeralds is Zimbabwe, with minor sources being Russia, India, and Brazil. But large, flawless emeralds are exceedingly rare from any source and are almost never found in a jewelry store. They appear only in private collections.

There is no such corner on the market of kindness. Large, flawless crystals of kindness can be found anywhere from the ghetto to the king's palace. The source of kindness is not a mine in some faraway land, but rather it is the throne of God, which is, according to our text, surrounded by a bow of emerald green—an unchanging hue symbolizing an eternal kindness that combines the justice and mercy of God.

THEY LIVE TO EAT

Who shall change our vile body, that it may be fashioned like unto his glorious body, according to the working whereby he is able even to subdue all things unto himself. Philippians 3:21.

They are veritable eating machines. When one of these creatures hatches from its egg, it begins to eat immediately. And it doesn't stop eating for all of its life, except when it is leaving one eating place and going to another. Can you guess what we are describing? This is actually a trick question, because this creature exists in three forms after it hatches from the egg; only in the first form does it eat without stopping. We are talking about a caterpillar—a relatively small creature that eats more than you can imagine!

Take the caterpillar of the polyphemus moth, for example. In its first twenty-four days this fat green caterpillar eats eighty-six thousand times its weight at birth! Think about that for a minute. If a baby person were born weighing seven pounds and ate at that rate, he or she would have to eat 602,000 pounds of food in twenty-four days—that's twelve and one-half *tons* per day!

A caterpillar eats so much and gains weight so fast that it has to change skin often. Some caterpillars change skins as many as forty times in their short lives.

Yes, the caterpillar lives to eat. Some of you might think that it would be great to be a caterpillar, but remember that it eats only one thing—a particular type of plant. It knows what it needs, and it goes after it with incredible dedication. And when its work is done, it rests for a few days, weeks, or months and then is transformed into a completely new creature of incredible beauty and with the ability to fly. What a difference!

Symbolically we, as Christians, are to eat the body of Jesus. "Whoso eateth my flesh, and drinketh my blood, hath eternal life; and I will raise him up at the last day" (John 6:54). When our lives are dedicated to receiving the life of Jesus into ourselves, we will be changed, and when He comes, we will wear new robes and fly like the butterfly.

ALEXANDER'S DARK BAND

I do set my bow in the cloud, and it shall be for a token of a covenant between me and the earth. And it shall come to pass, when I bring a cloud over the earth, that the bow shall be seen in the cloud. Genesis 9:13, 14.

If you have ever seen a double rainbow, then you also have seen Alexander's Dark Band. This is the area between the two rainbows, and it appears darker than the sky on the outsides of the two bows. As with the rainbows themselves, this phenomenon has to do with the bending of light rays as they pass through the droplets in the rain to produce the spread of colors.

There are interesting forms of rainbows that we rarely see. For example, if you see a rainbow in the twilight of the setting or rising sun, the bow will be entirely red because of the heavy bending of the light rays through the earth's atmosphere at that time of day. Then there is the "fogbow," which is a bow that occurs in the very fine mist of fog, especially in the northern latitudes; a fogbow is brilliant white. Moonbows occur very rarely at the rising of a full moon. Moonbows look white, but that is only because they are so faint. All of the colors are there, but we can't see them. You will see more than a hundred rainbows to every moonbow that you see. If you are lucky enough to see a rainbow at the edge of a placid body of water, such as a lake, you may see what is called a "reflection bow," which is the mirror image in the water of the bow above.

The brightness of a rainbow is controlled by the size of the rain drops through which the sun is shining. The larger the drops, the more brilliant the bow. As the droplets become smaller, the rainbow fades. Thunder is said to have an effect on the colors of the rainbow, but this phenomenon has not been studied.

Rainbows were a rare and beautiful gift from God to man at the Flood. With the bow went God's promise, and every time you see a bow of any kind in the clouds, you can be assured anew that God's promises are kept.

BIRDS HEAR INFRASOUND

"Perceive ye not yet, neither understand? have ye your heart yet hardened? Having eyes, see ye not? and having ears, hear ye not?" Mark 8:17, 18.

Have you ever put your ear to a railroad track to hear the sound of a train in the distance? Long before the sound of a train reaches you through the air, the sound can be heard in the tracks, because the tracks conduct the sound waves better than the air does. What if you could hear an approaching train many miles away without putting your ear to the track? Or, what would it be like to hear waves breaking on a beach hundreds of miles away or the sound of the wind made by a storm nearly a thousand miles away? Impossible, you say. Quite right, for you and me—but not for the birds.

In an earlier reading we mentioned that birds can hear infrasound—sound that is so low in pitch that human ears cannot pick it up. And we are told that some birds are sensitive to the sounds of such things as thunderstorms, earthquakes, and even noisy machinery, even when these sounds originate more than a thousand miles away. The birds apparently know how to adjust the course of their flight on the basis of what they hear of this sort.

How wonderful it would be to hear like a bird, for then our personal world would be greatly expanded! But just as there are physical ears, there are also spiritual ears—the ears within our souls by which we listen to the voice of God speaking to our hearts. Some of us may have become all but deaf to the sound of the still small voice. If so, we need only ask for our spiritual hearing to be restored, because Jesus has promised: "He that is of God heareth God's words" (John 8:47). Being able to hear God's infrasounds opens up the entire universe to us. You remember that when Jesus was baptized, God spoke His approval of His Son. Some heard the voice of God; others believed that it was thunder. Let's pray that we will always be able to hear God's voice.

HE BOUGHT THIRTY-TWO WOLVES

But he that shall endure unto the end, the same shall be saved.
Matthew 24:13.

Jack Lynch now lives on the Olympic Peninsula of Washington with his wolves. The way he came to own them began with a magazine story that Jack read in 1960. The article told of a Dr. McCleery who had decided to help save one of the Western subspecies of wolves from extinction. Back in the 1920s McCleery had purchased twenty-five wild wolves and had them shipped to his farm in Pennsylvania, where he began to raise them. After reading about the wolves, Jack wanted to meet McCleery, so he drove from Milwaukee to the Pennsylvania farm and found McCleery, feeble, 93 years old, and worried sick over what would become of his wolves. It seemed the next thing Jack knew, he had returned home, sold his home, quit his job, and gone back to McCleery, where he paid $1,000 apiece for all of the wolves—thirty-two of them! He began taking care of them, even though he knew little about wolves.

One incident will give an example of what Lynch had to endure in the beginning. Saber, one of the large male wolves, had a hole in his fence. Jack went into the pen to fix the fence, but he forgot to greet Saber. He started to fix the hole, but suddenly Saber had him by the leg and was dragging him around the pen. Mr. Lynch blacked out, but when he came to again, he found that he had been dragged outside the gate and left there. He was unharmed but shaken. The wolf was simply saying, "If you are going to come in here, you had better knock first!" Jack picked himself up and went to tell old Mr. McCleery what had happened. McCleery looked very pleased and said, "Well, it seems as though I found the right man."

Lynch endured much before he had successfully moved the whole pack to Washington, where they live today, but he says that the struggle was worthwhile.

Anything worth having is worth fighting for. And when we endure the tests of this life, Jesus notes our endurance with approval and says, "I've found the right person."

THE BEET LEAFHOPPER

And they shall turn away their ears from the truth, and shall be turned unto fables. 2 Timothy 4:4.

By eating the leaves of beets, tomatoes, and other vegetables, the beet leafhopper does more than 10 million dollars' worth of damage to these food crops annually. Entomologists (scientists who study insects) have been trying to control these harmful pests, but have been unsuccessful until recently.

Scientists soon discovered that the beet leafhopper's call was uttered only by males to attract females. This discovery was the major breakthrough that led to the only successful control technique to date.

The scientists recorded the mating calls of the males, then constructed insect traps in the fields and placed loudspeakers, and the females came by the thousands into the traps. You see, they knew it was mating time, and that call instinctively attracted them to mate with the males they thought were uttering the call. But they were being tricked by the sounds and led to their death.

Without the females there were no eggs laid, and the number of leafhoppers was drastically reduced, saving the farmers thousands of dollars.

The beet leafhopper, of course, acts instinctively and has little if any intelligence, so we aren't surprised that such a tactic works with these insects. But what if people acted the same way? Suppose that when they heard a song played over a loudspeaker, thousands of people dropped what they were doing and rushed blindly to the source of the music. Such people certainly would be foolish, yet we see people doing some strange things these days that aren't so different from the actions of these leafhoppers.

Without asking whether the words are true, literally millions of people are doing things and buying products that are suggested in a song on the radio, on television, on a record, or at a concert. Are we acting on the basis of wise counsel, or are we doing things without knowing whether they are based on truth or fable?

THE PAINTED BUNTING

Give unto the Lord the glory due unto his name; worship the Lord in the beauty of holiness. Psalm 29:2.

If you have never seen a painted bunting, you have missed a treat. Imagine a sparrow-sized bird with a deep-blue head, a bright-red breast, and a bright-green back. It has a cute little bill, and it looks sort of fat and very friendly. That is Mr. Painted Bunting—a feathered jewel. Mrs. Bunting has a delicate beauty all her own; she is light green all over, but when the sun is at just the right angle, her feathers seem to have a special glow.

I remember the first time that I saw a picture of the painted bunting in a bird book. I was about 10 years old, and I had just been introduced to the new *Field Guide to the Birds,* by Roger Tory Peterson. I still remember the wonder and amazement that overwhelmed me as I turned the pages of that book. Two birds made my heart pound with special excitement: the scissor-tailed flycatcher and the painted bunting. Now we live on a farm where both of them nest.

In spring the male painted bunting sits in the top of a tree and sings all day while his mate builds their cup-shaped nest of grass, leaves, strips of bark, rootlets, and small twigs, and lines it with fine grass and horsehair. The nest is about four feet from the ground in a small tree, bush, or vine. I will bet that our Mr. and Mrs. Bunting are building in the honeysuckle vines along our front fence.

Soon there will be from three to five tiny white or bluish eggs marked with reddish brown, lilac, or lavender-gray. While Mrs. Bunting sits on the eggs, her mate will continue to serenade her from the top of a nearby tree. In a few days those eggs will hatch, and then it will be worktime for Mr. Beautiful, as well as for his Lady Green. There will be little time for singing as they search for seeds and small insects to feed the hungry youngsters.

We never look at the painted bunting without praising the Creator whose holiness is seen in the beauty of its plumage and is heard in the beauty of its song.

107

A PLAGUE OF TOADS

And the Lord spake unto Moses, Go unto Pharaoh, and say unto him, Thus saith the Lord, Let my people go, that they may serve me. And if thou refuse to let them go, behold, I will smite all thy borders with frogs. Exodus 8:1, 2.

Back in the spring of 1982 the folks in Longwood, Florida, might have thought that they lived in Egypt during the plague of frogs. Because of the great rains that came earlier that year, there was an incredibly large crop of spadefoot toads. There was not room in the grass and weeds and woods for all of the toads, so they began to move out, looking for homes. During the heat of the day they would hide in the shade, but by evening (and again in the morning) they were hopping. The streets were choked with millions of these teeny hoppers.

One local resident said that they looked like "little soldiers." Another said, "They all seem to be going in the same direction—they don't run into each other." And yet another said, "They're just everywhere. They're yucky!"

Cars couldn't drive down the streets without smashing them. People had a hard time finding space to step without stepping on a toad. Being overrun by toads is something that people in Longwood don't want to see happen again. The only good words about the experience came from an agricultural agent who pointed out that the frog is "the best biological insect control that you can get." I suspect that there weren't many low-flying insects that made it through Longwood.

The people of Longwood weren't so badly overrun as the Egyptians were: "And the river shall bring forth frogs abundantly, which shall go up and come into thine house, and into thy bedchamber, and upon thy bed, and into the house of thy servants, and upon thy people, and into thine ovens, and into thy kneadingtroughs" (Ex. 8:3).

Yet, even with all of that, Pharaoh hardened his heart. What does it take to convince a hardhearted person that God is in charge and that He wants to take care of us?

THE DANDY DANDELION

For the earth which drinketh in the rain that cometh oft upon it, and bringeth forth herbs meet for them by whom it is dressed, receiveth blessing from God. Hebrews 6:7.

Of all the spring flowers, the dandelion is one of my all-time favorites. Perhaps it is because it is such a hardy little flower, or maybe it is because it looks like a burst of sunshine on the green carpet of new spring grass. I collect information about the dandelion.

It seems that most folks try to get rid of the dandelions in their yards; they seem to think that it is some kind of pest that detracts from the even green expanse of the grass. Every spring the yards are full of "dandelion diggers" out to win the war with this king of beast-plants. But not all are offended by the dandelion. There is a man in Maine who digs up all the grass in his dandelion patch. He cultivates the plant as a valuable herb for his table.

The scientific name for dandelion is *Taraxacum,* which means "remedy for disorders." Every part of the plant has been used for food or medicine—the leaves, the stems, the flowers, and even the roots. The Indians dried the leaves and made a tea that was used for indigestion and for a tonic. Dandelion leaves are rich in vitamins A and C. They are best cooked by stir-frying or steaming as greens.

Dandelion roots are used as a caffeine-free coffee substitute. After the dry roots have been roasted for several hours until they are crisp and brown all the way through, they are ground.

We even have a recipe for dandelion jelly made from the flowers! And it is said that the stems can be chewed like gum, although I have never tried this.

The dandelion's name comes from the French word *dent de lion,* which means "tooth of the lion" and refers to the indentations on the margins of the leaves. Other names for this plant include fairy clock, priest's crown, blowball, and poor man's spinach.

With its beautiful blooms and its many uses, the dandelion is truly one of God's choice herbs.

A SNAIL'S PACE

Wherefore, my beloved brethren, let every man be swift to hear, slow to speak, slow to wrath. James 1:19.

One of the surest signs of wisdom is the deliberation with which a person responds to a touchy question directed at him. For some reason, we have honored the fast answer. We play games to see who can get the answer out first, to see who can identify some unknown bird, tree, or flower before anyone else. This perhaps has helped to cause us to be too quick to speak in instances where we should take a bit more time to listen or think before we say anything.

One creature that has always been known for being slow is the snail. It is certainly no great honor to be called a snail, or to have someone tell you that you are as poky as a turtle or slow as a snail. But let's think about the lowly snail for a minute.

Snails are simply very deliberate about what they do. They are in no hurry. What would they gain if they hurried? Sometimes snails stay in their shells for a long time. No one knows why they do this, but evidently if they don't need to come out, they don't.

The story is told of a supposedly dead snail that was found in Egypt. It was glued to a card and displayed at the British Museum. Several years later, the snail emerged, much to the surprise of the observers—it was in no hurry!

A snail lays down a carpet of slime over which it moves safely, even if the path is down the edge of a razor blade. It takes time to produce such a carpet, and the snail takes all the time it needs.

There are few creatures on earth as strong as the snail. A snail weighing one third of an ounce is able to pull eight pounds—nearly four hundred times its own weight. This is similar to a ten-pound baby pulling an automobile! To generate such power takes time.

Wouldn't you like to be known for your wisdom rather than for your quick tongue? Take time to think before you speak. Consider the snail, and pace yourself accordingly.

JAY HELPERS

We therefore ought to receive such, that we might be fellow helpers to the truth. 3 John 8.

God's people on earth make one large family, and we will continue to draw closer and closer to each other as His coming draws near. Then, in heaven, the family will be complete and we will enjoy the full joy of being members of the household of God for eternity.

On earth there are creatures that exhibit family helping that is worthy of our notice. One example is provided by jays—saucy birds, but dedicated family helpers, nonetheless.

Mexican jays, for instance, maintain an "extended" family flock of eight to twenty individuals. While with most birds the male and female establish a territory, with Mexican jays it is the entire flock that sets up and defends its territory. Within the flock's territory are only one or two nests, and the entire flock participates in the housekeeping chores. In one flock of fourteen jays there were two nests. Every single member of the flock fed the young of one of the nests, and eleven of the fourteen jays fed the young in the other nest. About 25 percent of the feeding was done by the actual parents of the young; the rest was done by the relatives.

Then, after the young have left the nest, the flock continues to care for them, sharing equally in their training and feeding. Pinyon jays set up nursery areas where the young are established and surrounded at all times by adult sentries that guard them while the rest of the flock goes off to obtain food for the young. After the food gatherers return and feed the young, they take their turn as sentries, and the previous sentries take their turn at food gathering.

If we, as Christians, shared the responsibilities for all of God's children as do the jays, we would have a more secure and a much safer church for God's people to enjoy. The enemy of young Christians wouldn't stand a chance.

SUPERCHIP

But thou, O Daniel, shut up the words, and seal the book, even to the time of the end: many shall run to and fro, and knowledge shall be increased. Daniel 12:4.

The angel told Daniel that his prophecies would not be understood until the end of time, when two conditions would be present—intense travel from place to place and a dramatic increase in knowledge. I find it interesting that the angel did not tell Daniel that wisdom would be increased, only that knowledge would. To me, wisdom is the God-given ability to use our knowledge for the benefit of mankind; we are told that "the fear of the Lord is the beginning of wisdom" (Ps. 111:10). But I am afraid that some make the mistake of thinking that the more they know, the better their chance to be successful in this world.

Several hundred years ago it was believed that everything that you needed to know was contained in some books called the classics. Then knowledge began to increase, and the number of books you needed to read also increased, until today there aren't enough books to hold all the information that is available. So where can we keep all of that knowledge? In computers.

Computer tapes and floppy discs now store entire libraries of books on a single shelf. Inside a modern computer there are tiny chips, about the size of a pinhead, made out of silicon (the substance that makes up much of the sand in the world). One of these tiny chips can store all of the information on several typed pages.

But they are about to be replaced by a new chip (the "superchip"), composed of a chemical called gallium arsenide, that can hold ten times more information. Each superchip contains hundreds of millions of electronic parts that will allow us to process even greater amounts of knowledge. But will we be any better off? Not unless we learn to apply the wisdom of the Creator and to use the knowledge to serve mankind until He comes.

GREEDY CHIMPS

Take therefore no thought for the morrow: for the morrow shall take thought for the things of itself. Matthew 6:34.

When the children of Israel were on their way to Canaan and God saw fit to feed them manna from heaven, He also taught them and us a very important lesson—He will supply all of our needs, but no one should take more of something than he or she needs.

When manna fell the first day, Moses told the people that they would have more the next day and that they should take only what they needed at the moment. But there were greedy people there who filled every container that they had. Manna tasted like cookies made with honey, so you can imagine how much everyone liked it. Since there was no need to gather more than was needed for a day, manna was not designed to last. The "extra" manna was rotten by morning, and the tents of the greedy began to stink. All of a sudden people couldn't *get rid* of the spoiled manna fast enough. Only on Friday did God allow the people to gather enough for more than one day, and then the Lord worked a miracle to show the importance of keeping the Sabbath holy—He made the manna keep all night and all day Sabbath instead of becoming rotten.

Perhaps a good example of the greed that some people display when they don't need to is provided by the action of some chimpanzees at a feeding station in Africa. The station was stocked with bananas, and it was maintained every day so that there were always plenty of bananas for the chimpanzees. But the apes never seemed to learn that they didn't have to hoard the fruit. They would come to the station, load up, and depart with bananas in their mouths, under their chins, under their arms, in their hands, and even between their knees. Can you imagine how funny they looked when they were trying to walk away with such a load? Obviously, they didn't get far with that many bananas.

The chimpanzees are silly, but aren't we just as silly when we don't trust in Jesus to provide for our needs?

113

WRONG-WAY SKIMMERS

I have chosen the way of truth: thy judgments have I laid before me. Psalm 119:30.

Some black skimmers (black-and-white gull-like water birds) decided to set up housekeeping on one of the parking lots of a large chemical plant on the Texas coast. The lot was covered with crushed sea shells, and apparently the skimmers thought that it was a beach and established a colony there. Years went by, and the company ran national ads showing how the skimmers could live in the midst of the smoke and smells of a large chemical-producing complex.

Then one day an executive had the shells graded off. The lot produced a nice stand of goose grass. The skimmers, which don't nest in goose grass, went elsewhere, and the company was in for some bad publicity for not continuing to take care of its skimmers. The board of managers ordered that the lot be returned to the proper condition for skimmers. This was done, but the skimmers would not return.

A wildlife expert was hired to get the skimmers back. His technique was simple. He had a pair of plastic models made to look exactly like the skimmers. He placed the decoys on the new shell lot and waited. His plan worked. When real skimmers saw what appeared to be a pair of their own kind sitting on the lot, they stopped by for a visit. Soon the lot was again covered with nesting skimmers.

Additional experiments with the decoys showed that if the decoys were facing a certain direction, arriving birds would position themselves to face in the same direction, even when they would be facing into the wind—something that no skimmer would do naturally. When they wanted the skimmers to start nesting, they put the decoys off to themselves and very close together; the next day all of the skimmers began their nesting rituals.

Jesus came to earth to show us how to live. We won't go wrong by following His example, but when we look to the many decoys that are set up by Satan to confuse us, we will very often end up going the wrong way.

TULIP TREASURE

Lay not up for yourselves treasures upon earth, where moth and rust doth corrupt, and where thieves break through and steal: but lay up for yourselves treasures in heaven. Matthew 6:19, 20.

You may be surprised to learn that tulips aren't native to Holland. They arrived there in the late 1500s from Turkey. The Dutch people became obsessed with tulips. In the early 1600s tulip trading and tulip growing had captured the entire economy of Holland, and for several years there was a craze that has been called tulipomania.

When a new variety would suddenly appear (in the form of a freak caused by a virus), its owner could name his price. It could happen to anyone—even a peasant could become wealthy overnight if a freak tulip happened to develop in his garden. One such variety, called the viceroy, was traded for all of the following: two loads of wheat, four loads of rye, four oxen, eight pigs, twelve sheep, two hogsheads of wine, four barrels of beer, two barrels of butter, a thousand pounds of cheese, a bed, a suit, and a silver beaker.

Not everyone recognized the value of the bulbs, however. A wealthy Dutchman received a shipment of goods. A sailor informed the man that the shipment had arrived. The merchant was so pleased that he gave the sailor a plate of fish to eat. Taking what he thought was an onion from the shipment, the sailor added oil and vinegar and enjoyed a hearty meal. The "onion" turned out to be a tulip bulb worth enough to feed the entire ship's crew for a year.

Before long many Hollanders had their entire estates tied up in tulip bulbs. Then the market crashed, and all they had was their tulip bulbs that no one wanted anymore. The government of Holland was on the brink of bankruptcy.

God created flowers to demonstrate the lovely graces of His character. Sin takes that which is beautiful and makes it a curse. The simple beauty of Jesus is free to everyone, yet it is so valuable that it is worth more than all of the riches in all of the countries of the world.

LUTEMBE THE JUDGE

And I saw another angel fly in the midst of heaven . . . saying with a loud voice, Fear God, and give glory to him; for the hour of his judgment is come: and worship him that made heaven, and earth, and the sea, and the fountains of waters. Revelation 14:6, 7.

The day of judgment is fast approaching. Jesus, our High Priest, is at this hour performing the cleansing service in the sanctuary of heaven. We, His people, await the hour when He will lay down the scepter and say, "It is done; the judgment of all mankind is completed." "And, behold, I come quickly; and my reward is with me, to give every man according as his work shall be" (Rev. 22:12).

Throughout the history of the tropical regions of the world, to be eaten by a crocodile is considered the visitation of the curse of God. The belief is generally that if such an end should come to a person, that person is forever banished from any hope of another life. He cannot be resurrected or saved in any way. So it was that an amazing situation unfolded in East Africa some years ago.

Lutembe was a somewhat tame crocodile living in Lake Victoria, near the village of Entebbe, Uganda, during the 1920s and 1930s. I say "somewhat tame" because, as far as we know, it is not possible to tame a crocodile completely. This famous crocodile, like most large crocodiles, enjoyed eating a person now and then. But Lutembe was considered a sacred judge who ate only people who were guilty of some evil deed. As his fame spread, so did the reverence with which Lutembe was held. Before many years had passed, the villagers had started bringing suspected criminals to Lutembe to be judged. If he ate them, they were guilty; if he did not eat them, they were set free. It was judgment by the beast.

But when Jesus comes back as the judge, His justice is tempered by mercy. We are all guilty sinners, and the beast would like to consume us all; but if we believe on Jesus and let Him live in our hearts, then we are judged by His merits. The beast may breathe fire and smoke, but he can't touch us.

THE DEVIL'S HOLE PUPFISH

For God sent not his Son into the world to condemn the world; but that the world through him might be saved. John 3:17.

The fight to save the Devil's Hole pupfish has been called outlandish. Perhaps the spending of so much money, time, and energy on a drab-looking fish that lives in only one tiny pool in a Nevada cave is a bit farfetched, but consider for a moment what is at stake for the people who don't want to see any life forms lost.

There are only about two hundred of these little fish left in the world. Their species has lived for untold hundreds of years in this Nevada cave, and they have developed an ability to cope with the environment there—a trick that is not at all easy.

The battle is between those who don't want to see the pupfish lost and a rancher who wants to use the water to irrigate his land. If the rancher used the amount of water that he claims he needs, the pool where the pupfish live would be depleted, and the fish would probably become extinct.

The case has not only been taken to court, but the last I heard, the United States Supreme Court was to decide on the fate of the Devil's Hole pupfish. The case has probably been resolved by now, and I don't know the outcome, but the point remains the same—an awful lot of concern was generated over what some have called a "worthless" little insignificant fish, which had absolutely no control over its own fate.

When I read of the fight to save the Devil's Hole pupfish, I said to myself, "I am that pupfish!" I have nothing in me that is worth saving. The Bible even says that my own righteousness is no better than filthy rags—so why would anyone want to save me? Yet my case, and yours, is up before the Supreme Court of the universe. The difference, however, is that we can choose our fate.

117

THE THYNNID LOVE STORY

For this cause shall a man leave his father and mother, and cleave to his wife. Mark 10:7.

We have been to weddings, occasions when a man and a woman are united in the love of Jesus to live together as husband and wife and as father and mother to their children. Being married is a thrilling experience that requires years of planning if it is to work the way the Lord intended when He instituted marriage in the Garden of Eden.

Let me tell you about the marriage of the thynnid wasps. Every thynnid love story begins with a female who hatches underground and crawls out of her underground home to a grass stem or weed stalk. She climbs the stalk and gets into position to attract a mate. When she is ready, she daubs herself with perfume that is irresistible to the males and begins to sing the thynnid love song. The combination of the perfume and the song brings one or more males, who have been waiting for just exactly that combination. They know what they want, and they wait for the right signals.

Female thynnid wasps are unable to fly, and they do not have the time to hunt for food; they must go about their main business of raising a family as soon as the honeymoon is over. Therefore, the male must be strong, able to fly, and know where the food supplies are.

Responding to the female's enticements, the male arrives. He literally picks her up and flies away with her. I wish I could say that they live happily ever after, but their life together is rather short. The male feeds the female and carries her with him wherever they need to go in order to find enough food. She must be healthy and fat when she lays her egg. When the time is right, the female is released on the ground, where she burrows into the earth to lay her egg.

The book of nature is full of wonderful love stories. If we just watch and listen for them, they can help us to understand how God has provided for His many creatures.

118

VORTICELLA HOLDS FAST

Behold, I come quickly: hold that fast which thou hast, that no man take thy crown. Revelation 3:11.

Holding fast is a matter of life and death. There are forces in nature that push, shove, and yank to a point that if creatures did not have the ability to hold fast, they would be blown away, washed away and drowned, or otherwise removed. The same is apparently true in our spiritual life. Once we get hold of Jesus, we are told to hold fast!

Scientists are always looking for a better glue to work under various conditions. The Eastman Kodak Company hired Jim Elman to find a glue that would work quickly under water. Why they hired Mr. Elman is a story in itself. Ever since he was in high school, Elman has had a hobby of growing one-celled animals, or protozoans, as they are technically called.

Jim Elman especially enjoyed raising a type of protozoan called vorticella (pronounced vor-ta-CELL-a). And it was this little creature that caused the Eastman Kodak Company to become interested in Elman's work. Vorticellae grow in streams and stand on microscopic threads that are held fast to the objects they are growing on by an extremely strong glue. The force of a stream could easily carry away something as small as a vorticella, but this protozoan can produce this glue, which acts instantly, even under water. While Jim Elman has learned that this substance is similar to known chemicals, he has not been able to produce the substance in the laboratory. He hopes to duplicate the vorticella's formula for the Eastman Kodak Company, and that company will use the chemical in its production of multilayered photographic film. Vorticellae have something that Eastman Kodak wants and has not yet figured out how to get. Isn't that interesting?

Jesus knows that the pull of the world is strong and that only those who are able to hold fast will make it, so He has given each of us the ability to hold fast, just as He gave such ability to the vorticella.

119

VARIATION ON A THEME BY BIRDSONG

Serve the Lord with gladness: come before his presence with singing. Psalm 100:2.

Some birds sing a monotonous string of notes that never change, while others sing endless variations that seem never quite the same. Everyone knows what magnificent songsters mockingbirds and nightingales are, and nearly everyone would agree that there isn't much variation in the clucking of a hen or the crowing of a rooster. But there is more to the subject of birdsong variation than that.

Let's consider three related species: the song sparrow, the white-throated sparrow, and the dark-eyed junco. All three of these birds nest in the same areas in parts of North America, but the songs of the three types of birds are very different.

Song sparrows were correctly named. Their singing ability has been studied for many years, and the variation in the song patterns of song sparrows seems endless. White-throated sparrows, on the other hand, learn only one song. Each population may have its particular dialect, but all of the members of that population will sing that song, and there will be little variation, even though right next door there will be a song sparrow singing endless variations.

Now the dark-eyed junco is an example of individual variation. Where studied, each individual junco may have a repertoire of up to seven songs, but these will nearly always be distinct from the next neighboring junco, who will also have up to seven songs. So in the case of juncos the variation between different birds seems to have no limit, but the variation within one bird is limited to about seven different songs.

I think that the Lord likes variation within variation. That is certainly the way He has produced the symphony of birdsongs. We can be thankful for the variations that we see in all things, including you and me. Think of those variations that make us able to sing a particular song of praise to our Lord. He recognizes your song!

JILL-IN-THE-PULPIT

The Lord knoweth how to deliver the godly out of temptations, and to reserve the unjust unto the day of judgment to be punished.
2 Peter 2:9.

The jack-in-the-pulpit is a flower that grows in the woods of the Eastern United States. It hardly looks like a flower, because it is mostly green. One or two leaves appear first, just as the forest canopy is leafing out overhead; then a single stalk bearing a slender greenish tube with a hood grows from the leaf stems. Under the hood is the actual flowering part of the plant—a slender stalk of tiny white or purplish flowers. It is this stalk that represents Jack, and the green tube in which he stands is the pulpit.

As you know, many flowers are pollinated by insects that carry pollen from the male flowers to the female flowers; there the pollen causes the eggs to produce seeds. Most plants have pollen- and egg-producing parts on the same flower, but the jack-in-the-pulpit is different. The flowers on a single plant can be male or they can be female, but they can't be both. And you never know which it will be until the flowers open. The Jack-in-the-pulpit you see can actually be a Jill-in-the-pulpit. One year the plant can have Jack in its pulpit and the next year Jill.

These plants are pollinated by tiny fungus flies that are somehow attracted into the pulpits, where they light on the flowers. Once the fungus flies are in there, they cannot fly back out or crawl up the sides; all that they can do is fall toward the bottom of the tube. So how do they carry Jack's pollen to Jill? There is a tiny opening in the base of all Jack-in-the-pulpits through which the fungus flies escape in search of a Jill-in-the-pulpit. When they enter Jill's pulpit, however, they are doomed. Again they cannot fly or crawl back out the way they came in, so they fall, but this time there is no small opening, and they are trapped in there, where they die.

What example is provided for us by these two forms of the same plant?

BIRD DECOYS ARE BIG BUSINESS

[Those who hold the truth in unrighteousness have] changed the glory of the uncorruptible God into an image made like to corruptible man, and to birds, and fourfooted beasts, and creeping things. Romans 1:23.

Making, selling, and collecting bird decoys is a very profitable business these days. There are perhaps more people than ducks being attracted by decoys! At an auction in New York in 1981, a sandpiper decoy sold for $23,000. Can you believe that! At the same auction a plover decoy went for $17,000.

Decoys were originally produced to attract birds within range of the hunter's gun or bow and arrow so there would be food for the family to eat. About a thousand years ago American Indians used decoys made of birdskins stuffed with dry grass. The wooden decoy began to be used in the mid-1800s, when shotguns became common and when professional bird hunting became a popular and profitable occupation. In recent years decoys have become useful only for sport hunting. But now the decoys themselves have become the object of the hunt; it is far more profitable to hunt the decoys than the real ducks! What a turnaround!

The decoys that are worth the most are old ones, or antiques, and new ones that are the most lifelike. The decoy craze has become so widespread that wood carvers everywhere are turning out decoys that are made only for display. Carving birds as a form of art isn't bad, but as people get further and further removed from the natural world, they become satisfied with fakes—their heads are turned by decoys that are only replicas of the real beauty of wild things. A similar condition can develop when people get so far removed from the idea of a real, living, indwelling Jesus that they begin to make idols of various sorts to represent what they believe God is like. In ancient days such idols were patterned after birds and animals. Today the idols in our lives are, perhaps, different.

Can you name some of today's idols?

THE SNAKE HANDLER

And the serpent said unto the woman, Ye shall not surely die.
Genesis 3:4.

These words are often referred to as the world's first lie, and they certainly are that. Satan, speaking through the serpent, beguiled Eve with a lie.

Bill Haast, the director of the Miami Serpentarium, handles hundreds and hundreds of deadly poisonous snakes to extract their venom. Snake venom is as valuable as pure gold. It sells for hundreds of dollars per ounce, and Mr. Haast has the job of extracting the venom. This can be done only by hand, and it means holding the snakes and "milking" the venom drop by drop from their fangs into glass vials. Haast started this career in 1948 by smuggling snakes into Miami while he was in the Air Force. Today the serpentarium is the largest producer of snake venom in the world. Besides being used in the production of antivenin, the venom is used in the treatment of such rare illnesses as Lou Gehrig's disease.

Bill Haast has been bitten by his snakes more than one hundred times, and twice he came very near death. But he has been injecting snake venom into his bloodstream in very small doses for a long time, and his blood is now considered a valuable anti-snakebite serum. It is claimed that at least twenty people have been saved by Haast's blood. Some have referred to Haast as the "man with golden blood."

Bill Haast believes that he actually did die for a few moments during one of the near-death experiences. He believes that he left his body and floated into a corner from which he watched them lift his body from the stretcher onto the respirator. He concludes the description by saying that "no one should be frightened of death." Does that sound familiar? What he is really saying is "Ye shall not surely die"! Mr. Haast may have "golden blood," but he doesn't have eternal life. Only Jesus' blood can give us life after death.

CRICKETS BRING LIFE

Ye are all the children of light, and the children of the day: we are not of the night, nor of darkness. 1 Thessalonians 5:5.

Scientists who study caves are called speleologists (pronounced spee-lee-AHL-o-jists). One such scientist was Dr. Nicholas, who studied cave crickets in Kentucky. Over a three-year period Nicholas and his assistants carefully observed and recorded the actions of 3,750 cave crickets. The speleologists put a tiny daub of fast-drying paint on each cricket. The cave was divided into twelve sections, and the crickets from each section had a different color. And since the daubs were always of a slightly different shape, it was possible to tell that each cave cricket had its own particular place on the cave wall.

The cave cricket looks more like a grasshopper than it does the crickets that most of us are familiar with. It is light brown and has large hind legs used for jumping or hopping. I suppose that you could call them cave-hoppers. Unlike many cave-dwelling organisms, and even other forms of cave crickets, these cave crickets are not blind. The reason is that they don't spend all their lives in the cave. This is what Dr. Nicholas learned.

Every night, if the temperature outside was above freezing and the humidity was above 85 percent, one third of the crickets would leave their selected homesites in the cave and go outside to feed. They would return home before daybreak with their abdomens full, and would wait for two days while the other two thirds of the crickets took their turns—one third each night. But even though they would go out of the cave, they would do so at night, when the amount of light is least. These are creatures of the darkness and the night, taking their food from plants, which get their life from the sun during the day.

There are millions of God's children who live in spiritual caves. Let us allow Jesus to shine through us to them so that they may become children of the light.

HOW DO THEY GROW?

And why take ye thought for raiment? Consider the lilies of the field, how they grow; they toil not, neither do they spin: and yet I say unto you, That even Solomon in all his glory was not arrayed like one of these. Matthew 6:28, 29.

When Jesus was preaching on the hillside that spring morning, He didn't just say, "Oh, look at the pretty flowers! Aren't they lovely!" He used the word "consider" to tell us how we were to think about the flowers. When you *consider* something, you think about it, you analyze it—you give it a whole lot more than a passing ho-hum. That is what Jesus wanted His listeners to do. So let's do that.

You may take the growth of a plant for granted, but you would be amazed at how much is involved. There are thousands of scientists in this world who have spent their entire professional lives studying how plants grow. Yet there is still more that we don't know than there is that we do know; there are still more questions than there are answers. So there is plenty to think about in "considering how the lilies grow."

For instance, what starts growth? How does a seed know when to start? What ingredients are necessary for growth to begin? The process seems very simple on the surface, as every gardener knows: You prepare the soil, you plant the seed, you water the seed, the seed sprouts, you keep the weeds pulled, the plant grows, you keep the pests away, you water some more, the plant grows, the flower blooms, the bees and other insects help in the pollination, the fruit develops with seeds inside, and the process is ready to start all over again. Is it really that simple? Think about these things and talk about them with your family and friends. You will find that we don't know as much as we think we do.

Yet somewhere in that process are the secrets of a Christian's life: how we start growing, how we keep growing in Jesus, and how we flower and bear fruit. Can you figure it out? Start with Luke 8:5-15.

THE BIG DAY THAT FIZZLED

Without counsel purposes are disappointed: but in the multitude of counsellors they are established. Proverbs 15:22.

Birdwatchers have a game called the Big Day, on which a small group of persons (usually three or four) tries to find as many kinds of birds as possible in a twenty-four-hour day. The world record for a Big Day was set in Zambia in 1975, when 288 species were found. The U.S. record is 235 species, found in Texas on April 27, 1982.

One morning a friend called me and asked me to join in on a *really* big Big Day—one during which a team of five would travel across the country by chartered jet. I worked for months getting everything lined up. We would begin in Texas, fly to Arizona, then fly to San Diego for the grand finale. I went over much of the route in advance. I stationed cars at each airport so there would be no delays. I knew exactly what the flying time would be between stops. *Sports Illustrated* magazine sent one of their editors and a photographer to record the adventure. I had talked with just about everyone except the pilot, and I had contacted five of the six airports that we would use. I had done enough, I thought. But I was wrong.

The day came. At 2:00 A.M. we began what we hoped would become the new world's record Big Day. At least we would break the North American record. But we had overlooked two things—the time it takes to get up to flying altitude and down again, and whether there would be jet fuel at the Arizona airport. There wasn't, and we had to make an unscheduled stop in Tucson when we were already three hours late. So, instead of setting a record that day, we stood at the Tucson airport and watched the sun go down on our last bird—a Gambel's quail, No. 183. I had seen more birds than that on a Big Day in East Texas!

We had miscalculated and lost because we had failed to get the counsel of certain key people.

THE QUEEN WHO GIVES HER ALL

Take heed therefore unto yourselves, and to all the flock, over the which the Holy Ghost hath made you overseers, to feed the church of God, which he hath purchased with his own blood. Acts 20:28.

When a queen ant falls to the ground from her marriage flight, she begins a life of dedicated giving that has seldom been equaled. First, she rids herself of her wings. She will never fly again, and flight muscles will be needed for food, since she will get no food for many months. She must live and feed her first young on her own body reserves.

After losing her wings, the queen begins to dig a burrow. She can afford to dig only enough to get her out of sight of possible predators. The queen ant enlarges the end of the burrow to create a small chamber, and then seals off the exit, imprisoning herself within. She can no longer secure food by foraging and therefore ceases to eat.

Now the queen waits for the eggs that her body will produce. There will only be a few at first—too many eggs the first time would overtax the reserves, and the queen would die. When the eggs hatch, the queen feeds the ant larvae from her own mouth with a substance manufactured in her body. As the ant grubs grow, they need more and more of the queen's food. The queen is now feeding her young with the very last of her reserves. But her only hope of survival is in making sure that the little ants make it to adulthood, when they will be able to feed her for the rest of her life by putting food into her mouth. Amazingly, these first grubs are able to go into the pupa, or resting, stage long before the normal time for ants. If they did not, then their need for food would starve the queen to death.

At last the young emerge from their cocoons and begin immediately to serve the emaciated queen, who gave her last gram of energy and food reserves for them. Without her they would not exist, and now, without them, she cannot live.

THE POWER AND THE GLORY

For I am not ashamed of the gospel of Christ: for it is the power of God unto salvation to every one that believeth. Romans 1:16.

The text says that the gospel of Jesus is the "power" of God. What kind of power is that? Is God powerful? How would you measure the power of God? I have an answer for that question, but first let's talk a bit about power.

What kind of power runs your home? You may use natural gas or you may use electricity, or you may use some combination of both, but you undoubtedly have some type of electricity in your home. Is electricity powerful? How do you measure electricity? The electrician measures electricity in *volts* and *amps* (which is the abbreviation for amperes). Do you know how much electrical power is in one volt or one amp?

Electric power is caused by the flow of free electrons from one place to another, usually through a wire or some other type of conductor. Voltage is the pressure with which the electrons are moving, and amperage refers to the number of electrons moving. For example, when exactly 6 quintillion, 242 quadrillion electrons pass a point in a wire within one second's time, that is one amp. If you have a heavy electrical power source and you attempt to force electrons through the wire faster, or if you try to force them through a smaller wire, the voltage goes up because the "pressure" is greater. When both the voltage and the amperage is high, the power is tremendous.

Now, let's talk about God's power. His electrical power is illustrated in a bolt of lightning, and one lightning flash may measure up to 100 million volts and 160,000 amps! Our God is certainly powerful, but is that the way to measure God's power if the gospel is the power of God?

The answer to the question "How powerful is God?" is simply this: He gave Himself, the *Creator* of all the power on earth and throughout the universe, for you and me. Nothing else was powerful enough to save us.

THE HELIOSPHERE

[God] which commandeth the sun, and it riseth not; and sealeth up the stars. Job 9:7.

In this text Job tells of the absolute power of God to control the stars. I am not quite sure what Job meant by "sealing up the stars," but I want to tell you about how our solar system—our sun and all the planets—is sealed off from the rest of the universe. Our solar system is enclosed in a gigantic bubblelike space called the "heliosphere."

The heliosphere is somewhere between 10 and 20 billion miles across. It is shaped somewhat like a teardrop, with the sun in about the center of the fat end of the droplike shape. The bubble doesn't have a "skin" as such, but the edge of this space is the outer limit of the electromagnetic radiation from our sun. During periods of heavy sunspot activity, when the sun is bellowing forth with electromagnetic radiation, the bubble swells; when the sun's surface is relatively calm, producing very few sunspots, the bubble shrinks. It is as if the bubble were taking a breath every eleven years, when the sunspots reach their peak.

Right now the spacecraft *Pioneer 10* is racing through the outer limits of this bubble, sending back messages about the levels of solar radiation and other facts never before known. Sometime in October, 1986, *Pioneer 10* will be farther from the sun than the farthest planet, and by 1990, if all goes well, the space probe will penetrate the outer edge of the heliosphere and enter "interstellar space." Scientists consider that this achievement will be the crowning success of the *Pioneer* space launches.

When I read of the accomplishments of this tiny spacecraft, I couldn't help wondering what it might feel like if Jesus were to come in the meantime and if as we travel with Him to heaven we were to pass *Pioneer 10,* sailing silently along, sending its messages back to a dead planet, with no human scientists left to listen. It would seem like such a small thing compared to the glory and magnificence that we would be enjoying as we leave the heliosphere.

WOLF IN SHEEP'S CLOTHING

Beware of false prophets, which come to you in sheep's clothing, but inwardly they are ravening wolves. Matthew 7:15.

Jesus drew most of His illustrations from nature—from the things that people were familiar with. In that way, even if they might not be able to grasp what He was trying to teach them, people could remember the nature story or illustration, and the Holy Spirit could teach them the lesson as they thought about the words of Jesus.

When Jesus used the words of our text for today, He was quoting a familiar saying of the day. The idea of a "wolf in sheep's clothing" came from one of Aesop's six fables about wolves. By Jesus' time these stories had been told for several hundred years. According to legend, Aesop was a slave who won the favor of the king because of his clever sayings. When Aesop wanted to get a point across to the people, rather than insult them or hurt their feelings he came up with the clever idea of replacing people in the stories with animals. The trouble with that, however, was that after several generations, people began to believe that the animals in Aesop's fables behaved in the wild as they did in his stories.

When Jesus used the phrase so familiar to everyone, He was not even hinting that wolves would actually try to disguise themselves as sheep to catch a meal. He was using the same good method of telling stories used by Aesop, but Jesus wasn't afraid to let it be known that He was talking about people—about false prophets, in this case. Jesus' listeners knew about the wolves that came in and carried away their sheep if they weren't careful, and they knew about the fable. By putting two and two together, they could come up with the truth about their religious teachers—those who were teaching them error every day. Later Jesus came right out and identified the false teachers, but here in the Sermon on the Mount He simply left His hearers with the idea of the wolf in sheep's clothing.

THE PROMISE IN THE SAND

Fear ye not me? saith the Lord: will ye not tremble at my presence, which have placed the sand for the bound of the sea by a perpetual decree, that it cannot pass it: and though the waves thereof toss themselves, yet can they not prevail; though they roar, yet can they not pass over it? Jeremiah 5:22.

How would you describe sand? What is it? Would you say that it is tiny rocks? How many tiny microscopic rocks would you have to have before you had a sandy beach? Where did sand come from? How did it get where it is? What is sand made of? There are many questions about sand, but there is a promise that is present in every stretch of sandy beach. The promise is found in our text for today. The sand is God's boundary for the sea.

Did you know that sand is a more solid wall for the ocean than are rocks? Sand has the ability to absorb tons and tons of water between all the grains on the beach. The water acts as a glue, holding the sand together and making it impossible to move even in the heaviest pounding surf. Dry sand blows away and even washes out, but wet beach sand just washes back and forth and stays put.

Sand is made of many different kinds of rock. Some sand is made of quartz, while other sand is made of limestone. There is sand made of tiny pieces of shells, and there is jet-black sand made of obsidian. There is also sand made of pink coral and greenish sand composed of molten rock that came from volcanoes long ago. In Australia there is a unique type of sand that is composed entirely of tiny stars—the skeletons of one-celled animals called *forams.*

While the mightiest ocean cannot move the sand very far on the beach, the wind can move even the largest dunes of dry sand. God made the beaches to be a barrier, and His promises are sure. The beach will hold the sea. Sometimes tidal waves overflow the beach momentarily, but the sea returns and the sandy beach is still there.

ESTRILDID FINCHES AND WIDOWS

Let both grow together until the harvest: and in the time of harvest I will say to the reapers, Gather ye together first the tares, and bind them in bundles to burn them: but gather the wheat into my barn. Matthew 13:30.

The tares described in this text were probably a plant known as darnel. Some varieties of this plant are even poisonous. Darnel is indistinguishable from wheat until the harvest, when the difference between it and wheat is obvious and the poisonous weeds can be separated from the good wheat. Two bird groups in Africa exhibit the same difficulties during the growing stages.

The first group is the Estrildid (pronounced es-TRILL-did) finches, of which there are 125 different kinds. The nestlings of every one of the different Estrildid finches have a different set of markings on the inside of their mouths. The melba finch nestling, for instance, shows maroon, white, and light-blue markings in its mouth. The purple grenadier, on the other hand, has markings in white, yellow, orange, and blue—the blue is a different color blue from that of the melba finch, and it is in a different place. And so it goes; each species has its own special design for the mouths of its young. The adult birds will not feed young that don't show the proper colors.

The second group of birds is the widow birds. The widows lay their eggs in the nests of Estrildid finches, and let the finches raise their young. Each kind of widow bird lays its eggs in the nest of only one kind of Estrildid finch, and when the young widow bird hatches—guess what? Its mouth exhibits exactly the same colors as the other nestlings in the finch nest! The nestling paradise widow bird has the same colors as the melba finch, and the straw-tailed widow bird shows the same colors as the purple grenadier, and so forth.

Not only do the nestlings' mouths look alike, but the eggs and the bodies of the nestlings of the two kinds always look alike until they are grown. Then there is a remarkable difference.

VIROIDS AND DALTONS

And lead us not into temptation, but deliver us from evil: For thine is the kingdom, and the power, and the glory, for ever. Amen. Matthew 6:13.

They are so little that only large ones have ever been seen even with the most powerful microscopes, and they are so tiny that their weight is expressed in terms of the weight of hydrogen atoms—the world's lightest substance. They are viroids, named that because they are like viruses.

Have you ever heard of spindle tuber, chlorotic mottle, hop stunt, cadang-cadang, avocado sun blotch, or tomato bunchy top? These are all plant diseases caused by viroids. They are only a few of the many plant problems caused by these tiny but terrible germs.

Scientists measure the weight of such ultrasmall things as viruses with a measure called a dalton. One hydrogen atom weighs one dalton, and a hydrogen atom is the smallest atom, consisting of only one electron and one proton. Now, a virus is so small that it can get into a microscopic bacteria, and viruses weigh from 3.5 million to 40 million daltons. The viroid that causes spindle tuber in potatoes weighs only 130,000 daltons— you could put thirty thousand of them into one smallpox virus.

A viroid invades a healthy plant cell with a coded message that it presents to the cell's central office with orders to make more viroids. The healthy processes of the cell are suddenly reordered to turn out viroids, and before long there are untold millions of the germs overwhelming the entire plant. What that tiny coded message is continues to mystify scientists.

There is almost no possible way to keep viroids from spreading and doing their damage, and the problems they cause seem to be increasing all over the world. How much like sin these viroids are. There is no way that we can avoid the results of the sin that is all around us, but we do have the promise of our Saviour that He will keep us from being overwhelmed by the viroids of the devil.

EVERYBODY'S KEEPER

And the Lord said unto Cain, Where is Abel thy brother? And he said, I know not: Am I my brother's keeper? Genesis 4:9.

You remember the story. Cain had killed his brother and was lying to avoid the responsibility of what he had done. It is impossible to avoid responsibility for our actions, but it is also impossible to avoid some responsibility for our fellow men. All of nature teaches us that every living thing is in some way dependent on or responsible for all other living things. We share the same planet, we all breathe the same air, and we all share the natural resources of the earth. Also, throughout nature there are literally millions of examples of interdependency between different types of animal life and plant life.

There is a bird called the curlew, which is about the size of a Bantam chicken. A scientist captured a curlew and closely inspected it for feather lice. All birds have these lice, and they don't usually represent a significant problem to the bird. In this particular case the scientist wanted to find out just how many different kinds of lice were living on one bird. Although it is difficult to believe, the ornithologist reported that on that one bird there were about one thousand species of feather lice. That doesn't include all of the other microscopic creatures living on and inside the curlew. You can see why birds have been called flying zoos.

You would be amazed if you knew how many different kinds of microscopic organisms live on and in your body. Perhaps we could call ourselves walking zoos. But our carrying these organisms is normal; it is only when these body dwellers cause disease that they become problems.

There are many different kinds of people living on this one planet, and as long as they get along and don't become "disease-causing" there is no problem. However, there is one disease that is transmitted universally in this world—you could call it the sin disease. You and I have the option of being disease-causing agents on earth or of living together in harmony by the grace of Jesus. He is the only one who can heal us from the sin disease.

DECEIVED BLACKBIRDS

For there shall arise false Christs, and false prophets, and shall shew great signs and wonders; insomuch that, if it were possible, they shall deceive the very elect. Matthew 24:24.

Suppose someone who brought you a written note said that he was doing so at the request of your father. Would you simply take the messenger's word, or would you check the note and determine whether or not your father would send such a message? Suppose the message was contrary to everything that you knew about your father. Would you act on the message, or would you check it out?

Mockingbirds are well known for their ability to utter the calls and songs of other species. One ornithologist decided to see whether the mockingbird's calls were good enough to deceive the birds that were being mimicked. The scientist recorded a mockingbird singing the song of a red-winged blackbird. The ornithologist also recorded the songs of real red-winged blackbirds. He then took both recordings and played them in the territories of ten singing male red-winged blackbirds to see whether they would respond to a sound representing an intruder. In every instance, the blackbirds could not tell the difference between the call of their own kind and the call of the mockingbird.

There are many people in the world today who claim to have new light from our Father in heaven, but the various songs they sing don't agree. These people all claim to be singing the same song that Jesus sang, so to speak, and they claim that they know what Jesus teaches. How can you tell which song is right? Let's pray that we have more sense than the blackbird, who can be deceived by a mockingbird. Only by prayerfully studying the Word of God and comparing what people say and how they live to that Word can we know for sure. "To the law and to the testimony: if they speak not according to this word, it is because there is no light in them" (Isa. 8:20); they are mockers and deceivers.

WATER'S WONDERS

And the Spirit and the bride say, Come. And let him that heareth say, Come. And let him that is athirst come. And whosoever will, let him take the water of life freely. Revelation 22:17.

Water is perhaps the most important substance on earth. I am sure that it was no accident that water played the central role in the process of both the second and the third days of Creation week. We take water for granted, but without it we would be almost nothing.

Our bodies are 65 percent water. The body of a frog is 78 percent water, and that of a jellyfish is 95 percent water. Every living thing is dependent on water for its existence. Furthermore, we are dependent on water for the temperature that sustains life on this planet. An enormous amount of the sun's energy that strikes this earth is absorbed by the world's water. If much of the sun's energy were not absorbed by the oceans and lakes of the world, we would all bake under daytime temperatures of nearly 300 degrees Fahrenheit, and we would freeze at night. Water is essential to our lives!

We think that we know a lot about water, but there is far more that is not known. For example, why do water molecules behave the way they do in different situations? Most substances shrink when they become cold, but not water—it shrinks until it freezes, and then it expands. The expansion of freezing water has powers that are incredible. For example, if you take a hollow iron ball, with walls one quarter of an inch thick, fill it with water, and freeze it quickly in a dry-ice solution, the ball will explode like a bomb, and pieces of shrapnel from the iron ball will be shot with such force that they will penetrate deep into solid steel walls.

Just as water was important during Creation, it is also interesting that throughout the Bible Jesus used water as an example of His life-giving and life-sustaining ability. Jesus is water for a thirsty soul, and He also has all the power to destroy sin.

e a m e u

A NEST OF NAILS

And I will fasten him as a nail in a sure place; and he shall be for a glorious throne to his father's house. Isaiah 22:23.

In this text the nail represents Jesus, whom the prophet foretold would establish a sure government upon whom all His people could depend. In several places in the Bible the nail is used to represent Jesus.

I have a picture of a nest that was built by a pair of wrens in Mr. Kennedy's workshop in Kerrville, Texas. It is a remarkable nest built of almost nothing but nails. You could say that these wrens had heard someone say that in order to build a good house you have to have some nails. But since no one ever heard of birds building their nests with nails, why did these tiny wrens choose to build their home that way?

Mr. Kennedy had a small fan installed in the wall of his workshop. It was through this opening, between the blades of the fan, that the wrens got into the shop. But the opening wasn't large enough to allow them to bring in the sticks that they normally would use to build a nest, so they had to use the nearest thing to sticks that they could find. They looked around, found the cans of different sizes of nails, tacks, and screws, and began to use them. That makes sense, doesn't it?

When the nest of nails was completed, the wrens lined it with shavings and other types of softer material that they found in the shop. It was in this sturdy nest that their little ones were hatched.

We want very much to build a home in the earth made new. We can't take the things of this world with us to use in building our home there, so we will have to use whatever building materials Jesus provides. And just as Jesus has been called the Chief Cornerstone of a house, we could also say that we want our heavenly home built with the sure qualities of that nail that Isaiah described.

BEETHOVEN AND ICARUS

The Father loveth the Son, and hath given all things into his hand. He that believeth on the Son hath everlasting life: and he that believeth not the Son shall not see life; but the wrath of God abideth on him. John 3:35, 36.

Beethoven is a mountain gorilla. Until recently he was head of his band of fourteen gorillas living on Mount Visoke in Rwanda, Africa. He is at least twenty-five years old and was the undisputed leader of the group for at least thirteen years. To be a group leader in the mountain gorilla community, a gorilla has to be a male that is at least twelve years old—the age at which the hair on his back grows in silver. Such mature males are called silver-backs. The silver-back leader is responsible for the group, and he must see to it that all of the members of the group adhere to all of the rules of gorilla country.

Beethoven has been grooming the only other silver-back in the group to be his successor. The younger silver-back is called Icarus and is about 17 years old.

The "law of the jungle" is a rigid set of rules by which wild animals survive. In order for Icarus to show that he was ready for leadership, he had to perform an act in accordance with the law of the jungle. One of Beethoven's two old females became ill. Since she was no longer able to bear young, she was not needed in the group; now that she was ill, too, she was an unnecessary burden to the group. While Beethoven stood by, Icarus put the old female to death. Then Icarus took Beethoven's place in the center of the group, and Beethoven withdrew to the edge of the group, thereby giving up his leadership role.

I am glad that we don't have to live by the law of the jungle. Jesus came to this world, joined our group, and proved Himself worthy to be our leader, not by harming someone thought to be useless, but by dying Himself for every man, woman, and child—even for the person that some might think is useless. We have a wonderful group Leader.

THE RATHBUNI SALAMANDER OF PURGATORY CREEK

He turneth the wilderness into a standing water, and dry ground into watersprings. And there he maketh the hungry to dwell, that they may prepare a city for habitation. Psalm 107:35, 36.

One of the strangest creatures ever unearthed was found in 1895 near San Marcos, Texas, when some well-drillers were attempting to create an artesian well for a fish hatchery. The well-drillers sank a shaft 188 feet down to reach an underground stream called Purgatory Creek. With the water that came from the well came a creature never before seen by human eyes, and probably never seen before by any eyes.

There, living deep in the recesses of the earth, was a type of salamander not known even from caves. Rathbuni's salamander, as it was called, has no eyes; in fact, it has almost no head. Its body is extremely slender—grotesquely so—and tapered at the head end to a blunt, spoonlike snout. Its legs are abnormally long, helping it to search wide areas for food with minimal effort and helping it to stand tall and be better able to sense movements made by tiny swimming organisms that float by. The amount of available food in Purgatory Creek is incredibly low. Limnologists (those who study freshwater life) are amazed that such an animal can exist in such a food-poor environment.

Rathbuni's salamander has a much more highly developed lateral-line organ than most water-dwelling creatures. The lateral line is a line of special movement sensors along the side of most water-dwelling creatures. It is this organ that enables a group of fish to swim in such a well-schooled manner. The more sensitive the lateral-line sensors are, the easier it is to detect movement in the surrounding water.

The creative life force that came from God at Creation is so strong that it is constantly at work helping the descendants of Eden to survive in situations that seem impossible to us. Can we ever doubt that God will take care of us?

THE TERMITE FACTORY

Many, O Lord my God, are thy wonderful works which thou hast done, and thy thoughts which are to us-ward: they cannot be reckoned up in order unto thee: if I would declare and speak of them, they are more than can be numbered. Psalm 40:5.

Sometimes I am as amazed as the psalmist by the wonders that God has created. This is the way I feel about what goes on inside of termites. There are millions and billions of these tiny creatures all over the world, and each one of them is a microscopic factory with a number of different organisms working inside, each carrying out its own specific part of the task at hand. And with most termites the task at hand is eating and digesting wood.

How would you like to wake up every morning and have the table for breakfast or perhaps eat the kitchen cabinet or the bookshelves in the den. Regardless of what you chose to eat, it would always be wood and would be the most wonderful banquet that you could imagine. Termites look forward to spending their days chomping wood, but that is not the most amazing thing about termites.

Inside a termite are many different microscopic creatures: there is a protozoan, or one-celled animal, and a number of different kinds of bacteria. The protozoan has tiny hairlike paddles with which it moves about, digesting the wood that the termite eats and sends down to it. Sometimes among these hairlike paddles are found one of the types of bacteria, spirochetes (pronounced SPY-ra-keets), that live on the body of the one-celled animal and probably parasitize it (feed on it). The protozoan lives on the termite, the bacteria live on the protozoan, and the termite benefits from both. So the action going on inside the termite is a veritable factory, with many workers pulling together to get the job done. Isn't it amazing! God's creative genius knows no bounds!

BLUEBIRD HEAVEN

They helped every one his neighbour; and every one said to his brother, Be of good courage. Isaiah 41:6.

Isaiah's description of the way the island nations worked together against a common foe is also a wonderful description of how we, as Christians, should relate to one another. When a member of our community, our church, or our family suffers a tragedy, we should pitch in and help until that person is back on his feet. The family life of bluebirds is a perfect example of such assistance.

Bluebirds are unique in one respect: they seem to get along with one another extremely well. They spread themselves out over an area so that they don't have to fight for the same grasshopper, but when something happens to the parent bird of a nest, the others in the neighborhood come to help feed the babies.

One brood of bluebird nestlings lost its father. Did the babies suffer? Not in the slightest. Two other females came to the aid of the widowed mother bluebird; one was an unmated female from the area, and the other was a female from an earlier brood of the season—an older sister of the babies in the nest.

In another instance, a pair of bluebirds had just finished raising one brood and had another brood of nestlings seven days old when the mother bird died. In this case, the father bird was joined in caring for the brood by two of the males from the earlier brood; these two older brothers were only eight weeks old and were willingly helping Dad take care of the babies. Those boys worked from dawn to dusk every day for nearly a month until their little brothers and sisters had left the nest and were on their own. There is no lack for love around a bluebird house.

Evidently, when there is a loss of either parent in a bluebird family, not only the older children but all of the available neighbors as well come to help willingly, just as though it is their appointed task.

BUMBLEBEE MOTHERS

She looketh well to the ways of her household, and eateth not the bread of idleness. Proverbs 31:27.

Did you know that there are more than two hundred different kinds of bumblebees? They live all over the world, occurring from the barren mountaintops of the far north to tropical jungles at the equator.

Unlike the honeybee, which loses its life when it stings an enemy, the bumblebee can use its painful stinger over and over again. But this black-and-yellow bee uses its stinger only to protect itself.

Bumblebees live in colonies something like honeybees, but more often than not their nest will be underground in a hole excavated by another animal, such as a field mouse. The queen, who establishes a new colony each spring after hibernating all winter, may also choose a hollow tree or other secluded spot in which to nest.

At first the queen has to do all the work herself, but when the first workers hatch she has lots of help, and the colony may produce as many as four hundred children, not one of whom needs to be told to do the chores. When there is a rare complaint the queen, with a quick butt of her head, puts the negligent child back into line swiftly but kindly. She is a good mother, and she takes the best care of her nestful of baby bumblebees.

In writing of the virtues of a good wife and mother, Solomon could just as easily have described the industrious ways of the queen bumblebee. Mothers have a way of working tirelessly, with little or no thanks, taking care of the house, preparing the food, and rearing the children. There is little time to rest. Solomon goes on to say of such a mother, "Her children arise up, and call her blessed." The next time you see a bumblebee, ask yourself whether or not you are doing your part to help your mother take care of the many things that she has charge of as queen of your house.

GREEN BLOOD

And to every beast of the earth, and to every fowl of the air, and to every thing that creepeth upon the earth, wherein there is life, I have given every green herb for meat: and it was so. Genesis 1:30.

It was way back in 1818 that two French chemists discovered *chlorophyll*. The name of the substance means "green leaf" because it is the green substance that makes leaves green. Later experiments showed that this mysterious substance is involved in the production of glucose, which is the combination of water and carbon dioxide that plants produce as the basic food source for all the animals on earth. But the makeup of chlorophyll was still unknown for almost one hundred years after its discovery.

In 1912 the chlorophyll code was cracked to reveal that a molecule of this miracle substance is composed of exactly one atom of magnesium linked to 136 atoms of nitrogen, carbon, and oxygen. That in itself was not so startling, but another fact that was already known made the composition of chlorophyll a stunning discovery. If you take that one lone magnesium atom and replace it with one lone iron atom, you have essentially produced a molecule of red blood! The formulas are so close to the same that scientists nicknamed chlorophyll "green blood."

One of the greatest arguments in favor of Creation by God, as set forth in the book of Genesis, is the fact that there is so much similarity between all forms of life. God apparently started with a basic formula for living things, then varied it just enough to give us all the different animals, birds, fish, flowers, trees, butterflies, moths, and every other kind of life that was created on the third, fifth, and sixth days of Creation.

Jesus likes variety, but He also likes order. Although He made us all different, there are basic rules of living that keep us happy and healthy.

HELICONIAN HYPOCRITES

And when thou prayest, thou shalt not be as the hypocrites are: for they love to pray standing in the synagogues and in the corners of the streets, that they may be seen of men. Verily I say unto you, They have their reward. Matthew 6:5.

Some of the most beautiful butterflies in the American tropics are the many different kinds of heliconian butterflies. This family of butterflies is perhaps best known for its practice of mimicry—copying one another. The caterpillars of many heliconians feed on plants that provide them with an internal chemistry that is poisonous or very distasteful to birds. A bird usually needs only one taste of these caterpillars to learn not to bother heliconians again.

Other kinds of butterflies and even various families of moths mimic some of the heliconians that have such safety from the birds that would prey on them. But that is not all—the protected heliconians are even imitated by other heliconians that would taste delicious to birds, but since they look just like their distasteful cousins, birds generally leave *them* alone, too.

You could say that the bad-tasting heliconians have their protection inside. By their beautiful outward appearance they let the enemy know that they are not to be touched. But the heliconians who mimic their safeguarded cousins can only put on the *appearance* of being protected. They go about their tropical paradise in showy display of something they are not. They are true hypocrites in the butterfly world, for they do not have the true protection on the inside. Oh, they are beautiful! They dance in the sunshine like the best of those that are protected from within, but when the enemy happens to take a peck at them, which happens now and then, they are quickly consumed. The heliconians that are protected from within are almost never eaten, because their bad taste is sensed immediately, and they are dropped.

STRANDED ON ATTU

And it shall be said in that day, Lo, this is our God; we have waited for him, and he will save us. Isaiah 25:9.

The island of Attu is the outermost island of the Aleutian chain in Alaska, and it is the westernmost point in the United States. It is actually in the Eastern Hemisphere, it is so far west, if you can figure that out.

In the spring of 1978, several of us visited Attu to study the migration of birds there and to enjoy the beauty of this remote piece of God's world. The only people who permanently occupy the island are several dozen men on temporary assignment at a Coast Guard station. Otherwise, the only living things are the birds, a few imported foxes, several tiny trees planted during World War II, and an endless ground cover of tundra plants.

We had originally planned to stay two weeks, but the weather was so bad that all but one of us decided to leave on the eleventh day. There was a runway on the island but no radar or lights, so the plane's pilot had to be able to see clearly to land. Often, for days at a time, Attu is covered with fog so thick that no plane can land.

There was drizzling rain on the day when we were to leave, and thick fog surrounded the island. We feared that the plane from Anchorage, 1,400 miles to the east, would not be able to land and would have to return without us. As the time for the plane's arrival approached, I thought about how we are stranded on this world. There was no way off the island of Attu except by taking a plane. There is no way off this world except through Jesus.

Anxious eyes watched the sky, and I praised the Lord when, at the last hour, the fog cleared just enough to let the sun shine through and give enough visibility for the plane to land. First we heard and then we saw our plane coming through the golden haze of the clearing in the sky. A cheer went up from everyone waiting, and I thought how much more significant will be the cheer when Jesus comes in the clouds of heaven.

Carmen

21-DEGREES-NORTH VENT FISH

*And though they hide themselves in the top of Carmel, I will
search and take them out thence; and though they be hid from my
sight in the bottom of the sea, thence will I command the serpent,
and he shall bite them. Amos 9:3.*

Amos is telling of the complete ability of God to locate His
creatures on earth. While it is quite unlikely that Amos knew
much about the ocean, certainly God was aware of the depths of
the sea. The only sea that Bible writers knew much about was
the Mediterranean Sea, but since there were no submarines or
other means of going down to the bottom, they related to the sea
as a place where the bottom was so deep that it was known only
to God and to the sea creatures that He had made. They couldn't
even imagine how deep it might be.

There are still millions of square miles of the ocean's depths
that not only are unexplored but have not even been touched. No
one knows what might be there. Every year new and
astonishing things are found on the bottom of the oceans. For
example, three eellike fish were recently brought up from 8,500
feet below sea level about 120 miles south of the tip of Baja
California. These fish were like none ever before seen, but they
died on the way up from the bottom, so their habits remain
unknown. All that is known about them is that they are
pinkish-white, they are eight to twelve inches long, and they
have two eye-spots and small, prickly teeth.

Since they were taken near volcanic hot-water vents on the
ocean floor, 21 degrees in latitude north of the equator, they
have been named the 21-degrees-north vent fish. When they are
studied more thoroughly, they will probably be given a more
appropriate name, but for now, that is what they are called.

The all-seeing eye of the Creator knows all about the
21-degrees-north vent fish, living there in the depths of the sea.
Jesus knows why the fish is there, what it eats, and how it came
to be there. He knows everything!

mama

THE MOUNTAIN THAT EXPLODED

Therefore be ye also ready: for in such an hour as ye think not the Son of man cometh. Matthew 24:44.

At exactly 8:31 A.M. on May 18, 1980, Mount St. Helens exploded with five hundred times the force of the atomic bomb that ended World War II. The entire top of the mountain was blown away, leaving it 1,300 feet lower than it had been. A cloud of ash rose twelve miles high above the mountain, and tremendous slides of mud made of ash mixed with snow flowed down the slopes, crashing through the valleys and causing death and destruction beyond belief; what the mud didn't destroy, the clouds of ash and poisonous gas did.

Harry Truman lived with his sixteen cats just five miles north of the peak. As the threat of eruption grew greater, he was told repeatedly to leave. But his words were, "No one knows more about this mountain than Harry, and it don't dare blow up on him." On the eve of the eruption Harry was watering his lawn, apparently unconcerned about the danger. No one ever saw Harry or his cats again. The next morning his lovely camp by Spirit Lake was nothing but a steaming mass of gray mud and water.

David Crockett, a TV photographer, was at the base of Mount St. Helens when she blew. He heard a roar and looked up to see a wall of mud coming directly at him. Because he was on slightly higher ground, the wall of surging mud divided and swept past him on both sides. As the ash cloud settled over him, he spoke these words into his tape recorder, "I am walking toward the only light I can see. I can hear the mountain rumble. ... The ash ... burns my eyes. ... It's very, very hard to breathe and very dark. If I could only breathe air. God, just give me a breath! ... It's either dark or I am dead. God, I want to live!" Crockett lived. He was picked up by a rescue helicopter.

Jesus is coming soon; the rumblings are all around us. We must be ready. We can't survive by ignoring the warnings any more than could Harry Truman. And, as did David Crockett, we must move toward the only light that we can see in this dark world. That light is Jesus.

147

Jose

INDICATOR PLANTS

For he shall be as a tree planted by the waters, and that spreadeth out her roots by the river, and shall not see when heat cometh, but her leaf shall be green; and shall not be careful in the year of drought, neither shall cease from yielding fruit. Jeremiah 17:8.

In the Bible, God has used plants, particularly trees, to indicate types of persons—the types that we should be and the types that we should avoid being. You would have no trouble recognizing the type of person being described in this text, because he or she is like a well-watered tree.

Plants can also be used to indicate the presence of certain minerals in the soil in which they grow. These plants are called *indicator plants*. Explorers and dwellers of the dry lands of the world learned quickly to locate water by looking for indicator plants. In Central Asia, for instance, a plant called Syrian rue has been used for thousands of years to find water sometimes as deep as one hundred feet below the surface.

In 1810 a geologist on the Maryland-Pennsylvania border noticed areas where the holly leaves were yellow with green veins. He guessed that these holly plants were feeding on high concentrations of one or more minerals underground. The geologist was right; the mineral was chromite—a chromium-containing ore that later was mined commercially there.

Scientists have learned to read the plants in order to discover ores of a number of minerals. For example, large amounts of nickel or cobalt will cause white patches on leaves. Soil rich in manganese will produce plants that are larger than usual, and where uranium is present the plants may be either very small or very large. In the early days of exploration for the development of atomic energy, plants were used as primary indicators of uranium in the Western United States.

Did you know that our lives also indicate what we have been feeding upon, "for out of the abundance of the heart the mouth speaketh" (Matt. 12:34).

Cornen

THE LAKE OF LOT

All these were joined together in the vale of Siddim, which is the salt sea. . . . And they took Lot, Abram's brother's son, who dwelt in Sodom, and his goods, and departed. Genesis 14:3-12.

The Dead Sea is one of the world's natural wonders. The Arabs call this sea the Lake of Lot, because it occupies much of what was the fertile plain that Lot chose for the home of his family. It was here that a rain of fire and brimstone destroyed the wickedness of the cities of the plain. But first, God provided a way of escape for Lot and for anyone who would join him in leaving the cities. The extent of the wickedness in those cities is perhaps illustrated by the fact that even angels from heaven could convince only Lot, his wife, and two daughters to leave Sodom. Even Lot's wife was loathe to leave and, in her longing to be back in the city, lagged behind and became a pillar of salt.

We don't know exactly what happened that day on the plain, but the result apparently left a deep canyon in the earth, with no outlet to the sea. The canyon filled with water and today is called the Dead Sea—1,300 feet below sea level!

From the river Jordan and other streams that flow into it, the Dead Sea receives an average of about 6.5 million tons of water daily. Because the region is so hot and dry, almost that much water evaporates from the sea surface daily, so there is only a very slow increase in the size of the lake. While the water evaporates, the minerals are left behind; there is now so much salt in the water that it is impossible for a person to sink in the water. You can literally float in a sitting position with your head and shoulders and feet out of the water.

We are told that in the last days the whole world will be as wicked as was Sodom. Again, God has sent His angels—three of them (Revelation 14)—to warn us of the coming destruction. This time the result will be a dead earth, not just a lake. How many of us are ready to leave without a backward glance?

Montecito (handwritten)

SUNDI

For the Lord himself shall descend from heaven with a shout, with the voice of the archangel, and with the trump of God: and the dead in Christ shall rise first. 1 Thessalonians 4:16.

Let me tell you the story of Sundi, a purple martin who broke a wing when she flew into the side of a house in Wisconsin one Sunday afternoon in August. She was rescued by the couple next door.

It was late in the season, and Sundi's relatives, who lived in the martin houses in the yard, would be heading south soon. Her wing could not heal fast enough for her to join them, but with the help of a very sensitive veterinarian Sundi improved quickly, and before long she could sit on a perch and twitter to the martins. Soon the martins left—or so the people thought. Sundi was placed outside one day and a tape recording of her twitters was played to make her feel at home. Suddenly ten martins appeared and sat twittering to her from a wire. Sundi was placed up on the martin house, and the other martins flew around, swooping past her and twittering excitedly, as though inviting her to join them on their trip south. Sundi spread her wings and tried, but she couldn't fly; she fluttered to the ground. The martins left, and Sundi continued to heal.

She would make practice flights again and again. Every day she could do a little better, and before long she could fly as far as eight feet. Then one day Sundi flew into the wall during one of her exercise flights. She was injured internally and died quietly in her cage.

Sundi had been a member of the household for only forty days. She had given every ounce of her being in an attempt to fly again. Some of God's children on this earth are with us for only a short time, but they give us so much, and we look forward with such longing for the joy that we will know when we meet them each one in the resurrection.

THE EXACT ORBIT

For the Lord God is a sun and shield: the Lord will give grace and glory: no good thing will he withhold from them that walk uprightly. Psalm 84:11.

As you may know, the earth revolves around the sun. The orbit that Planet Earth travels in its trip around the sun is extremely exact. In fact, it is so exact that it is hard even to imagine. Let me try to explain it.

As the earth moves through space this gigantic ball of rock, water, dirt and all the rest is also rotating—spinning like a top. I learned in astronomy class that the earth is moving in a number of other ways also, but for the present it is enough to make our *heads* spin when we just try to imagine how it works with only two sets of motions. So the spinning earth is moving along through space on an imaginary line that will take it around the sun in a year. Well, surely it must wander just a bit as it moves through space: after all, it is twenty-five thousand miles in diameter, it is spinning, and the moon is pulling on it, making the trillions of tons of water swish back and forth. Surely it must "wobble" out of line a little bit!

Well, Earth does vary a little bit in its path. It doesn't follow an exactly straight line. In fact, Earth departs from a straight line orbit by one ninth of an inch every eighteen miles. That's right! That is only one inch in 162 miles. But that variance is part of the exact orbit that the earth follows; in other words, it's supposed to wobble—but wobble precisely.

If Earth were to wander out of line by as much as one eighth of an inch in eighteen miles, we would all burn up. And if it were to move from a straight line by only one tenth of an inch in eighteen miles, we would all freeze to death. For life to continue on Planet Earth, the orbit has to be slightly off a straight line by exactly one ninth of an inch in every eighteen miles of the orbit around the sun.

I am sure that with that kind of accuracy to His credit, I can depend on the Lord God to provide for my needs.

151

Josita

THE LOST EGG

Let nothing be done through strife or vainglory; but in lowliness of mind let each esteem other better than themselves. Philippians 2:3.

California condors, the largest flying birds in North America, are rapidly nearing extinction. Soon there may not be any more left. There are no more than about two dozen of them left in the rugged mountains of southern California. In years gone by, this species ranged across much of the West, but California condors like privacy and don't do well where there are humans to disturb them—and there are now just too many people around to suit them.

The government has hired scientists to see whether it is possible to save this magnificent bird from extinction. These scientists have to observe the condors without disturbing them, so they set up lookout hiding places, called blinds, a long way from the condors' known nest sites. The scientists sit in these blinds day after day, and use telescopes to watch the condors.

In the winter of 1981-1982, among all the condors only one egg was produced. It was laid in a nest that was located in a shallow cave on the side of a cliff. The men watched the nest with that egg from a blind about a half mile away. They were excited that there would be yet one more California condor. But then something happened.

The parents of the one lone egg got into a fight over who was going to get to sit on the egg.

"It's mine; I laid it," said Mrs. Condor.

"But it's my turn," said Mr. Condor.

Several days of this squabbling went by, and then, as it often does, the fussing turned to pushing, and the two condors began shoving each other off the egg. Their fight became so intense that the egg was pushed to the edge of the cliff, and then, sadly, in the continued tussle, the egg went over the edge and was smashed on the rocks below. The ravens had fresh condor egg for dinner.

Do you think it was worth the fuss for the condors to lose the only egg that they had produced in years?

TACHYONS

At the beginning of thy supplications the commandment came forth, and I am come to shew thee; for thou art greatly beloved: therefore understand the matter, and consider the vision. Daniel 9:23.

This text indicates the presence of some fantastic natural laws about which we know nothing. Daniel has been praying. His prayer begins with verse 4, and when he gets to verse 21, the angel Gabriel arrives and says, "When you began praying I was commanded to come and explain the vision that is troubling you, and here I am."

No matter how you read it, Daniel's prayer did not take more than a very few minutes, and there are two time periods implied by the angel's message. First, how long did it take Daniel's prayer to get to heaven? The angel said, "At the beginning of thy supplications the command came forth." That means that Daniel's prayer was transmitted to heaven instantly. And in that same instant the command was given from the throne of God to the angel Gabriel. Now, we assume that Gabriel was beside the throne of God, but the angel could just as easily have been anywhere in the universe on another mission from the throne. At any rate, Gabriel received the message at the beginning of Daniel's prayer and probably set out immediately for Planet Earth, arriving several minutes later! Until recently, science has not even had a theory to explain such speed in space travel, let alone the instant reception of Daniel's prayer in heaven.

Recently a Columbia University scientist proposed the existence of some hitherto unknown rays in the universe, which he called tachyons. According to the theory, the slowest that tachyons can travel is the speed of light, or 186,000 miles per second, and there is no upper limit whatsoever to the speed of this particle. That means that it would be possible for a tachyon to leave the earth and be anywhere in the universe instantly. Now, I can't understand that, but I do know that Jesus hears and answers my prayers, and I can hardly wait to ask Him how He does this.

153

Cornen

TO MOVE OR NOT TO MOVE: THAT IS THE FOOLISH QUESTION

But avoid foolish questions, and genealogies, and contentions, and strivings about the law; for they are unprofitable and vain. Titus 3:9.

It is quite amazing how many foolish questions we can find to fuss about. If you stop and listen to most arguments, you will be listening to utter foolishness. Try it sometime. It happens in families, in churches, in government, and even between governments. The basic issues are rarely discussed. Arguments usually descend very quickly to vain and unprofitable contentions about foolish questions. A good example is provided by ants, who decide, for no good reason that anyone has ever been able to determine, that they want to move the nest.

It is usually a small group of radicals in the ant colony that want to move. By some means that we don't know, this minority has found another nesting site that they want to be their new home. So they just begin picking up the furniture, the eggs, the ant larvae, and the cocoons and start moving them to the new house.

Now, the conservative ants—those who don't want to move to a new house—don't want their furniture and babies moved, but by the time they realize what has happened, the movers have already left with a load or two of their precious contents. So they go after them and bring back what they lost. Not to be outdone so easily, the movers return and pick up the contents and cart it off again. Soon the whole nest is engaged in this amazing foolishness. The entire ant colony is on one trail either taking their nest contents one way or taking it the other. They are even passing each other on the way. Two streams of ants, both carrying the same cargo—one group carrying it away, the other group carrying it back. Like people having an argument, they don't even know what they are fighting about. This contention can go on for days, but eventually one side or the other gets tired of the unprofitable action and gives up.

FEATHERED FLYING SAUCERS

And then shall appear the sign of the Son of man in heaven: and then shall all the tribes of the earth mourn, and they shall see the Son of man coming in the clouds of heaven with power and great glory. Matthew 24:30.

One spring day, as I was birding on the South Texas coast, I noticed what looked like a tiny round cloud in the sky out at sea. It was moving steadily along and seemed to be coming closer. I could see through my binoculars that the dark little cloud was bobbing slightly as it moved. Then I saw another one farther out, and then another. These clouds were so far away that I could barely make them out, but they all seemed to be coming closer to land. When they came close enough, I could see that the dark shapes bobbing along were made up of hundreds of tiny specks—birds! I had never seen birds fly in flocks like that before.

One of the clouds of birds swept overhead and dropped in a fluttering mass into a nearby tree. Finally, the birds could be identified as dickcissels—sparrow-sized finches that live in the Central United States and winter from southern Mexico to South America. The dickcissels were returning to their summer homes. But what was the meaning of their flying in those cloudlike balls? I had seen many dickcissels before, but I had not noticed this behavior.

Research revealed that birds flying in a tight group conserve energy for long flights over the sea, where there is nothing to eat; when birds fly as one, they use one of the laws of the aerodynamics of flight: each bird in a flock has to work less than it would if it were flying by itself. The ball shape is especially suited to give the flock the greatest amount of flying efficiency. The flock is, in a very real sense, a single unit—a feathered flying saucer.

When Jesus comes, we will first see a small cloud in the distance. As the cloud nears, it will be seen as thousands and thousands of angels accompanying Him, all flying together as one ethereal spaceship, coming to take us to our summer homes in heaven.

CHAMELEON COLOR

Can the Ethiopian change his skin, or the leopard his spots? then may ye also do good, that are accustomed to do evil. Jeremiah 13:23.

We have all heard that chameleons can protect themselves by changing color to match their background, but they do not actually have the ability to change colors at will. Instead, the chameleon's skin color is controlled by its emotions and by the air temperature. Each kind may be colored differently, but basically a chameleon's colors change from light to dark, depending on how it uses a substance called melanin, which is present in its skin cells.

Melanin is present in human skin also, and the amount of it varies by race and heredity. In the chameleon the melanin molecules can get together in one spot or they can spread out evenly in the skin cells. There are a number of layers of skin on the chameleon, and the action of the melanin in the various layers determines its color. One species, for instance, will turn yellow when it becomes too warm and a dull gray if it becomes cold; if an intruder comes near, it turns pale; and in a fight the loser signals its defeat by turning dark. These colors have little to do with the background on which the chameleon is perched.

Humans can change colors to some degree. Some of us can get a tan, but the process takes quite a while. Sometimes we blush, and our face and neck turn red. We turn pale quite rapidly when we are frightened, and when we are very cold we even turn bluish. All of these colors are caused by changes in the action of our blood just under the skin. But we cannot change our skin color as the chameleon does, by rearranging the melanin.

Today's text tells us that as sinners we can't, in our own strength, be good any more than we can change our skin color. But the chameleon shows us that the Creator also allows for change, and Jesus has promised to move into our lives through His Spirit to change us from within. When that happens, it won't be just an emotional experience—it will be a permanent one.

MAYFLIES

But, beloved, be not ignorant of this one thing, that one day is with the Lord as a thousand years. 2 Peter 3:8.

The word *ephemeral* (pronounced ee-FEM-er-al) means that something lasts for only a very short time, such as one day, and is gone. Some flowers are ephemeral in that they bloom one morning and close up their blossoms that same evening, never to open them again. When we put the word *ephemeral* together with the Greek word for wing, *ptera* (pronounced tera), we get the word *ephemeroptera* (pronounced ee-fem-er-OP-ter-a), which is the scientific name for a group of winged insects that live for only one day. These ephemeral insects are the mayflies. Actually, mayflies live for several years as larvae, or wormlike creatures, under water, but on that great day when they grow up and become adults, they become ephemeral.

Crawling out of the water, the mayfly larvae emerge from their old bodies and unfold shimmering wings in flight. They have less than twenty-four hours, however, to complete the mating cycle. The eggs are laid and then, true to their ephemeral natures, the adult mayflies die. This seems like a sad love story, but that is the way of mayflies. The eggs will hatch, and the young will start the cycle over again in their homes under water.

Compared to mayflies, other types of animals live a long time. The record for old age in an animal is held by a Marion's tortoise, which lived for 152 years or more. Of course, that is nothing compared to the age of Methuselah, who was 969 years old when he died (Gen. 5:27).

But compared to eternity, even Methuselah's age was no more than a day. He lived nearly a thousand years, and yet the Bible tells us that such a long time is as a single day with God. One day is all the mayfly needs to complete its mission, and a lifetime is sufficient to complete the tasks God gives each of us. The length of time doesn't matter nearly as much as the way we use that time in fulfilling God's purpose for our lives.

KOJAK THE MOUSER

For the scripture saith, Thou shalt not muzzle the ox that treadeth out the corn. And, The labourer is worthy of his reward."
1 Timothy 5:18.

It is rare indeed to find a lazy animal. Every creature has its work to do, and it does it with determination. Perhaps the most notable exceptions are the pets of man. It isn't unusual to see a pet cat or dog that does nothing but lie around all day. I suppose that there is nothing particularly wrong with that, except that the Creator gave every created being a work to do, and after sin entered the world, work became more important, partly as a means of keeping us properly occupied so that we wouldn't get into trouble. But let's go back to the lazy pet cats for a minute.

Did you know that the British Government has had cats on its payroll for more than a hundred years? It seems that the British postal system had a problem in the mid-1800s. Mice were eating the mail! The postal employees tried poison and traps, but the mice continued to nibble on the nation's important papers. In 1868 the secretary of the post office, in London, ordered that three cats be hired to tackle the problem at a weekly wage of fourpence. "But," said the secretary, "if the number of mice is not reduced in six months, the cats are to be fired."

The cats went to work. The number of rats and mice was so drastically reduced that the secretary gave his approval to hire additional cats. Even now there are cats working at the post offices in London, but the pay has improved considerably. One of the highest-paid mouse hunters is Kojak, a tailless employee who earns one pound and eight shillings per week. His boss says that "most weeks Kojak leaves a couple of rats and an array of mice on my desk."

Remember Kojak and his fellow workers the next time you feel lazy. "Whatsoever thy hand findeth to do, do it with thy might" (Eccl. 9:10).

GERTIE THE GREAT

O Jerusalem, Jerusalem, which killest the prophets, and stonest them that are sent unto thee; how often would I have gathered thy children together, as a hen doth gather her brood under her wings, and ye would not! Luke 13:34.

No one knows why the female mallard decided to nest in the middle of downtown Milwaukee, but the spot she chose for her eggs was on top of some pilings beside the Main Street bridge, where more than eighty thousand people passed every day. It was April, 1945, near the end of World War II, and the folks of Milwaukee were ready for some warmhearted news. So, when the first story about the duck appeared in the local paper, she was dubbed Gertie the Great and became the center of attention for more than a month. Gertie became famous worldwide through daily news releases. The news of each new egg flashed around the world. Streetcars would stop for a look to get the latest news. Schools took field trips to the bridge. Gertie began to receive presents.

Unfortunately, there was a potential problem. When the babies hatched, they would naturally jump into the water—water that was so polluted with oil that the ducklings would certainly die. To prevent this tragedy, city officials ordered that great pumps be started to supply more than 2 million gallons of fresh lake water every hour to wash away the oil. On May 30 the Memorial Day parade was routed past Gertie's egg-filled nest, and at 5:30 P.M. the word went out: GERTIE'S FIRST DUCKLING BORN. Through that night and the next day the vigil was held, while one by one the babies hatched. In the middle of the second night a terrible storm struck, and all the hatched ducks were blown into the water. Rescue crews found Gertie and all of her babies. Several days later Gertie the Great and her family were transported to a local park.

Jesus placed us here on this earth, and sin came along and made this planet a pretty terrible place to be. But Jesus also made every possible provision to help us survive, and He watches over us with even more love and devotion than the citizens of Milwaukee watched over Gertie.

159

HOW MANY COLORS?

Now Israel loved Joseph more than all his children, because he was the son of his old age: and he made him a coat of many colours. Genesis 37:3.

This was a special coat for Joseph, probably pieced together with many different pieces of cloth of different colors. All the colors represented a special love that Israel, also called Jacob, had for Joseph. I think that it was just such a special love that God had for us when He created the world in so many colors.

How many colors can you name? We all know the primary colors: blue, red, and yellow. We can mix these to get such colors as orange, purple, green, and brown. But we also know that all these colors can be varied in an endless variety of different hues.

Scientists have divided color into about 2.5 million hues within the visible color spectrum. Each of these hues has its own electromagnetic wavelength that makes it different from all the others.

An interesting recent discovery is that when each different hue is seen through our eyes, it affects our brain in different ways. It appears that God created color in nature as a way of guiding our behavior. Greens and blues relax your body, whether you like these colors or not. Reds and oranges excite your brain and the rest of you into action. Is it any wonder, then, that throughout nature the dominant colors are blue sky and green grass and leaves? There is very little bright color—just enough to excite us at the proper level for good health.

Dr. Alexander Schauss has studied the effects of color and reports that pink calms mental patients. As he says, "It's cheaper and better than sedatives." He also reports that orange stimulates your appetite, and black tends to depress you. Dr. Schauss has identified a color that he says makes people stronger, but he is afraid to tell anyone about it because of how it might be used.

God created the world with a coat of many colors.

SOAP

Wash me throughly from mine iniquity, and cleanse me from my sin. Psalm 51:2.

Do you know why you use soap to help get you clean? Soap has been called a "molecular middleman" between water and oil or grease. And it is because of this connection that we use it to get ourselves clean. "But," you say, "I am not greasy! So why do I need to use soap?" Many children would like to be told that they didn't have to use soap, wouldn't they? But I'm afraid you can't get away with the statement that you aren't greasy.

Our skin is just naturally greasy. That's right, you *are* greasy. One of your body's primary defenses against disease is the production of various substances in your skin to keep out alien creatures such as disease germs. So you have a thin coating of oil and grease all over your body.

When dirt gets mixed into the natural oils of your skin, it is impossible for the water to wash it away. You need soap. Soap works like this: one end of the soap molecule is attracted to oil molecules, and the other end of the soap molecule is attracted to the water molecule. So when you scrub your skin with soap, you break up the natural oil and grease into small particles that become attached to the soap molecules that get washed away by the water molecules. It is simple!

When you don't use soap, all you are doing is scrubbing— very little cleaning is taking place. Increasing the flow of water or rubbing harder will not help get you clean without soap. Even if you could stand under Niagara Falls, you would never get clean without soap. You've got to have soap!

It is the same way with sin. We sin, and we are stained with the dirty deeds until Jesus comes and makes us clean again. Jesus is like the soap. When we want to be clean, we can try and try and try to get rid of the sins in our lives, but it is a useless exercise without Jesus. Because He overcame sin, He can take hold of our sin and wash it away. If you want to be clean, you've got to have Jesus.

PROUD EARS

Hear ye, and give ear; be not proud: for the Lord hath spoken.
Jeremiah 13:15.

Not too many of us are proud of our ears, because we usually think they are too big, too small, stick out too far, or are not shaped attractively. But whether or not we are proud of the way our ears look, we can still suffer from proud ears. If we refuse to hear something that is for our good because we are too proud to do what we hear that has to be done, then we have "proud ears."

When our son, Michael, was 3 years old, he would sometimes act as if he didn't hear us when we asked him to do something. Even when we asked, "Michael, do you hear?" he would shake his head, and say "No." He didn't want to hear, and in his immaturity he felt that if he said he didn't hear, then he wouldn't have to do what we had asked him to do. Michael was demonstrating a form of proud ears.

There aren't many of us who are deaf, and even the deaf can have proud ears, because hearing in the sense that I am talking about is "understanding" more than it is the physical ability to hear sounds. But just for the sake of interest in the physical ability to hear, let me share a couple of facts with you about our eardrums.

All sounds that we hear reach our eardrums as sound waves. The sound waves cause the eardrums to vibrate. The vibrations are picked up by very tiny bones in the ear and are transmitted to a nerve center, which is somewhat equivalent to the amplifier in your stereo. There, nerves take the sound to our brain, where the sounds are translated into meaning that we can understand.

It is interesting to note that a human eardrum is so sensitive that the faintest high note that you can hear causes your eardrum to vibrate back and forth by less than the diameter of a single hydrogen atom! God has given us ears that can hear! But He gave them to us so that we could hear what He had to say, and then act accordingly. Are your ears working properly, or do you suffer from proud ears?

THE COWBIRD
AND THE OROPENDOLA

Can two walk together, except they be agreed? Amos 3:3.

In Central and South America two kinds of birds have learned to live together in a remarkable way. The oropendola (pronounced o-ro-PEN-da-la) and the giant cowbird are cousins in the blackbird family. The oropendola builds magnificent hanging-basket nests that swing like pendulums from the overhanging branches of the tallest trees. These nests, each hanging about three feet from its anchor on the limb, are built in colonies, so you often see a group of the nests hanging high overhead.

The cowbird builds no nest at all, but lays its eggs in the nest of the oropendola and lets the oropendola raise the young. To make the egg more attractive to the oropendola, the lady giant cowbird lays an egg that is very close to the same size and shape of the egg of her host.

Having to raise "adopted" children, as well as its own, might be a burden to the oropendula except for one thing. A type of botfly, living in the same region, lays its eggs on baby oropendolas in their nests. When the botfly eggs hatch, the larvae burrow into the baby birds and kill them. Oropendolas like to build their nests near the nests of bees and wasps because, for some reason, the botflies don't seem to bother the birds when there are bees and wasps around. But there aren't enough bees' and wasps' nests around to provide safe nesting places for all of the oropendolas—this is where the cowbirds come into play. When there is a cowbird egg in the nest, it generally hatches first and gobbles up the botfly eggs and larvae as fast as it can find them. So by giving the baby giant cowbird a home, the oropendola parents are actually saving their own babies.

When you see strange partners in nature, you may not know the reason for the partnership. The same goes for people: there are friends for everyone—you may not be able to see anything attractive in a person at first, but when you understand him better, he becomes a friend.

THE ~~BLUE YELLOW BROWN~~ GREEN TREE PYTHON

Now the serpent was more subtil than any beast of the field which the Lord God had made. And he said unto the woman, Yea, hath God said, Ye shall not eat of every tree of the garden? Genesis 3:1.

In New Guinea there lives a nasty green snake. But it isn't always green, and therein is a mystery. The snake is called the green tree python. It is not poisonous, and it is not very large, as pythons go, seldom growing to more than six feet in length, but it certainly has a mean disposition. The primary mystery about the snake, however, is the fact that when the eggs hatch, the newly emerged snakes can be any one of three colors, blue, yellow, and brown, but never green. Green is the color of only the adult snake, and regardless of what color they start out with, all of the green tree pythons turn green when they are about a year old.

Karl Switak went to New Guinea to collect specimens of the green tree python for zoos in the United States. He had to go into the mountains and contact the people of the local tribes, many of whom were cannibals. He needed the help of these people in catching the snakes. When he showed them the pictures of the snakes in different colored forms and told them that the snake came in different colors, the natives only laughed at him. They knew the snake well, but they would not believe that the brown and yellow ones would turn green.

The tribespeople brought Mr. Switak all sorts of wildlife in the process of looking for the snakes. Whatever he did not want, they ate: snakes, rats—everything. As Mr. Switak says, "They can't go to a supermarket to buy their meat."

When the first green tree python was brought in, Mr. Switak opened the cage that it was in and it came out and bit him on the nose. He was more careful after that. On the way home, one of the females laid twelve eggs, which hatched into ten brown and two yellow babies.

Why do you suppose the serpent in the Garden of Eden didn't bite Eve on the nose?

164

LUCIFERIN

How art thou fallen from heaven, O Lucifer, son of the morning! how art thou cut down to the ground, which didst weaken the nations! Isaiah 14:12.

Lucifer's name means "light-bearer," and before falling into sin, this son of the morning stood at the side of God's throne. The light-producing agent in fireflies is called "luciferin," because it also is light-bearing.

Fireflies, or lightning bugs as we called them when I was a boy, use special cells called photocytes connected to tiny air tubes that supply oxygen to produce flashes of light. In the photocyte cells there are chemicals that can be excited by a nerve. When the firefly wants to start flashing, it sends an electrical message by way of the nerves to the photocyte cells and opens the air tubes at precisely the right moment to provide the oxygen. As a result, the chemicals react to become high-energy molecules. The firefly then stops the flow of electrical nervous energy and stops the supply of oxygen. The high-energy molecule breaks up, and the chemicals return to a low-energy state, but in the process light-energy is released. That is what you see when a lightning bug flashes.

There are about one thousand different kinds of fireflies in the world, and each of them has its own particular pattern of flashes, measured by the number of flashes per minute and the amount of time between flashes.

An interesting aspect of the light produced by luciferin in fireflies is that it is often called "cold light," whereas light from such sources as electric lights has warmth. I think it is very significant that the cold light is named after Lucifer and that the warm light is more often associated with Jesus, who told us that He is the Light of the world. In the last days Satan will appear as an angel of light, seeking to deceive the righteous into believing that he has the truth, but his message will be cold and lacking in the warmth of Jesus' love.

PLANTS THAT "CLICK"

O God, thou art my God; early will I seek thee: my soul thirsteth for thee, my flesh longeth for thee in a dry and thirsty land, where no water is. Psalm 63:1.

Some plants tell us when they are very thirsty. An Australian botanist named John Milburn discovered this not long ago by listening to castor beans. What did the castor beans say? They said *click;* that's all—just *click.*

To be fair to the scientist, we should tell you that he was listening to the plants by way of a special microphone hooked up to the stems. Dr. Milburn's mini-microphone is so sensitive that he tests it by hitting it with a human hair. The resulting sound is "like two logs banging together," he says. That is how powerful the tiny listening ear is when it is placed on a plant's stem. When the plant speaks, or clicks, the microphone has no trouble hearing it. The sound is then amplified so that Dr. Milburn has no trouble hearing it either. Now, how does the plant produce those clicks?

In every plant there are tiny tubes, called xylem cells, that carry water from the roots to the leaves. When there is plenty of water in the ground these tubes are full of water, and the plant literally pulls the water up from the roots and out into the leaves. During a severe drought, when there is no water at all in the soil around the roots, the tubes become empty. But the plant keeps trying to draw water from the roots when there isn't any. The plant exerts such effort under these conditions that the tubes break under the strain. When they break there is a snap that is heard by Dr. Milburn's microphone as a "click."

What a wonderful example of faith these plants provide us. They never give up! Jesus has promised us living water through His Holy Spirit—we need only to ask for it. But sometimes we become discouraged, and it seems as if there is no water. David longed for Jesus, the way a thirsty person in a desert wants water. Jesus has promised that whosoever will may take the water of life freely, but sometimes we have to become quite thirsty before we realize our need.

THE GRACKLE AND THE STARLING

But God commendeth his love toward us, in that, while we were yet sinners, Christ died for us. Romans 5:8.

In Texas we have a lot of great-tailed grackles—noisy birds that are a little smaller than crows but are just as black. These birds not only have great big tails (from whence they get their name) but also have great big appetites. There are millions of them, and they wander around the cities and towns devouring bugs, garbage, and even small birds if they can catch them. If they find the nests of smaller birds unattended, grackles will more than likely eat all the baby birds. So, while these bold and aggressive grackles may have great impressive tails, they aren't such great birds otherwise.

One rainy day I was driving in Austin when a grackle flew across the street in front of the car and attacked a baby starling that was stranded and wet in the gutter. The baby was jumping and jumping, trying to get over the curb. If it could just get up there, it could escape into the brush and be safe. But the grackle grabbed it just as I drove past. My car splashed water and apparently scared both birds. The grackle flew away, and the young starling finally made it over the curb to safety.

All of this happened in a matter of two or three seconds, at the most. I was relieved for the little starling, even though when it grows up it too will become an aggressive bird, capable of kicking other birds out of their nests so it can live there. But at the moment I didn't want to see any harm come to that baby bird, and I was glad that my big car took care of the situation.

I thought of Jesus, who loves us so much, even though we may grow up to be rascals. He died to save us. When the devil tempted Adam and Eve and they sinned in the Garden of Eden, he thought that he had them for sure. But Jesus made a way so that not only they but each of us can escape.

THE WHOLE MEADOW OR A SINGLE FLOWER

Hast thou not known? hast thou not heard, that the everlasting God, the Lord, the Creator of the ends of the earth, fainteth not, neither is weary? there is no searching of his understanding. Isaiah 40:28.

My favorite place on earth is a mountain meadow. I don't have a particular meadow; almost any will do as long as it is quiet. But I have a problem in the meadow that I would like to share with you. Should I concentrate on the whole meadow or on a single flower?

You see, there is so much to experience there. If I just relax on my back in the thick grass and luxuriate in the warmth of the sunshine, I will feel the firmness of the earth beneath me, I will hear the symphony of birdsong and insects calling around me, and I will be spirited away, so to speak, to think that this must be as close to what heaven is like as anything on earth.

But perhaps I am missing the essence of the meadow by not focusing on each one of the myriads of tiny flowers—each one perfectly shaped and delicately painted by the Creator. Most flowers in the meadows of the world bloom and fade without anyone's ever seeing them. What a terrible loss, I say to myself. So I decide to study the beauty of one flower until its qualities will be forever etched in my mind. I will watch it as the gentle mountain breeze causes it to sway slightly. I will watch an alpine butterfly visit it and drink the nectar that it has produced for that visit. Then a tiny bee might happen by for a visit.

I wish I could see the flower growing. If I just had microscopic eyes, perhaps I could study the tiny pollen grains that have been brought by the bee and by the butterfly from other flower visits in the meadow. Perhaps I could see the seeds beginning to form as the petals fade and drop. But, alas, I cannot see any of these things. My eyes are so dim. I long for heaven, where I will have enough time to study every flower in the meadow so that when I look at the meadow, I will know the meadow as I know a family of friends.

MOON WITNESS

It shall be established for ever as the moon, and as a faithful witness in heaven. Psalm 89:37.

As I write this, I can see the round moon shining in the perfectly clear Texas sky. The sun has just set, and the sky is still blue. The coyotes will probably howl tonight; they love the bright moonlit nights, and so do I. Do you remember the song with the words "The moon shines full at His command"? Such a witness, this moon of ours; it takes the sun's light and gives it back so freely and fully.

Just after sunset on June 18, 1178, some men were looking at the new moon's crescent near Canterbury, England, when the moon appeared to be rocked by a gigantic explosion that caused the crescent to writhe "like a wounded snake." The explosion itself was like a "flaming torch" spewing "fire, hot coals, and sparks" into the sky. These words are the description written by a local monk, who wrote down the story as the men related it afterward.

Dr. Hartung, an astronomer at the State University of New York, read the story and guessed that the explosion might have been caused by the impact of an asteroid. Using the monk's description, Dr. Hartung calculated the probable impact site on the back side of the moon, then he went to the Planetary Institute in Houston to check the map of the far side of the moon. He wanted to see whether a crater exists where he expected it to be. In exactly the right place, Dr. Hartung found a fresh crater, twelve miles across and twice as deep as the Grand Canyon. There were splatter marks radiating out from the crater for hundreds of miles. Hartung theorized that to make a hole like that, the asteroid would have had to have been as large as the Astrodome and must have hit the moon at a speed of forty thousand miles per hour.

It would be inconceivable to think that any blast such as the one sustained by the moon in 1178 would cause it to stop reflecting the sun. The moon is an eternal witness. I want to be like the moon—an eternal witness to the light of Jesus, the Sun of Righteousness. Don't you?

BAT HABITS

Train up a child in the way he should go: and when he is old, he will not depart from it. Proverbs 22:6.

Sometimes children don't understand why parents have certain rules. We often tell our children, "When you grow up, you will understand." Childhood is the time for learning how to live. Usually you learn faster when you are a child, and you remember what you learned longer. Being a wise grown-up is little more than learning many things so well as a child that doing the right thing has become a habit.

Bats rely completely upon their ability to move through the darkness. They have to be able to avoid trees, wires, buildings, and other obstacles as they pursue their food. They are unable to see as you and I do, but they use sonar—sound signals sent forth and bounced back—to let them know what is in their path. Since they can't spend all of their time worrying about hitting things, the Creator has given the bat an incredible memory.

Some bats were released in a dark room that contained a maze of wires through which they had to fly to obtain food. It took a while for the bats to learn where all the wires were, but once they had learned the location of each wire, they appeared to fly without hesitation around each obstacle. To test whether they had learned where the wires were or whether they were still using sonar to feel their way around, all of the wires were removed and replaced by photoelectric beams, like those used in doors that automatically open when you walk through the beam. The amazing discovery was that even in the room with no wires at all, the bats still avoided the places where the wires had been. They had memorized the location of every obstacle so well that they could fly through the room full of imaginary wires without flying through a single photoelectric beam!

As young Christians we need to learn to recognize the devil's wires so well that we will instinctively avoid the danger at all times.

THE GIANT NEST OF THE SOCIAL WEAVER

And Jesus said unto him, Foxes have holes, and birds of the air have nests; but the Son of man hath not where to lay his head. Luke 9:58.

It is highly significant that the Creator of every living thing, the God who gave every creature a home, had no home when He walked among men as our Saviour. I believe that Jesus wanted a particular home, but before we talk about that, let me tell you about the social weaver of Africa—a small bird that builds a huge nest. Social weavers are members of a large worldwide family of birds.

Social weavers like company, so, instead of building a single nest, they build an apartment house that may hold as many as one hundred pairs of weavers. You can't imagine how big these nests are unless you have seen one. From a distance you might think that the nest is a native hut or a haystack up in a tree. The nest can be twelve to fifteen feet in diameter and can attain a volume of about two thousand cubic feet. Every year the colony of weavers adds to its nest. Sometimes the weight of the nest becomes so great that the tree falls!

In 1924 the American Museum of Natural History, in New York, asked a man to find one of these nests and bring it back for display. A fine specimen was located, and it cost a small fortune to keep it intact by a number of very specialized methods, while transporting it to New York. This nest has recently been revitalized and can be seen at the museum. It hangs in a man-made tree and requires three or four people working full time for a month to clean it, but there are no birds in it. When the social weavers lived in it, they kept it clean, aired out, and repaired at all times. One such nest will last the weavers for at least one hundred years.

I think that Jesus wanted an apartment house also. He didn't have a home of His own, because He is very social and wants to live with each of us. He wants to dwell in our hearts, and He is building a huge apartment garden in heaven where we will dwell together with Him in harmony and peace.

171

THE FLY THAT BLINDS

*And there were certain Greeks . . . that came up to worship at
the feast . . . saying, Sir, we would see Jesus. John 12:20, 21.*

Tens of thousands of people in West Africa are the victims of
"river blindness," a disease that is caused by a tiny black fly
called, not surprisingly, the blackfly.

The blackfly feeds on human blood, and while sucking its
meal, the fly deposits tiny parasites into the blood. These tiny
parasites set up house under the skin, causing horrible-looking
bumps that itch. The parasites breed rapidly and move
throughout the body, even entering the cornea, which is the
clear covering of the eye that covers the iris and the pupil. Some
of the parasites die in the cornea, leaving a tiny spot. The spot is
opaque, meaning that light will not pass through it. As more
and more of the parasites die, more and more of these tiny blind
spots accumulate. Eventually the spots cover the cornea and it is
permanently destroyed, leaving the victim blind for the rest of
his or her life.

In areas where the blackfly is the most abundant a person
can be bitten as many as thirteen hundred times a day, so it is
pretty hard to avoid the painful and blinding parasite that
comes calling with the fly-bites. The victims often have painful
itching sores over every inch of their bodies.

Blindness is a sad condition to endure, and we look forward
to Jesus' coming, when the blind shall see—some again, and
some for the very first time in their lives. Won't His coming be a
wonderful first sight for them!

But there is a blindness that is even worse than not being
able to see with our eyes. Little sins can creep into our lives and,
if allowed to grow, can destroy our spiritual eyesight, so we don't
see how much Jesus loves us, and our hearts do not respond as
willingly to Him.

Let's always be as eager as the Greeks were to see Jesus, and
let's not allow any little thing to blind us to His wonderful
presence.

STRIFE ON THE LOOSE

A froward man soweth strife: and a whisperer separateth chief friends. Proverbs 16:28.

The word "froward" means disobedient, willful, obstinate, perverse, not easily managed. Such a person is no fun to be around at all! And a "whisperer" is a talebearer, or gossip. Another proverb along this line is "Where there is no talebearer, the strife ceaseth" (Prov. 26:20). Listen to a story of strife.

Back in the past century, the seeds, or perhaps even the plants, were accidently brought by ship to North America. But no one noticed. It has only been within the past twenty years or so that the plant was noticed as a problem. It is a plant called purple loosestrife. For the wetlands of the northern United States, the plant does in fact represent strife on the loose, although I doubt that that has anything to do with the origin of its name.

Purple loosestrife is an attractive plant that grows about five feet high, with a mass of rose-purple blooms. Unfortunately, wherever purple loosestrife has gotten a good stand, it reproduces wildly. For example, in 1951 what was an acre of lovely purple wildflowers in upstate New York had by 1956 taken over more than one thousand acres! In the process the invading plant pushed out such native plants as cattail, smartweed, and various sedges and rushes. The plant is beautiful, but one thousand acres is more than too much of a good thing.

Attempts to control purple loosestrife have included pulling it up, mowing it down, burning it, flooding it, and spraying it with chemical poisons, but nothing seems to stem the overwhelming growth. Each year a stand of the stuff produces eighty thousand stalks per acre, and these stalks can produce 24 billion new seeds. Multiply that times one thousand acres in the one New York patch, and you get 24 trillion seeds that are taking over the neighborhood!

It would be hard to find a better example of the results of unchecked talebearing and willful disobedience.

COMPOST

And he answering said unto him, Lord, let it alone this year also, till I shall dig about it, and dung it: And if it bear fruit, well: and if not, then after that thou shalt cut it down. Luke 13:8, 9.

There are things in the Bible that are pretty terrible when you think about them—all sorts of meanness, killings, vice, cheating, stealing, and the like, even among God's chosen people and messengers. I used to wonder why all of that corruption was in the Bible. Why didn't God just talk about the good things? Well, there are a number of answers, but the other day as I was working on the compost for my garden it occurred to me that one answer to this question was right in front of me. I was shoveling manure to mix with hay to make compost to put on the garden.

First I put down a layer of grass and weed cuttings, and then I placed a layer of manure on top. I keep it all properly dampened to encourage the growth of the bacteria. The action of the bacteria causes heat, and the combination of heat and moisture breaks down all the ingredients into nutrients for the plants when the compost is placed on the garden. When the inner workings of the compost pile are finished, the result is perhaps the best fertilizer known. If a tree or garden of plants doesn't do well with the application of such assistance, then there is probably little that can be done.

Perhaps the Bible has the same effect, for in it are the effects of sin, as well as the demonstrations of the character of Jesus. By considering all the aspects of this world as presented by God, and with the aid of the watering of the Holy Spirit, we should produce much fruit. The disciples on the road to Emmaus had this experience with Jesus: "Did not our heart burn within us, while he talked with us by the way, and while he opened to us the scriptures?" (Luke 24:32).

THE GYPSY CATERPILLAR

I said in mine heart, God shall judge the righteous and the wicked: for there is a time there for every purpose and for every work. Ecclesiastes 3:17.

When the egg of a gypsy moth hatches, the tiny caterpillar that emerges climbs the tree on which it was born. Reaching the topmost twig, the tiny creature tries to keep going higher, but can't, so it falls. A thread, like a mountain climber's rope, catches the caterpillar. Then as the caterpillar starts climbing back up, a gust of wind is apt to catch the silk thread and its passenger and carry it aloft. Soon the airborne traveler lands on another tree, only to start the whole story over again.

After a number of such parachute rides, the baby gypsy caterpillar decides to settle down and begins eating small holes in leaves. After about a week of eating, the caterpillar sheds its skin. Now it begins to consume entire leaves. It will shed its skin five or six times in about two months before it is a full-grown, 2½-inch gypsy caterpillar, and with each change of clothes its appetite increases. Eventually the caterpillar stops eating and spins its cocoon. About two weeks later a full-grown gypsy moth emerges from the cocoon, mates, and lays its eggs, to start the cycle all over again. After laying its eggs, the adult moth dies.

The gypsy moth's life plan goes something like this: hatch, climb, fall, climb, sail, land, climb, fall, climb, sail, land, climb, fall, climb, sail, land, eat, shed, eat, shed, eat, shed, eat, shed, eat, shed, eat, spin, sleep, wake up, fly, mate, lay eggs, die. There is a specific time for each of the gypsy moth's duties, and it does every one of them without one complaint. Even more important, the caterpillar doesn't try to change the schedule and do things for which it is not yet time.

God has a schedule for each of us, and we too have definite times for all of our appropriate activities. Will we be as faithful to the tasks before us as is the gypsy caterpillar?

THE MATAMATA TURTLE

For we have made lies our refuge, and under falsehood have we hid ourselves. Isaiah 28:15.

Isaiah is rebuking the descendants of Ephraim for their wicked ways. Some people get so used to living with falsehoods that lying becomes a way of life. They can rarely be trusted to tell the truth, and they practice their deceit knowingly. There are many creatures that obtain their food by deceitful means, but one of the strangest is the matamata turtle of the freshwater rivers of northern South America.

The matamata turtle is a "side-necked" turtle (there are only a very few different kinds of these strange turtles in the world). That name comes from the fact that the matamata cannot withdraw its head into its shell like most turtles; furthermore, it has a long neck, so it must bend its neck into an S curve and fold it in under the shell to the side, like a bird tucking its head under its wing.

When this turtle is threatened by an enemy, it will feign death by going limp, leaving its long neck and head hanging with jaw slack. The matamata is unable to render a bite of any strength, because it has a very fragile jaw structure. It cannot obtain food by any direct means.

The way that the matamata turtle gets its fish dinner is by falsehood. On the sides of its long neck are appendages that look like pieces of vegetation floating in the water. The turtle will float in the water with the tip of its pointed nose above water like a snorkle and with the rest of its neck and shell held rigid like a piece of wood with attached water plants. When an unsuspecting fish takes refuge under this "piece of wood," the matamata suddenly opens its large mouth, gulping in the fish with the water that rushes into the cavity.

It is sometimes such a temptation to take advantage of others, to let someone else do our work for us. But further on in Isaiah's discussion of the tribe of Ephraim he writes, "Hail shall sweep away the refuge of lies, and the waters shall overflow the hiding place."

CARDINAL TO THE RESCUE

He delivereth and rescueth, and he worked signs and wonders in heaven and in earth, who hath delivered Daniel from the power of the lions. Daniel 6:27.

These are the words of Darius to the people of the whole earth, after he had seen with his own eyes how God had saved Daniel in the lions' den.

On another scale, I believe that the story told by Louis Jacobberger, of Omaha, Nebraska, is also a remarkable rescue. In 1979 he wrote of the experience in a letter to the *Nature Society News*.

The setting was a purple-martin house where several pairs of martins had set up housekeeping. A male northern cardinal was perched overhead singing his heart out, as is usual in the spring. As Mr. Jacobberger watched, five house sparrows suddenly arrived and began systematically to cast out the martins and to take over their house. This is a regularly occurring problem for purple martins, and they often lose the fight and have to go elsewhere. As Mr. Jacobberger reports, "The martins fought long and hard but seemed to be losing the battle against those persistent, die-hard sparrows."

Just when all looked hopeless, the cardinal joined in the fight. In a red flash, he grabbed a sparrow in his beak, flew straight to the ground, and slammed the sparrow on the ground so hard that it lay there for a while before getting up.

The cardinal then flew back up to the house and got another sparrow. He "repeated this action over and over, until the sparrows had had all they could take, and gave up, never to return again."

Louis Jacobberger says, "We probably would not have believed this incident, except that my wife and I had actually witnessed it with our very own eyes."

Darius was also sharing his own personal witness. Jesus has rescued each of us. Let's tell the world what we have witnessed in our own lives.

THE INDESTRUCTIBLE RAT

But thanks be to God, which giveth us the victory through our Lord Jesus Christ. 1 Corinthians 15:57.

One pair of rats living in a cellar, garbage bin, sewer, or city dump today can have more than fifteen thousand descendants by this time next year. Since as long ago as ancient Egypt, man has been trying to win the war against rats, for health and economic reasons. More than twenty different diseases are carried by rats, including the dreaded bubonic plague, which has taken the lives of millions of people. And rats eat more than one fifth of all the food crops that man plants. Millions of dollars are spent each year in trying to get rid of rats, but still the rodents thrive and seem to be increasing by leaps and bounds, even under the most adverse conditions. When a Pacific island was all but blown out of the sea by an atom-bomb test, the rats remained alive.

We are talking mainly about two kinds of rats: the brown rat, which weighs up to a pound, and the black rat, which weighs about half a pound. Both species live virtually all over the world.

There appear to be no known ways to win the war against rats. All that we can do is control them so that their numbers don't get too great. They reproduce unbelievably fast, and they become immune to poisons and then pass on the immunity to their offspring. The rat seems indestructible.

Learning these facts about rats brings to mind an even bigger problem, the one that caused the rat problem in the beginning: No matter what we do, sin seems to increase. There is more spiritual garbage and filth in the world today than ever before, and sin seems to survive our greatest efforts to overcome it. "But thanks be to God, which giveth us the victory through our Lord Jesus Christ," we may yet win the war against rats. With Jesus there is no question that we can win the war against sin and live in an earth made new, where there will be no rat problem.

HOT BACTERIA ON MOUNT ST. HELENS

Thy faithfulness is unto all generations: thou hast established the earth, and it abideth. They continue this day according to thine ordinances: for all are thy servants. Psalm 119:90, 91.

Living right in the boiling-hot crater of Mount St. Helens are some bacteria that are almost identical to those found at volcanic vents in the depths of the sea, as well as to those that are known from fossils that evolutionists claim are 3 billion years old.

The fact that these tiny microbes can survive in such temperatures led one scientist to surmise that they are all related and have their heritage in a common ancestry in the beginning of time. We have no problem agreeing with that, do we? It takes no calendar of billions of years to put together the conditions that provide deep-sea volcanoes and mountaintop volcanoes, such as Mount St. Helens.

What the bacteria need for food is chemicals: manganese, sulfur, and carbon dioxide. Under the conditions of a volcanic eruption these elements and compounds are found in abundance.

The mystery that remains, however, is how those bacteria got to the top of Mount St. Helens when the only other known location is the depths of the sea and the fossil rocks. No one knows the answer to that question, but the theory is that the bacteria have been growing for eons deep within the fissures of the mountain, within the volcanic cracks and crevices that were left over from the many previous eruptions. One thing is sure: If these microscopic creatures can suddenly appear in a place never before known, their fossil history certainly isn't likely to support a theory that requires billions and billions of years of development.

All living things are servants of the Creator, and Jesus takes care of all of them, from the smallest microbe to the largest whale. We can depend on Jesus to take care of us according to His ordinances, because it is His rule.

manie

SOLAR MAX

Truly the light is sweet, and a pleasant thing it is for the eyes to behold the sun. Ecclesiastes 11:7.

We are blessed beyond measure by our own star, the sun. But there is far more to the sun than meets the eye.

Solar Max is studying the sun and is able to look directly at it, when you and I would go blind if we tried to look at the sun for more than a few seconds. Solar Max also has the advantage of conducting this study from the comfort of a satellite traveling high in space. You have probably guessed that Solar Max is a robot on a satellite. Studying the sun from its vantage point 356 miles above the earth, Solar Max uses its electronic eyes to scan the sun's surface for sunspots, which are gigantic swirling storms on the sun.

Solar Max is also looking for solar flares, immense flaming arches rising hundreds of thousands of miles above the sun's surface. These ribbons of fire, which are associated with sunspots, often break away and lash out into space; while the fire goes out, the intense radiation remains and moves like an invisible wall of charged particles through space. When a solar flare collides with the earth, most of it is deflected by the earth's magnetic field. But the little bit of radiation that does make it into our atmosphere causes strange and awful things to happen. First X-rays arrive, disturbing radio transmission and causing ghost images on radar screens. Then, within an hour, protons and electrons direct from the sun's blowout arrive, causing communication blackouts that may last for days. So much electricity enters our atmosphere that the polar skies light up like fluorescent lights, causing the phenomenon that we call the northern lights. Tremendous amounts of electricity pass through man-made wires with unusual results. In 1854, for instance, during one such solar blast, telegraphs could be operated without batteries.

We can only begin to imagine the power that is in the sun. But that power is no greater than the power that is available to you and to me through Jesus, the Son.

EAGLE MOTHER DIES—
HATCHLING LIVES

As an eagle stirreth up her nest, fluttereth over her young, spreadeth abroad her wings, taketh them, beareth them on her wings: so the Lord alone did lead him, and there was no strange god with him. Deuteronomy 32:11, 12.

This story took place in the spring of 1977 in northern Wisconsin. A group of ornithologists were making their annual aerial survey of eagle nests in the area and noticed, as they flew over one nest, that something seemed wrong. The pilot banked and made another and then another pass over the nest. They couldn't tell for sure, but it appeared that there was a dead eagle on the nest.

A few days later the men visited the nest site to determine what they had seen. When they arrived, two adult eagles began flying around scolding, and the men noticed signs of at least one young eagle in the nest. By this time the men were really confused. Climbing the tree to the nest, they found just what they thought they had seen: The mother eagle had been dead for nearly a month. But, alive and very healthy, there was a young eagle. How could this have happened?

The men studied the tree and the ground beneath and suddenly found the answer to their question. Lightning had struck the tree. There was evidence that a portion of the top of that tree had literally exploded when hit by the bolt of lightning. Limbs from three to five inches in diameter had been ripped from the tree and were strewn about on the ground. The telltale signs of a lightning strike were noticed just under the nest and all the way to the ground.

By some miracle, the young bird had survived while the mother, probably with her wings stretched to cover the nest from the fury of the storm, had been killed. And by some fortunate blessing, the father eagle had been able to recruit another mate almost immediately to help with the very arduous task of feeding a growing eagle.

What a perfect example of the love that Jesus has for us. He was quite willing to risk death to save us.

jou

BUG MOATS

Thou preparest a table before me in the presence of mine enemies. Psalm 23:5.

Some plants manufacture chemicals that taste terrible to insects—they may even be poisonous to the insects. In others the distasteful chemical isn't produced until the bug bites the plant, so the plant doesn't waste energy making the chemical if it isn't needed. This system of using chemicals has been carefully studied as it affects the various insects, but some bugs have a way of outsmarting the plant, as you will see.

A bug lights on a plant that it wants to eat, and at the bug's first bite, coded chemical messengers are sent through the plant's circulatory system. Bug repellant is produced within minutes and transported to the site of the bug's invasion. Normally bugs would be repelled and would have to move on to a more tolerant plant. But there are some insects that are not repelled. These bugs chew a trench around themselves, isolating a portion of the leaf that they will now eat at their leisure, since the distasteful chemical cannot get past the trench that has been dug to protect their food supply. In the meantime, the plant is producing large quantities of repellant and sending it to all nearby parts of the plant to ward off a possible invasion of insects.

When the bug finishes the meal within the circle it flies to another plant or a spot on the same tree that is at least twenty feet from the last point—far enough so that the chemical repellant did not get that far—and there the insect chews another trench and feeds, safely surrounded by a protective moat.

It is interesting that these insects first dig the trench before they set to enjoying their dinner. They seem to understand the concept of "first things first." Jesus will surround us with His protective care. And as these bugs have their task, so we have ours. We must trust Jesus, believe on Him, and ask Him to take care of us.

DICK T. O. STELIUM

So we, being many, are one body in Christ, and every one members one of another. Romans 12:5.

Dick T. O. Stelium is a name I made up to help you pronounce the name of a strange organism that lives on the forest floor. His scientific name is *Dictyostelium,* which is pronounced "dick-T-O-stelium." Dick is a form of plant called a slime mold.

Under normal circumstances Dick is a tiny microscopic organism that looks like an amoeba. He lives alone and feeds on bacteria that live on the debris of the hardwood forest floor—rotting leaves, wood, and the like.

But for a reason that no one knows, the time sometimes comes when Dick wants company—and for a very special purpose. So he sends out a chemical signal into the air. Other individuals of his species begin arriving, and soon there are tens of thousands piling up around and on top of him to form a stalk less than one sixteenth of an inch long. When about 100,000 of Dick's relatives have aligned themselves in this manner, the stalk bends over and begins to crawl along like a slug. It now appears that each of the individual creatures has become a part of one much larger organism that is looking for the sun. Since all of this usually happens under leaves and clutter on the ground, the new organism may have to go quite a way, but eventually it crawls out from under a leaf and feels the sun above.

When it senses the sun, the organism changes again. Most of it forms spores, which are on top. The remainder forms a stalk that pushes the spore cells up into the air. Wind catches these spores and blows them to happy hunting grounds where they will each form new individuals like Dick.

Sometimes we wonder why we can't each worship God in our own way all the time. While we each need to have a personal relationship with Jesus, it is also important that we get together as a church, which Jesus likened unto His body. In this way each of us contributes to a larger body that is able to help us toward a wonderful new world.

183

WATERMELON HEARTS

And of Joseph he said, Blessed of the Lord be his land, for the precious things of heaven, for the dew, and for the deep that coucheth beneath, and for the precious fruits brought forth by the sun, and for the precious things put forth by the moon. Deuteronomy 33:13, 14.

In the above text, Moses is giving a blessing to the tribe of Joseph, and he promises precious fruits brought forth by the sun. The watermelon is certainly such a fruit. The hotter the sun and the drier the weather, the better the watermelon tastes. If there is too much rain, the watermelon will tend to taste flat. But when the watermelon sits in the patch and endures the sun through a dry spell, the water content is used up and more and more of the sweet is left, so that it tastes like heavenly fruit.

Ever since I can remember, way back to the time when I was little more than a toddler on a farm in Georgia, I loved watermelon. Big ones, little ones, red-meated ones, yellow-meated ones, round ones, oblong ones, striped ones—it didn't matter. I still can eat watermelon for every meal of the day. It is one of those fruits that I believe is a special gift from the Creator. After we left the farm, we nearly always had to buy our watermelons. They were expensive, so we would eat every speck of red (or yellow) that we could get, right down to the white rind. Everyone that I knew ate watermelons that way; we thought that that was the only way to eat them.

But the farmers where we now live raise so many watermelons that some rot in the fields. They have more than they can eat, sell, or give away. There are so many that people in these parts eat only the hearts of the watermelon. A neighbor told us that she was surprised to learn that folks up north eat so much of the watermelon, because she had always eaten the heart down to the seeds and then given the rest to the cows.

It is like a little piece of heaven to eat watermelon hearts until you are full. It is as though we are enjoying the blessings of Joseph.

184

FISH DOMINIONS

And God said, Let us make man in our image, after our likeness: and let them have dominion over the fish of the sea. Genesis 1:26.

Man has taken this command quite literally throughout history. We are talking about the domain that you set up when you establish a fish pond or an aquarium. If you have even so much as a fish bowl, you have your own little domain—your own special kingdom to take care of. In a very real sense, the fish are your subjects—subject to your watchcare and keeping.

One week in church the preacher told us what he had learned from watching the fish in his aquarium. He talked about his concern for each kind of fish and for each individual fish, about how important it is to have the proper ingredients and the right plants in the water, and about how important it is to keep the temperature just right. Having a domain of fish takes thought and work.

The ancient Sumerians kept fish as a hobby more than two thousand years before Christ. The ancient Egyptians kept fish for pleasure and for study. Montezuma, the Aztec ruler of what is now Mexico, kept freshwater and saltwater ponds for fish. Today, keeping fish is a most active and thriving hobby, with millions of dollars invested each year in its maintenance. There are many organizations that cater to those with fish domains. The first aquarium society in the United States was organized in 1893, and today there are associations for fanciers of almost every type of fish—the International Fancy Guppy Association is an example. There is something fascinating and relaxing about watching the fish go about their routines.

I am sure that Adam and Eve enjoyed the fish in the river of the Garden of Eden in the same way that we enjoy the fish in our aquariums. Having an aquarium is a good method to enjoy, in a small way, the original charge that Jesus gave man in the beginning. It was to help us to understand how much He loves and cares for us that He gave us dominion over the fish.

THEY DIED LAUGHING

Who satisfieth thy mouth with good things; so that thy youth is renewed like the eagle's. Psalm 103:5.

Have you heard someone tell about an experience that was so funny that people "died laughing" hearing about it? This common saying is used to describe something that is extremely funny—but the real thing can happen. Members of a tribe in New Guinea literally died laughing when they contracted a disease called laughing sickness, a very rare disease caused by a virus that gets into the brain. This *isn't* funny.

Dr. Gajdusek went to help the tribe find a cure for the disease, which, strangely, affected only women and children; men never contracted the disease. The doctor believed that the disease was connected to a particular tribal ritual. This tribe held their departed dead in such reverence that they ate their brains. Gajdusek suspected that when the brains were eaten, the virus invaded the eater—but why, then, did the disease affect only the women and children?

The tribesmen all live together in a large house in the center of the village. The women and children live in separate houses surrounding the men's house. The men ate their food in the large house, but it is cooked for them by the women and children in *their* houses. Before the brains of the departed were eaten, they were cooked, and the women and children would sample the stew to see whether it was done. When it was thoroughly cooked, the delicacy was taken to the men's house, where the men enjoyed a meal that they thought would give them great strength and health. By the time the dish was completely cooked, the heat had destroyed the virus, so the men did not get the disease. But in the early stages of cooking, anyone tasting the dish would become sick.

Sometimes we wonder why we send missionaries to help primitive people. If someone had come to this tribe's village and helped the people to know that the Creator of all things loved them and provided them with the best diet, they would have been able to overcome the disease and also receive the happiness that comes from meeting Jesus.

THE TEMPERAMENTAL WEATHER BEAST

For they have sown the wind, and they shall reap the whirlwind. Hosea 8:7.

The "temperamental weather beast" is the tornado—awesome in its power and destructive force, and unpredictable in the path it takes. A tornado occurs when cold, dry air at higher altitudes meets warm, wet air below, while the cooler air is moving generally southeast as the leading edge of a "cold front." The resulting clash between airflows sometimes produces a freak motion in the winds, and a twister is born.

Normally a tornado moves northeast as it bounces or plows along at up to forty miles per hour. But the wind whirls around the center of the twister at up to three hundred miles per hour, giving the tornado its beastly power. This weather beast may snake its way out of the sky and literally explode one building in a town while leaving the other buildings intact. A tornado struck my mother's hometown in Wisconsin; it destroyed the theater, jumped a church, and leveled the next building.

In Codell, Kansas, having a tornado visit on May 20 was an annual event at one time; one struck there on that date in 1916, 1917, and 1918. I imagine that the folks in Codell were happily surprised by the lack of a visit from the weather beast on May 20, 1919. On May 30, 1879, two tornadoes, forty-five miles apart, hit Irving, Kansas, and sucked all of the water out of the Blue River for a mile—fish and all. In 1931 a tornado picked up an eighty-three-ton train with 117 passengers, lifted it eighty feet into the air, and then hurled it into a ditch. But sometimes the twister just plows steadily along as a continuous force of destruction. According to one account, the record for duration was set by a tornado that occurred on May 26, 1917; it moved 293 miles across Illinois and Indiana, lasting seven hours and twenty minutes.

Tornadoes are called "whirlwinds" in the Bible, and in today's text, the prophet Hosea tells us that playing with sin may at first seem like dealing with just a small wind, but later we reap trouble and destruction more like that of a tornado.

187

THE OSPREY'S NEW HOME

And he that sat upon the throne said, Behold, I make all things new. And he said unto me, Write: for these words are true and faithful. Revelation 21:5.

Sadie Hawkins was an osprey that decided to build her nest on top of the foremast of a $125,000, seventy-foot yacht in Newport Harbor, California, in 1978. Until she set up housekeeping at that location, no one noticed her at all or cared whether or not she had a name. But since there had not been an osprey nesting in southern California since 1912, the new guest was most welcome and was named by her admiring public.

However, there was a serious problem. The boat belonged to the Levis family, and Dr. Levis was paying $1,200 a month to maintain the boat in the harbor. He wanted to move it to a dock for repairs before selling it. Since ospreys usually select a nest site and use it for the rest of their lives, which could be ten years or so, Dr. Levis simply couldn't afford to pay Sadie's rent. So what was he to do? His first solution was simply to tear down the nest and move the boat, but his six children vetoed that idea.

A local firm came to the rescue by buying a tall cedar pole and having it driven into the harbor beside the Levis' boat. Then, with the aid of a crane and telephone company linesmen, the nest was carefully wrapped and moved to the platform on top of the new cedar pole. Within minutes, Dr. Levis had his boat towed away; he had it taken to a mooring several miles away.

Now the townspeople, who had cheered the move, waited to see whether Sadie would take to the new nest site. She didn't come around for a day, and the people feared the worst. Then she reappeared, sitting on a TV antenna nearby. And then there were two ospreys. Apparently the new home was accepted. It certainly was superior to the old one.

Sadie had built her home on an unsteady foundation. There was no security to her old home. But her new home, like our new home in heaven, is built on a solid foundation that can't float away.

manni

THE PROTON TEST

Heaven and earth shall pass away, but my words shall not pass away. Matthew 24:35.

Scientists have dug a giant hole at the bottom of a salt mine in Ohio. When the hole is finished it will be filled with ten thousand tons of the purest water that can be found. On all sides of the chamber, photocells will be installed. These are instruments that detect even the minutest amount of light. You might wonder why they would think they could detect light in an airtight, water-filled chamber some two thousand feet underground. Well, that is what the experiment is all about.

After the project is set, the chamber is filled, and the photocells are in place, the scientists will take readings for one year. If those photocells pick up a sudden flash of light during that year, the scientists tell us that it will be the disintegration of a proton—one of the parts of an atom. Now why would that be important? The scientists say that if a proton disintegrates in that chamber under the ground in Ohio, it will mean that the world will come to an end someday.

Isn't it amazing! The Bible tells us very plainly that the world will come to an end—"The elements shall melt with fervent heat" (2 Peter 3:10). But science—in its infinite skepticism—must prove all things for itself. The theories and speculations upon which such experiments are based require years of study to understand, but, basically, the scientists are studying about what everything is made of and how it all continues to be. They are studying about what they call matter and energy.

God understands matter and energy and the relationship between them. He works through His laws and guides planets and suns in their courses. He will destroy this old world in one sense, but He may simply be converting the sinful matter into energy and then back to its perfect state by His creative power. "I saw a new heaven and a new earth: for the first heaven and the first earth were passed away" (Rev. 21:1).

189

carmen

RISING WITH THE WHIRLWIND

Then the Lord answered Job out of the whirlwind. Job 38:1.

As you drive across the prairies and deserts of the West, it is common to see one or more whirls of wind, or "dust devils." They usually travel north and slightly east in our latitudes, and they are most visible as they stir up the dust and leaves in their paths. They are associated with rising currents of hot air and often lift dust and debris to great altitudes. There is a lot of energy being expended in such a whirlwind, and apparently some birds have learned to use them to gain altitude.

One day in Oklahoma a meteorologist was out looking for dust devils to photograph. Upon noting a particularly large one to the east, he sped northward in his car to pass it and then eastward to intercept it. The whirlwind was plainly visible as a swirling column of dust. As it crossed a small patch of woods, the whirlwind disappeared because there was no dust to pick up and make it visible. It was then that the meteorologist noticed several vultures in the air. They seemed to have been heading for the dust devil, but when it disappeared they began circling low over the ground.

Then the whirlwind reappeared as it reached the plowed field on the near side of the woods. Now it stirred up the dust again, and the vultures immediately sped with great flaps of their wings toward the rising column of dust. When they reached it, they flew directly into it and were rapidly lifted by the rising air until they were completely out of sight in the sky above.

It was as though a voice from the whirlwind spoke to the vultures saying, "I will lift you up easily to great heights." The same voice of God that spoke to Job from the whirlwind speaks to us through His Word. Jesus says to each of us, "I, if I be lifted up from the earth, will draw all men unto me" (John 12:32). All we need do, as we think of those birds that hurried to the whirlwind, is to hurry to Jesus and let Him take us to heights that we can't even imagine now.

THE ELEPHANT WEPT

Jesus wept. John 11:35.

You will recognize this text, of course, as the shortest one in the Bible, but it is in many respects also the longest because of the amount of love that is wrapped up in those two small words.

We can't know, of course, the degree to which animals feel the way we do about things, and it is a mistake to attribute much in the way of human emotion to the feelings of an animal, but there are some experiences that we observe in animals that are difficult to describe in any other way.

Take, for example, the way elephants act when they come upon a fallen member of their herd. It is common knowledge that other members of the herd will make every effort to rehabilitate a dying elephant. And after death, there appears to be a number of behaviors that resemble mourning their departed family member. The elephants often seem to be burying their dead by placing sticks and grass over the body.

When elephants come upon the bones of an elephant long since dead, they will often gather around the skeleton and tenderly pick up various bones, especially the tusks, hold them up in the air, walk around with them, and sometimes carry them some distance, before putting them down again.

The most remarkable exhibition of emotion from an animal that I have ever read is found in a book called *The Dynasty of Abu,* by Ivan Sanderson, the famous jungle explorer. He tells of a circus elephant named Sadie that couldn't perform and tried to leave the ring, only to be ordered back. "At this, Sadie sank to her knees and then lay down on her side. The two men . . . stood dumbfounded for a few moments, for Sadie was crying like a human being. She lay there on her side, the tears streaming down her face with sobs racking her huge body."

Fortunately for all of us, Jesus was able to carry out His appointed task on earth. He wept on numerous occasions, and always because of the depth of His love for you and me.

191

m Am!

BLOODSTONE WISDOM

But one of the soldiers with a spear pierced his side, and forthwith came there out blood and water. John 19:34.

Jesus died of a broken heart. His anguish was so great with the load of sin that He carried for you and for me, that His human, physical body broke up inside. No one has ever known such grief. The closer we come to Jesus, the more we feel that grief with Him. It is painful, and He suffered it all for us.

There is a gemstone called the bloodstone, which is a form of quartz that is dark green in color, with bright red splotches throughout. When polished, it makes a highly prized gem and is one of the birthstones for the month of March.

A folk myth of the Middle Ages said that the bloodstone was created when the blood of Jesus fell on a green stone at the foot of the cross. According to other myths and legends, wearing a bloodstone is supposed to provide the wearer with wisdom.

When we put the two stories together, we find the suggestion of a truth that is no myth. The Bible clearly says that "the Lord giveth wisdom" (Prov. 2:6). Does the Lord give us wisdom by giving each one of us a piece of bloodstone to wear somewhere on our body? Of course not!

The apostle Paul, writing in his first Letter to the Corinthians, compares the wisdom of men with the wisdom that God gives us and concludes by speaking of "Christ Jesus, who of God is made unto us wisdom, and righteousness, and sanctification, and redemption" (verse 30).

Yes, we get wisdom from God's act at the cross. It comes from the provision made by Jesus in shedding His blood, and is a true wisdom that confounds the greatest worldly wisdom. It is available to everyone, and it is free. You need not pay the high price of a gemstone to receive the wisdom that Jesus would give you free. "If any of you lack wisdom, let him ask of God, that giveth to all men liberally, and upbraideth not; and it shall be given him" (James 1:5).

"NO MORE PLAGUES"

And I heard another voice from heaven, saying, Come out of her, my people, that ye be not partakers of her sins, and that ye receive not of her plagues. Revelation 18:4.

In modern terms a plague is usually a deadly disease. In the Bible the term is used to describe a number of disasters, among which are diseases and other deadly natural events. In olden times natural catastrophies were considered to be acts of God serving one purpose or another—usually a punishment of some kind. Now that science has become so advanced it is generally believed that God has nothing to do with such disasters. What do you think?

During the Middle Ages the word *plague* usually referred to the bubonic plague, or Black Death. Millions of people died from that plague. Cholera is another disease that has been referred to as a plague. This disease can kill a person in a single day, and when an epidemic breaks out, if no medicine is available it is reported that at least half of a population will die of the disease.

The most recent worldwide plague was the 1918 flu epidemic, which killed more than 20 million people. As a result of this experience, as well as the advancement of medical knowledge and such precautions as immunization, it appears that such outbreaks are not as likely to occur now as they were in the past. Government agencies, such as the U.S. Center for Disease Control, in Atlanta, Georgia, have been established to help ward off any such epidemics.

When experts at the Center for Disease Control were asked whether there would ever be another plague they answered "probably not." Is that an encouraging statement?

If you believe your Bible you know that there will be at least one last disease-type plague (Rev. 16:1, 2). The Center for Disease Control will have no power whatsoever over this outbreak. We can't place a lot of security in the statements of man, but when God says that "neither shall any plague come nigh thy dwelling" (Ps. 91:10), that's a form of security that I can depend upon.

FIVE DUCKLINGS AND THEIR LOON PARENTS

But as many as received him, to them gave he power to become the sons of God, even to them that believe on his name. John 1:12.

One summer, on the coast of Alaska, a pair of spectacled eiders nested about forty feet from a pair of Arctic loons. The story that I am about to relate is amazing for a number of reasons, but primarily because adult Arctic loons will normally eat baby ducks. The fact that the two nests were this close together was unusual, since the adult eiders are quite able to protect their young against any attempt on the part of the loons to harm them. The location of the nests were noted by an ornithologist studying in the area.

Both nests were occupied by their respective pairs of adult birds when visited on July 6 and again on July 13. But on July 27 the ornithologist found a very interesting situation. For reasons unknown, the five eider ducklings, which had hatched in the meantime, were being attended by the pair of adult loons. The eider parents were never seen again, and the loons had produced no young of their own.

The adult loons were observed to care for the ducklings just as they would care for their own. They fed them from the nearby pond, they called softly to them but clucked loudly when there was danger. The baby ducks would go running to mother and father loon when the adoptive parents called. Occasionally a duckling would climb up onto the loon's back and stand like a little captain on a proud ship as the loon paddled around the pond. These birds of widely different and usually antagonistic species seemed to have no trouble at all communicating with each other, and the adoptive family seemed to be as happy and peaceful as any family could be.

As sinners we are alien to the family of God, but by believing in Jesus we become part of God's adopted family. And as Christians we have a newfound love for all of God's people, which helps us to live together in peace and harmony.

THE HOGNOSE IS ALL BLUFF AND NO BITE

And Jesus answered and said unto them, Take heed that no man deceive you. Matthew 24:4.

There are many nonpoisonous snakes that try to deceive an enemy into thinking that they are some sort of poisonous snake. I was frightened once as a small boy when, walking ahead of my family, I happened upon a black racer that lifted its tail and began to vibrate it like a rattlesnake. I went screaming back to my father, calling, "Rattlesnake!" After my father calmed me down and took me back to look at the harmless snake, I felt better, but I never forgot the ability of that snake to get rid of me in a hurry.

The hognose snake is a wonderful example of the bluffing that a snake can do. The hognose is perhaps the most harmless and docile snake in North America. It grows to a length of about three feet but wouldn't think of attacking a person and has rarely been known to bite even when captured. The rare instances when a hognose has bitten people was when the person bitten was also carrying a quantity of frogs or toads and the smell of these amphibians led the snake to believe that the person's thumb or finger was dinner—so it bit. But normally the hognose will not bite, even if teased. I have handled them in Florida, and it is a most delightful snake for handling.

The most famous bluff of the hognose is to swell up, spread the head and neck, hiss, and lunge at the intruder. If this fails to intimidate, it will roll over, hide its head under its coils, and go limp, as if dead, with the mouth open and the tongue hanging out. This action has earned hognose snakes the title of "puff adders" by country folk, many of whom are convinced that the snake is deadly poisonous.

Satan, the original deceiver, lied to Eve when he spoke through the harmless serpent in the Garden of Eden. Sometimes Satan tries to make you believe that he is harmless, and other times he bluffs you into thinking that he is more powerful than he is. A Christian will not be affected by either the scary bluffs or the deceptions of Satan.

195

AFTER THE GYPSY MOTH IS GONE

Therefore if any man be in Christ, he is a new creature: old things are passed away; behold, all things are become new. 2 Corinthians 5:17.

In the northeastern United States there is a small insect called the gypsy moth. Those of you who live where the gypsy moth dwells don't need to be told about the problems that it causes.

In spring, when the gypsy moth eggs hatch, there may be billions and billions of tiny caterpillars, all of which must eat in order to grow up to be gypsy moths. So up the trees they go, and they literally eat up the forest. Before long all the leaves of every tree have been devoured by the insatiable appetites of the hordes of caterpillars. I have seen entire mountains in New York and Massachusetts where it looked like winter—even worse, because there weren't even any evergreen trees with leaves.

Caterpillars that find enough leaves to eat so that they make it through the caterpillar stage are the lucky ones. But for the rest, when all the leaves are gone, there is no more food. They let themselves down from the trees on a strand of silk, and when they reach the ground they go off in search of a tree with leaves. The caterpillars may become so thick on the ground that you can't walk without stepping on them. One day in June, 1981, there were so many swarming over the railroad tracks that the trains couldn't get up a hill in Massachusetts. But when there aren't any more trees with leaves, all the caterpillars die looking for food. What happens to the woods after the caterpillars are all gone? The trees look dead.

Then a miracle happens on some trees. Tiny buds appear, and new leaves come forth. It looks like spring again. Before long the trees are covered again with living green leaves.

Sometimes we are tempted to feel that our lives have been so messed up by things—even little things—that the future looks bleak. But the same Creator who brings life to the apparently hopeless woods can come into our lives, and "Behold, all things are become new." Isn't He wonderful!

THE OUTSIDER

When once the master of the house is risen up, and hath shut to the door, and ye begin to stand without, and to knock at the door, saying, Lord, Lord, open unto us; and he shall answer and say unto you, I know you not whence ye are. Luke 13:25.

There is a word we use sometimes to describe someone who is not a church member—*outsider*. I'm not sure that we should use this word in this way. It might be very discouraging to someone who is thinking of being a member of the church to hear us talk about the outsiders. It might sound as if we believe we are somehow better because we think we are safe on the inside. Don't misunderstand me; there is certainly such a thing as being outside of the hope in Jesus, but we can be a member of the church and still be outside. Let me explain by telling you about the blue-footed booby—a seabird of tropical oceans.

The blue-footed booby nests on the ground on various islands in the eastern Pacific Ocean, most notably on the Galápagos Islands. Each nest consists of a shallow scoop in which the female lays several eggs. While sitting on the nest and when coming and going to and from the nest, the bird leaves droppings that form a ring around the nest. After the young hatch, this ring becomes critical to their survival.

It is the nature of the mother booby to serve only those nestlings that are inside that ring. Any young bird that is outside the ring is considered to be from some other nest and not the mother's responsibility—an outsider for sure. Usually there are no problems, but when food gets scarce, the largest chick often pushes the younger, and therefore smaller, chick out of the nest—and outside the ring.

You see, that assures the remaining chick of all the food, because the mother no longer recognizes the chick that is outside the ring. The "outsider" will die of starvation.

While it is true that we must be inside the company of Jesus, aren't you glad that He is constantly going out after those who stray from the nest?

m Ami

A SUPERGALAXY

For as the heavens are higher than the earth, so are my ways higher than your ways, and my thoughts than your thoughts. Isaiah 55:9.

You know that the earth revolves around the sun along with the other planets, and you may know that we call the sun and all its planets a solar system. You also know that there are many other suns—millions and millions of them, in fact. Each of these suns may have planets, making more solar systems. The stars that you see at night are these other suns. We can't see the other planets. Most of the suns that you see as stars are parts of giant systems called galaxies. A galaxy is like a giant swirl of suns all rotating around a center, very much as our earth and the rest of the planets revolve around the sun. We call our galaxy the Milky Way because the ancients called it that, not knowing what it was. There are perhaps millions of galaxies out in space, each with billions of stars or suns.

Now, you may have known most of what you just read, but here is a new thought for you. Scientists have recently decided that groups of galaxies may be traveling together in a giant system that they are calling a supergalaxy. One astronomer figures that our Milky Way is part of a supergalaxy composed of about 20 galaxies. These 20 galaxies are revolving around a common center; we, with our galaxy, are traveling at about one million miles per hour through space around this center.

I can't help speculating that somewhere in the midst of all the universe is the throne of God and that perhaps all of these systems—solar systems, star clusters, Milky Way systems (or galaxies), supergalaxies, and maybe even super supergalaxies are revolving in magnificent splendor and perfect order around that throne.

Just thinking about these things makes my head spin like one of those systems. Won't it be wonderful when we can listen to the Master Scientist, Jesus, explain it all.

HEAVEN-SENT BAT SCENT

But my God shall supply all your need according to his riches in glory by Christ Jesus. Philippians 4:19.

This is one of my favorite texts. The great God of the universe, Owner of all that there is, will provide me with what I need, because Jesus loves me and I love Him. What a promise! I need lack for nothing, and I never need to be afraid that I will go without something that I really need. That is a promise in the Word of God, and we can claim it. If you are ever tempted to doubt it, then I suggest that you consider the case of the long-nosed bat and the century plant.

The century plant, native to the southwestern deserts of North America, is dependent upon the long-nosed bat to pollinate its flowers in order to produce seeds. But why would the long-nosed bat want to pollinate the century plant? It so happens that the long-nosed bat is dependent upon the century plant for two amino acids that are essential to its survival. But how does the bat find out that it can get these essential nutrients from the century plant? Well, this is perhaps the most amazing part of all. The Creator has provided the century plant with the ability to produce a special "bat scent." The century plant flowers give forth tyric acid, which just happens to be the same substance that attracts male and female bats to each other.

So long-nosed bats are attracted to the scent of tyric acid coming from century plant flowers. When the bats get to the flowers they probe with their very long tongues deep into the flowers to extract the nectar. In the process, the century plants are pollinated, and the bats receive two essential nutrients: proline, which helps produce the connective tissue in their wings, and tyrosine, which stimulates the growth of their babies when it is received through the mother's milk.

If the Creator has such tender regard for the needs of baby bats and century plants to work out such an intricate arrangement where both are benefited, then need I worry?

DOUBLE-NESTING DICKCISSELS

If a bird's nest is lying on the ground, or if you spy one in a tree, and there are young ones or eggs in it with the mother sitting in the nest, don't take the mother with the young. Let her go, and take only the young. The Lord will bless you for it. Deuteronomy 22:6, 7, T.L.B.*

God is a conservationist. Here is a text to prove it. The Creator has always been concerned with the livelihood of His creatures. In man's search for food, it is sometimes tempting to take more than is needed, and God was presenting to man some rules to go by in taking fowls of the air for food.

Another example of God's concern for the nesting mother bird is provided by a unique habit of a North American bird called the dickcissel—the name is derived from the bird's song, which somewhat resembles the sound of the name. Dickcissels nest primarily in the prairie mid-section of the United States and Canada, although a few of them nest farther east.

In spring, the male dickcissels precede the females in migration. They reach locations from Texas to the Dakotas, establish their territories, and await the arrival of the females. When the females arrive in Texas on their way north, most of them seem to stop and set up housekeeping. All indications are that the females raise a single brood in territories that have been set up by the males in Texas. When the young are able to fend for themselves, the females pick up and fly north to the males awaiting them there with other choice nesting sites ready for their domestic touch.

Consequently, the dickcissel females raise two broods per year—one in the south before it gets too hot, and the second in the north, still before it gets too hot. It is quite an efficient system.

We don't know why female dickcissels have chosen this method of increasing the population of the species, but I feel certain that the Creator, who watches over the mother bird and her young, had a hand in directing the behavior.

---

* Taken from *The Living Bible*, copyright 1971 by Tyndale House Publishers, Wheaton, Ill. Used by permission.

THE AXOLOTL

When I was a child, I spake as a child, I understood as a child, I thought as a child: but when I became a man, I put away childish things. 1 Corinthians 13:11.

Don't worry about pronouncing *axolotl* correctly. It is an Aztec Indian word meaning "water toy." The axolotl is a salamander that lives in Mexico and the western U.S. It has a very peculiar trait. Many axolotls never grow up. They remain axolotl children for their entire lives—perhaps 25 years.

Every salamander begins life as an egg. From the egg hatches a water-dwelling form, called a larva. In frogs and toads, these larvae are often called "tadpoles." Young salamanders, like tadpoles, usually grow legs, and climb out onto the land, where they live their adult lives. But in the case of the axolotl, the young often fail to mature. For some reason they do not exchange their water-breathing gills for air-breathing lungs, as do other salamanders. The axolotls that do not mature are destined to remain water creatures for the rest of their lives, crawling around on the pond bottoms like baby axolotls.

The reason some axolotls don't mature seems to have to do with the amount of food and water available. Where there is more food on land but the ponds dry up, more axolotls mature; but where the land is parched and dry but bodies of water remain available, more axolotls remain immature in the water. If conditions are right for maturity they mature; otherwise they don't. I think there is a lesson in that.

The author of the book of Hebrews compares our need for spiritual food to the difference between milk and meat. A baby drinks milk, and that is about all that a new Christian can stand from the Word of God. But when we grow up in our Christian lives we need more—we must mature! There is more to God's Word than milk: "strong meat belongeth to them that are of full age, even those who [can] . . . discern both good and evil" (Heb. 5:14). Jesus has made it possible for us to grow to be fully mature Christians. It would be foolish to remain babes in the Word when there is so much food available.

201

Carmen

JULY 12

THE MIMOSA GIRDLER

And we know that all things work together for good to them that love God, to them who are the called according to his purpose. Romans 8:28.

Even if you have a mimosa tree in your yard, you may not know about the mimosa girdler. We have two beautiful mimosa trees by our house, and the hummingbirds love to feed at the hundreds and hundreds of pink fluffy flowers that are just dripping with sticky nectar. But mimosa trees don't live very long, and if we want to keep them around, we must make sure that the mimosa girdler is alive and well and working in our mimosa trees.

The mimosa girdler is a small beetle that lives only on mimosa trees—it cannot live anywhere else. The mouth of the mimosa girdler is specially constructed to help it cut through the bark of small limbs on the tree as it girdles the limb with a ring that kills the branch. That the mimosa girdler does this may seem, at first, like a bad thing for the tree, but, as you will see, the tree benefits in the end.

When a female mimosa girdler is ready to lay her eggs she crawls out to the end of a limb, makes a slit in the bark, and lays her eggs there. Then the beetle crawls back toward the tree a short distance and begins her girdling by chewing a groove in the bark all the way around the limb. The groove is just deep enough to cut off all of the incoming sap to the branch beyond that point. Soon the branch dies and a gust of wind will break it off and blow it to the ground, scattering the eggs. When the eggs hatch, the baby girdlers seek out a mimosa tree and start the process all over again.

This natural pruning process doubles the life of the mimosa tree. So what may seem like damage to the tree is actually prolonging its life. The mimosa gives off a special scent that attracts the beetle. Do you think that we could think of our little problems from day to day as part of God's pruning process to help us live forever?

BABY GULLS LEARN TO PRAY

And it came to pass, that, as he was praying in a certain place, when he ceased, one of his disciples said unto him, Lord, teach us to pray, as John also taught his disciples. Luke 11:1.

You may think that the above title is a bit strange. After all, birds can't pray! But didn't Jesus tell His disciples, as a part of the Lord's Prayer, that they should say, "Give us this day our daily bread"? (Matt. 6:11). I think you could say that the baby bird is praying for its food when it asks the mother and father bird for food, but we usually reserve the word *prayer* for talking to God. So it isn't entirely correct to say that a bird prays. Yet the Creator, who provides for the birds, is ever watchful of the needs of even the baby birds; so the feeding cries of a nestling aren't all that far from prayer.

Take the baby laughing gull, for example. When the bird first pecks its way out of the egg it needs to begin eating, but it doesn't quite know how to go about it. It is apparently born with one bit of knowledge, that being an attraction to the color red. Somehow the baby laughing gull knows that there is food where the color red is located. But the baby bird isn't too talented in aiming his beak, so the parent birds have to help a bit by holding their reddish beaks (the source of the baby's food) down in front of the hatchling. When the baby bird sees the red beak it begins pecking at it. At first the baby misses the red beak about as often as it hits it. But soon, with practice, the baby is able to clasp the parent's red bill in its tiny beak and give it a gentle tug, which is the signal for food to be delivered.

Is the baby gull's method of obtaining its daily food that much different from our method of praying to God for our daily blessings? When we are young Christians, God has to show us the way and teach us how to ask Him for what we need. How happy it must make Him when we learn to trust in Him enough to ask for the things that we need.

203

YOUR LAWN

He shall come down like rain upon the mown grass: as showers that water the earth. Psalm 72:6.

This text refers to the way Jesus, the Messiah, will come to His people like a gentle rain on the grass. There is something special about green grass. A lush, soft grassy meadow invites you to walk barefoot on it. A grassy hillside invites you to lie down and roll. The "green pastures" spoken of in Psalm 23 have always been symbols of peace. Yes, we are drawn to green grass, and we put forth great effort to see that we have a nice grassy yard wherever possible.

It is estimated that there are more than 20 million acres of grass yards in the United States, representing about 2 percent of the total land area. That is a lot of real estate to keep watered, weeded, and free of insect pests.

Few people understand the teeming life that is present in the grass of their yard. You may think that your yard is made up of a single kind of grass. The truth is that your yard, like all others, actually contains many different kinds of grass *in addition to* the type of grass that you have planted there. In spite of all of your efforts, there are also many different kinds of weeds growing in your yard.

Amazingly, there are also more than 100 different kinds of insects living in the average American yard, and that doesn't count the snails, spiders, spider mites, pill bugs, earthworms, and the like.

The amount of plant growth in a yard is nothing short of phenomenal. There is more new plant growth in the average lawn than in a tallgrass prairie or coniferous forest of equal size. And all it takes to get such output is water and sometimes a little fertilizer.

It was Jesus' custom to take His followers out into the countryside and seat them on the grass while He taught them. There is enough going on in your own lawn to provide quite a few lessons from the Creator.

SPACE-CHIPS

And I saw the dead, small and great, stand before God; and the books were opened: and another book was opened, which is the book of life: and the dead were judged out of those things which were written in the books, according to their works. Revelation 20:12.

The invention of computers has changed the way almost everything in the world is done. Suddenly, with computers, man is able to perform feats that would have boggled the minds of our predecessors. There seems to be no limit to what can be done with the help of these memory machines.

One of the secrets of computers is the ability to store vast amounts of information in extremely small spaces in a way such that all of the information can be used when it is needed. And the secret to such storage has been a tiny silicon crystal, carefully prepared with microscopic circuits that I can't begin to describe. A piece of this silicon not much larger than a pinhead can hold the amount of information on four typed pages—it is called the 64K chip. By the time you read this, there will be computer chips that will hold far more than that. A 256K chip has just been announced by IBM, and there is already an experimental chip made from the crystals of a mineral called gallium arsenide that will contain ten times what the silicon chip can hold. Before long, entire libraries will be stored in less space than is now occupied by one book on the shelf!

One of the problems in producing the better chips is that, here on earth, gravity gets in the way of perfect crystals. So what science intends to do is build a factory in space where there is no gravity; there they can build near-perfect chips and transport them to earth by way of a space shuttle.

If man has already managed to create computers that can store almost everything known, it is certainly not difficult to imagine that God can keep a record of everything that we do. Won't it be interesting to see God's "books"? Do you suppose that God uses some type of "space-chips"?

THE WORLD'S FASTEST-GROWING PLANT

Who covereth the heaven with clouds, who prepareth rain for the earth, who maketh grass to grow upon the mountains. Psalm 147:8.

God provides everything that is needed to live on this earth, and for those who trust in Him, His promises are sure. For the people of Oriental countries, there is a special plant that they especially depend upon. It is a grass, but not an ordinary grass such as grows in your yard. This grass is the fastest-growing plant in the world. It can grow about 18 inches every day—that's three quarters of an inch every hour. You can almost see it grow! In Japan, where this plant is extremely important, there is a joke that the plant grows so fast that you can *hear* it growing. The plant we are discussing is bamboo.

Bamboo does all of its growing in a short growing season at the beginning of summer, but the result is a tender, though very tall, shoot that takes the next three years to mature and become hard enough to use for most of the many products that are made from it. In Japan, for example, bamboo has been the most staple building material for centuries. Almost every part of this valuable plant is used. Even the leaves are used for making paper.

You rarely see a blooming bamboo, but the plant does flower and bear seeds. A bamboo plant goes for as long as sixty years without flowering. In fact, a few kinds of bamboo that you see, unless they are flowering, have never had a flower, because when the flowers come the plants will die. In Japan, a flowering bamboo is the sign of bad luck, and you can readily see why. When the source of so many of their necessities dies, that is bad luck indeed. But even in death there is life, for the seeds, which usually look like rice or barley grains, are ground and eaten as flour. I wonder whether the people make bamboo bread?

The grass that God makes to grow upon the mountains for the Japanese is bamboo.

BEES AND VOLCANIC ASH

Blessed are the undefiled in the way, who walk in the law of the Lord. Psalm 119:1.

One thing about lessons from nature that is hard to accept sometimes is that natural laws are hard and fast. When the laws are broken the price has to be paid; there are almost no exceptions to this rule.

When Mount St. Helens erupted in full force several years ago, the air was filled with microscopic particles of ash that had been blown from the volcano. The region around Mount St. Helens contains some of the most fruitful country in the world; flowers and fruit abound, and, of course, there are millions upon millions of bees to help pollinate the flowers and produce the fruit. And when those bees left the safety of their hives after the eruption, they were unaware that they were doomed by the ash that they couldn't see and had never before experienced.

Bees are covered with tiny barbed hairs that protect them from bumping into things and serve as the pollen traps used to help cross-pollinate the flowers that they visit. On the days following the eruption these tiny hairs became traps for ash particles instead of pollen. And, while the bees have natural brushes and combs to clean the pollen when it becomes too thick, their brushes and combs were powerless against the ash that accumulated to a point where it weighted them down; they couldn't fly. The ash also got into the bees' breathing tubes and suffocated them, or it damaged the waxy coat on their bodies that prevents them from dehydrating in the heat of the day. And, interestingly, when the bees were in this condition they became irritable and were more prone to sting.

Untold millions of bees died in those few days following the eruption. They simply could not cope with the unusual conditions that were present. Beekeepers in the State of Washington alone lost millions of dollars' worth of bees. There was no savior for the bees. They went out into the world completely helpless, and they were lost.

207

THE CRY OF DISTRESS

In my distress I called upon the Lord, and cried unto my God: he heard my voice out of his temple, and my cry came before him, even into his ears. Psalm 18:6.

It is natural for a healthy person to run fast to answer a sincere cry for help. I know the fear that grips my heart when I hear a child scream in the pain of some distress or injury. I drop everything and go running. This impulse also seems to be true for birds.

I used to capture birds in traps and nets, place numbered bands on their legs, and then release them. It was commonplace for some birds to start screeching loudly as soon as they were captured.

There are people like that. When something goes wrong some people howl in distress, while others endure it all patiently. But I think there is a time to howl and a time to keep silent. And the birds seem to have figured this out. The aggressive birds that seem to play the role of patrolmen, are the screechers. Birds such as the bluejay, the vireo, and the cardinal, almost always screech when they are picked up from the trap or plucked from the net where they have become entangled. What they are apparently doing is trying to bring in other birds to attack and evict or intimidate these mean monsters who are catching them.

I read of a situation where bluebirds were netted and immediately set up a screech that brought a whole flock of bluebirds from the surrounding area. The arriving flock immediately set to attacking the person who was holding a captured bluebird. It seems that, with little thought for themselves, other birds come in mobs to help drive out what they instinctively think might be a snake, an owl, or maybe a cat. So the screeching cries uttered by captured birds are apparently not cries of fear or pain, but, rather, cries of warning and cries for help. And the cries work. Other birds come running, just as I do when I hear someone calling for help, and just as Jesus does when we call upon Him.

JACKSON'S CHAMELEON

And God made the beast of the earth after his kind, and cattle after their kind, and every thing that creepeth upon the earth after his kind: and God saw that it was good. Genesis 1:25.

It looks like a prehistoric monster. It has three gigantic horns on its head; a row of dragonlike ridges down its back; and large bulging eyes in sockets, each of which operates like a turret on a tank. It is such a hideous-looking creature that the people of East Africa, where it lives in trees and thickets, once believed that it had supernatural powers. Its one attractive feature is its beautiful skin, colored in varying shades of green, blue, and red. It is Jackson's chameleon—a lizard only eight or nine inches long, and actually quite harmless to humans.

The most amazing thing about a Jackson's chameleon is its tongue, which is slightly longer than the lizard's entire body! The tongue is a deadly accurate insect trap, darting out to catch an unsuspecting grasshopper in one twenty-fifth of a second.

When a Jackson's chameleon gets hungry it stations itself on a perch and waits. Nothing moves but its eyes. Each eye can act alone, or the two eyes can focus together on a target. It is strange indeed to see each eye looking around on its own.

When an insect is seen within range by one of the eyes, a message is flashed to the other eye, "OK, other eye, I've got one." The other eye swings around, and both eyes focus on the intended prey, giving the chameleon binocular information about the exact location and distance of the target insect. Now, even if you are watching, if you blink at the wrong time you will miss the catch; it will look as if the insect simply disappeared into thin air.

We don't know why this wonder of creation now looks so forbidding, and we don't know what its original ancestors ate in the Garden of Eden. But the chameleon still depends on the Creator for its life and health, just as we do.

CHASED BY 5 TONS OF WATERMELONS

For he shall give his angels charge over thee, to keep thee in all thy ways. Psalm 91:11.

It is 4:00 A.M. and dark, when Mark, his father, and three boys leave the farm with five tons of watermelons. His father drives ahead, and Mark is driving the truck. The three boys are asleep in the front seat. Before leaving, Mark's family had knelt to ask for the Lord's watchcare and protection over them.

The route includes a long slope where one highway dead-ends into another. Mark is driving at a safe speed down the slope when his father's brake lights flash. But when Mark applies his brakes, a cold realization hits him—he has no brakes! There is no time to pray now, only time to trust. Straight ahead is a dirt bank; to hit it anytime would be bad enough, but with five tons of watermelons behind the four young men, they will be crushed. Mark must attempt the turn. His speed is too great, and he can't possibly make it; but he must try. Mark carefully pulls the steering wheel to the left, but the truck with its heavy cargo wants to go straight. Somehow, the truck begins to turn; the tension on the tires is so great that grooves are gouged in the pavement by the rims. Mark knows that the truck is going to roll over if he keeps on trying to turn, and five tons of watermelons will be on top of him and his three young friends. Suddenly, he notes the bank is somewhat lower ahead. Perhaps he can make it. Mark straightens the wheel, and the truck rockets up the bank, leaving the ground as it catapults into the field beyond.

As the truck lands upright the boys awaken and ask, "What happened?" Mark is still at the wheel, and the truck is still moving across the field, where it finally comes to a stop. In the process, three watermelons were lost and a few more were broken when the truck hit the ground—that's all.

No one knew until daylight that if Mark had held on to the turn for a fraction of a second longer, the truck would have landed in a canyon instead of the soft field. The angels were busy for a few seconds, don't you think? Mark thinks so!

WE HAVE A BUILT-IN CLOCK

Whoso keepeth the commandment shall feel no evil thing: and a wise man's heart discerneth both time and judgment. Ecclesiastes 8:5.

Most of us wear a watch of some kind to tell us what time it is, but have you ever noticed that you often have an inner sense of what time it is, even without looking at your watch. When a person sets his alarm at night for a certain time in the morning, it is a common thing for that person to awaken just a few moments prior to the alarm. There is good reason for this: we have a built-in clock. Its existence has long been suspected, but only recently has its location been discovered. You might even be able to guess where it is.

Your built-in clock is in your hypothalamus, which is a part of your brain that lies on the underside, right in the middle of your head. It would not be a good idea to try to check your hypothalamus instead of looking at your watch the next time you want to know what time it is!

So far all that is known about this built-in clock is what a group of Harvard Medical School researchers have learned. The clock consists of a cluster of brain cells that, according to the scientists, probably send out regular spaced pulses like the ticking of a clock. This has not been verified yet, but this is the theory.

When the brain clock is damaged in animals, their sleep patterns become confused. Such animals will sleep at irregular times throughout the day or night, and there is no longer any rhythm to their daily life.

Scientists can't experiment with humans the way that they do with animals, but there is no reason to believe that these clocks don't operate in at least as complicated a manner in humans as they do in animals. Wouldn't it be interesting to know what our bodies use to set the correct time? There has to be a standard time for all of God's creatures, and we are programmed in accordance with God's time when we keep our body temples in order. The same is true when we keep all of God's laws.

211

CROCODILE BABIES

And when she could not longer hide him, she took for him an ark of bulrushes, and daubed it with slime and with pitch, and put the child therein; and she laid it in the flags by the river's brink. Exodus 2:3.

In the same waters that sheltered baby Moses in his basket, baby Nile crocodiles are sheltered in a unique and fascinating manner. First, the mother crocodile lumbers ashore, finds a likely place, digs a hole about a foot deep, and lays her eggs in it. She carefully covers the eggs with soil and stands by to guard her nest for up to three months, just as Moses' mother hid him for his first three months. The hot tropical sun bakes the dirt that covers the eggs until it is just about as hard as rock. In fact, the dirt is so hard that when the eggs hatch and the baby crocodiles emerge they are trapped in what would be their graves if their mother weren't waiting outside. They let forth with a chorus of yelps, which the mother hears, and she rips open the nest to let them out.

But the strange story is just beginning. As each baby emerges from the ground the mother crocodile takes it gently in her jagged teeth, and gulps. One by one, the youngsters vanish, but they are alive and well in a special pouch in the mother's throat. After all twenty or so of the babies are safely inside this special crocodile transport, the mother lumbers heavily back into the water. There she releases her offspring into the safety of their watery home. It is comforting to know that even the predatory crocodile mother has a very tender regard for her offspring and sees to it that they are safely cared for.

Once the future seemed to be an unhappy one for baby Moses, for Pharaoh had ordered that all baby boys be killed. But God had a job for Moses, and He led Jochebed to place the baby in the water, where the old "crocodile's"—Pharaoh's—own daughter would find him and rescue him. We also have a special work to do for God. We have to help lead His people to the promised land, away from the worst crocodile of all—the devil.

A COLLECTION OF 20,000 BUTTERFLIES

They shall not hurt nor destroy in all my holy mountain: for the earth shall be full of the knowledge of the Lord, as the waters cover the sea. Isaiah 11:9.

Bernard D'Abrera of Australia has a butterfly collection that is one of the largest in the world. He has more than twenty thousand different kinds of butterflies in his collection! Can you imagine that? But that's not all. Not one of his butterflies was killed or is mounted in the usual way of butterfly collections. All of Dr. D'Abrera's butterflies have been captured on film. He is producing a massive five-volume series called *Butterflies of the World.* He feels that butterflies should be flying free—not pinned in dusty museum trays with the odor of moth balls. What do you think?

Have you ever made an insect or butterfly collection? When I was a boy I spent a lot of time every summer collecting butterflies and moths. My parents helped me make butterfly nets and drying boards, and they even had a special display cabinet made for me so that I could safely store my specimens. Collecting was fun, and I enjoyed chasing the insects night and day. But eventually all of my insects crumbled and broke into pieces, even in the special cases that had been prepared for them. Besides that, the butterflies, and especially the delicately colored moths, lost their living colors. Eventually they faded and weren't very pretty anymore, and I wondered why I had enjoyed making the collection.

I have decided that it was the collecting that was fun, not having the collection. I agree with Bernard D'Abrera. There is no need to catch the lovely creatures that Jesus created for us to enjoy; there is no need to kill them and pin them in a box in order to appreciate their beauty. And if I must have a collection I can take my camera and take pictures of them as they fly freely about and feed on the beautiful flowers. What kind of butterfly collection do you think Jesus would have made as a boy?

THE TREE-SWALLOW PARENTS

As birds flying, so will the Lord of hosts defend Jerusalem; defending also he will deliver it; and passing over he will preserve it. Isaiah 31:5.

A woman in Maine had a bird house in her yard. A glossy greenish-blue male tree swallow was able to claim the house, and his mate built a lovely nest. She laid three eggs, and soon the babies hatched. They were hungry from the start, and off went both parents looking for food. Again and again they returned to the nest with food.

But one day another pair of tree swallows showed up. They were not so brightly colored, so the woman could tell them from the first pair. The drab female decided that the three babies were hers and moved into the house while the real parents were hunting for food. A terrible battle took place when the true parents returned, and the true mother was so badly injured by the drab female that there was nothing that she could do but sit on top of the bird house, with one wing drooping. Her mate was heroic, but having worked so hard to find enough food for the babies, he was no match for the intruding pair. The real parents took up a vigil where they watched as the intruders seemed to have the young all to themselves. The drab female stayed in the house guarding, while the drab male had to do all of the feeding that the natural parents had shared.

Days passed. The natural mother's wing was healing. The true parents waited for the day when they would be able to take wing with renewed strength. It was just before the young birds were to leave the nest that the final battle took place. With feathers bright and with new zeal, the true parents attacked the intruders. The drab male was worn out from having to do all of the feeding and was now no match for the true parents, who drove him and his drab mate away in short order. In the end the true parents saw the young safely out of the nest and into the air on their first flight.

There could hardly be a better example of the way Jesus created the world and lost it temporarily to Satan. In due time, after a final struggle, He will take it back.

THE CRAZY-MONKEY CAPER

Let all things be done decently and in order. 1 Corinthians 14:40.

Your room should be a place where you like to go and where you have fun, but there is no question that a tidy room makes you feel better when you are there. The story of Coco provides a good-but-horrible example of a messed-up room.

Coco is a capuchin monkey—the kind used by organ grinders. Mr. and Mrs. Brandt owned a pet shop in Chicago, which they kept neat and clean for their customers and pets. The Brandts had just purchased Coco, and they placed him in a presumably monkeyproof cage for the night. They left the shop and locked the door, planning to return later in the evening to check on Coco.

Several hours later the Brandts returned to an awful sight: four police cars were there with lights flashing, and a crowd of people standing 14 deep were outside the pet shop straining to see what Coco would do next. Coco had gone ape!

"You've got a monkey in there wrecking the place," an officer said to Mr. Brandt.

What an understatement! Coco had opened the cage by unfastening a plate on the bottom. Now free, he was opening jars, overturning cages, breaking glass, and even opening flip-top cans. He was bouncing off the walls and hurling himself at the crowd on the other side of the shop window. He seemed to be using the pet shop as his private gymnasium.

Mr. Brandt unlocked the door and went inside. Coco came right to him as if nothing had happened—as if to say, "Daddy, I like this new place, there are so many neat things to play with." The Brandts were up all night cleaning up the mess. They fixed Coco's cage and put three padlocks on it. Mr. Brandt remembers the experience as the crazy-monkey caper, and he doesn't want to have another one—ever!

Such a mess might be understandable for a monkey that doesn't know any better, but when our rooms look like the results of Coco's antics, what is our excuse?

STORM PETRELS

And Peter answered him and said, Lord, if it be thou, bid me come unto thee on the water. Matthew 14:28.

Storm petrels are small seabirds that spend almost their entire lives far out in the ocean. Occasionally, a storm will blow them ashore, where people see them; that is why they are called *storm* petrels. The name petrel comes from the way some of them appear to be walking on the water, as Peter did. Actually, they are patting the water with their feet while holding themselves in the air with their wings. This odd action is part of their feeding behavior.

There are about twenty different kinds of storm petrels inhabiting the world's oceans; they vary in size from about six to ten inches in length. They are all drably colored in various shades of brown, black, and white. It is very difficult to tell some of them apart, because they look so much alike.

One of the best ways to identify the different kinds of storm petrel is to watch their feeding behavior above the water's surface. One author, writing about storm petrels, describes some of them like this: "The Wilson's and Elliot's storm petrels show the most foot-pattering;" the grey-backed storm petrel "skips and bounces from side to side;" the white-faced storm petrel "has a habit of dangling its legs and swinging as a pendulum set at two-second intervals and simultaneously hitting the water with both feet;" the white-bellied storm petrel "springs from side to side over the surface on outspread wings, using both feet as springboards;" the white-throated storm petrel "appears to kick off from a wave, glide for approximately 20 to 30 seconds, then kick off again;" Harcourt's storm petrel "hops, runs, and dances along the surface." Don't those descriptions make you want to see these remarkable birds?

When Peter stepped from the boat and began to walk toward Jesus on the water, his behavior also was very significant. As long as he feasted his eyes on Jesus he was safe, but when he looked away to others, he began to sink.

STRANGE APPAREL

And it shall come to pass in the day of the Lord's sacrifice, that I will punish the princes, and the king's children, and all such as are clothed with strange apparel. Zephaniah 1:8.

The term *strange apparel* probably referred to the people wearing things that made them look like the heathen of the surrounding nations. The sins of the tribe of Judah had become many, and, as is often the case when people depart from God, their unbelief was obvious in the way that they dressed.

Goldfish provide an interesting example of strange apparel. All of the ancestors of today's goldfish were drab, silvery-gray fish that lived in the freshwater streams of eastern China. Somewhere in history, these drab fishes became the object of fish culture, and beautiful golden varieties were created by selective breeding. These beautiful little fish soon became prized by the Japanese, as well, and because at first only the rulers and the wealthy of Japan were able to afford them, they were called royal fish. Still today, goldfish breeding and showing is more popular in Japan than anywhere else in the world.

As goldfish became more common, breeding them for special varieties became a hobby. Some of these varieties are beautiful, but recent varieties, or "fancies," are misshapen, grotesque, and helpless. There is the "lionhead," for example; it is a large, fatheaded goldfish that is a clumsy swimmer and cannot feed itself. The lionhead has to be hand fed all its life—the Japanese breeders feed it with chopsticks!

Another fancy example is the "bubble eye," which has huge sacs around its eyes, causing the eyes to bulge out like grotesque bubbles on its head. Owners of the bubble eye must remove all sharp objects from its aquarium.

We don't have to look drab. God wants us to be handsome and beautiful, but our apparel should glorify Jesus instead of being strange and grotesque.

on one

DODDER

Keep me as the apple of the eye, hide me under the shadow of thy wings, from the wicked that oppress me, from my deadly enemies, who compass me about. Psalm 17:8, 9.

Dodder is only one of many names for this strange plant. It is also called love vine, spaghetti plant, angel's hair, tangle gut, witches' shoelaces, devil's gut, and strangle weed. It is a common plant, growing the world around, but especially in the Americas. It is a member of the morning glory family, but has none of the lovely traits of that flower, except that it too is a clinging vine. There are many different species of dodder, but they all have the same unfortunate trait—they are parasites, taking all of their sustenance from other plants.

Farmers are particularly harmed by dodder, since the plant attacks such crops as clover, alfalfa, lespedeza, and other legumes. This parasite is not even able to make its own food. The dodder plants attach themselves to their host plants by tiny suckers that draw forth the juices from the host into their own hungry, vinelike growths. They often completely cover their host plant with orange or yellow tendrils, giving bloom to small white flowers. The tangled mass of dodder vines can easily overcome and kill the host plant.

There are dodder people, I am afraid. Have you ever heard someone called "a clinging vine"? It is not usually a compliment. Sometimes people don't receive enough love and feel as if nobody likes them. So they cling to you or to someone else in the hope the closeness will help them feel loved. We should not shun such people, although they do become a bit tedious at times. We need to introduce them to Jesus and let them know that there is someone who loves them. Try to help them cling to Jesus instead of clinging to you, and remember that we are all clinging vines, drawing every ounce of our strength from Jesus.

PRAYER AND PRAISE AT DAWN

And in the morning, rising up a great while before day, he went out, and departed into a solitary place, and there prayed. Mark 1:35.

To be waiting when the world wakes up in the morning is a great thrill. If you haven't tried it, I urge you to experience the exhilaration of dawn's first light. As I sit here writing, it is 5:30 A.M. The mockingbirds just woke up a few minutes ago, and I am warmed by their songs of anticipation as the day begins. Sometimes in the spring mockingbirds can't wait for morning, so they sing all night.

There is something about a morning that is special. Most of the world's people miss this time of day, but most of God's other creatures enjoy it, or at least it seems to me that they do. It is a time of intense activity. The night creatures hurry to finish their chores before retiring for the day, and the day creatures warm up for their activities. Flycatchers, for example, have special dawn songs that they sing only in the first light of the fading darkness. These songs are sweet warbles and twitters, unlike their raucous calls of the day.

Most small birds start the day with a song. Before eating, birds sing or call in some way. Then they set out to find breakfast.

Of course there is no way for the animals and birds to know what the day holds for them. There may be danger or delight ahead. Some may be injured, and some may die. Some unsuspecting bird may discover our bird feeder for the first time and find an unlimited food supply. The day ahead will bring all sorts of adventures, but now, in the breaking light of dawn, there is always time for a special song or call.

Our days are just as uncertain; each is a new adventure. Do we remember to take time every morning to lift our hearts to Jesus in prayer and praise?

219

NATURAL SUNSCREEN

The Lord is thy keeper: the Lord is thy shade upon thy right hand. The sun shall not smite thee by day, nor the moon by night. Psalm 121:5, 6.

The next time that you want to lie out in the sun to get a nice tan, remember what you are about to read. The suntan is your body's defense against the ultraviolet rays of the sun. Too much sun ages the skin prematurely, and people who spend hours lying out in the sun to get a tan are not doing their bodies any favors.

Our skin comes equipped with myriads of tiny cells called melanocytes. The purpose of these cells is to monitor the amount of ultraviolet radiation that is being received by the skin and to produce a natural sunscreen for the skin if the level of radiation becomes too high. The natural sunscreen is called *melanin*. Melanin is the brown pigment that causes the suntan.

Every person on earth, regardless of apparent skin color, has about the same number of melanin-producing cells. The difference between the fair-skinned person from northern Europe and the dark-skinned person from equatorial Africa is not the number of melanin-producing cells, but the amount of melanin that these cells produce. The African's melanocytes produce melanin at a persistently rapid rate, whereas the Swede's melanocytes produce melanin at a restrictedly slow pace.

Each melanocyte has a few skin cells that it watches over. When the ultraviolet rays of the sun strike the skin cells a message is transmitted to the melanocytes, and more dark granules of melanin are formed and begin to flow into the surrounding cells to form a protective covering for the cell's nucleus. The destructive ultraviolet rays are absorbed by the melanin.

A good tan looks great, but even more desirable is the sunscreen that Jesus provides for those who rely on Him for protection from the world's scorching heat. The Lord provides a physical protection for our skin, and He provides spiritual safety for our souls.

WORLD'S STRONGEST MAGNET

And I, if I be lifted up from the earth, will draw all men unto me. John 12:32.

We measure distance in such units as inches, centimeters, and miles. We measure time in such units as minutes, hours, and years. But you know all that, don't you? Maybe you don't know the name of the unit that scientists use to measure the pulling power of a magnet. This unit of measure is called a gauss (pronounced to rhyme with house), and it was named after the German mathematician Karl Gauss. The plural of the word is also gauss. The amount of magnetic power needed to make your compass needle work is about one-half of one gauss—the strength of the earth's magnetic field.

The largest man-made magnet is one recently produced at the Massachusetts Institute of Technology. At full power this magnet can produce a magnetic field of 300,000 gauss. What a force that is! It takes 4.5 million watts of electricity to power this magnet. (An average light bulb takes only 60 or 100 watts.)

We have all played with small magnets, and we know that in one way magnets attract and in another way they repel, and that many substances have no response to the magnet at all. Have you ever held a strong toy magnet over a pile of small nails or tacks and watched the nails almost leap up and cling to the magnet? The magnetic field surrounding the magnet is extremely attractive to materials containing iron. And when a nail is attracted to the magnet that nail also becomes magnetized, so other nails become attracted to it. But if you take the nail away from the magnet it loses most of its magnetic power. Only when the nail is connected to the magnet does it also have strong magnetism.

Jesus, when He came to earth and died for you and me, established a spiritual magnetic field as powerful as the whole universe and would make the MIT magnet seem like a toy compass in comparison. When we accept Jesus as our Saviour, His magnetism begins to draw us to Himself, and we not only receive His blessings ourselves but we also become magnetized and able to attract others to Jesus.

C̶o̶n̶v̶i̶e̶w̶

THE JESUS BIRD

Who gave himself for our sins, that he might deliver us from this present evil world, according to the will of God and our Father: To whom be glory for ever and ever. Amen. Galatians 1:4, 5.

If you were to ask me to pick a bird to represent Jesus, I wouldn't choose the eagle or the dove. I would select the bluebird. My choice isn't based on the lovely color of the bluebird or its wonderful song, though both of these characteristics would be fitting honor for my Lord.

The reason I would choose the bluebird as the bird to represent the Creator is simple: the bluebird demonstrates such devotion to its family and to the families of its neighbors that it will defend them to the death.

One of the primary enemies of bluebirds is the house sparrow. House sparrows can nest just about anywhere, but they seem almost to delight in taking over a bluebird's house and ousting the bluebird family. If there are eggs, the sparrows peck holes in the eggs; if there are young, the sparrows kill them by pecking them on the head and then either throw them out the door or proceed to build their own nest right over the top of the little bluebird bodies.

Now, the father bluebird doesn't just sit by while the sparrows massacre his young. He fearlessly goes into the box to do battle with the intruders, but he is at a disadvantage inside the nest box; the smaller and more robust sparrows are able to maneuver better, and the bluebird is often overcome by the same type of hammering blows to the head. The sparrows leave him where he falls. Famous bluebird specialist Lawrence Zeleny, says that it is fairly common to remove a sparrow nest from a bluebird box and find the remains of an adult male bluebird under the sparrow's nest—and the "bluebirds almost always show the fatal peck marks over most of its head."

Our Saviour dared to come into this world, the stronghold of the devil, to rescue His children. He gave His life in the attempt, but, praise His name, He rose again!

SAUROLOPHUS

And it repented the Lord that he had made man on the earth, and it grieved him at his heart. And the Lord said, I will destroy man whom I have created from the face of the earth; both man, and beast, and the creeping thing, and the fowls of the air; for it repenteth me that I have made them. Genesis 6:6, 7.

According to the newspaper his name was Saurolophus (pronounced saw-ROL-o-fus). A native Californian, he lived near Fresno. He was a peace loving vegetarian with more than a thousand teeth, and he weighed about 6,000 pounds. Rumor has it that when Saurolophus and his family began to talk, the vibrations would literally rattle your bones if you were nearby. He was built a bit like a kangaroo, with powerful hind legs and a long powerful tail. He had a long, S-shaped neck and a hornlike crest on the back of his horselike head. He was 30 feet long. Was Saurolophus a monster? Well, I don't know about that, but if you saw him today you'd probably call him a monster.

Saurolophus was a dinosaur. His bones were discovered not long ago in the San Joaquin Valley. He lived with other members of the Saurolophus family on the shore of what was at that time the ocean, and he and his friends ran around in packs in search of plants to eat.

I don't know where Noah and his family lived, but if it was near California, maybe when they were boys, Shem, Ham, and Japheth saw Saurolophus. Then again, maybe all the dinosaurs lived in areas where there weren't any people. We just don't know, do we? Even though the dinosaurs were perhaps monsters formed in some way by the workings of Satan, I feel certain that Jesus was very sad when they had to be destroyed, for He is the Creator of all life. Even though He didn't make dinosaurs, as such, their life had come from Him, and I believe that the loss of the dinosaurs also contributed to the grief in His heart. When He comes again, Jesus will again grieve over the lost ones.

SHE HAS AN EAR ON HER KNEE

Give ear, O my people, to my law: incline your ears to the words of my mouth. Psalm 78:1.

How would you like to have an ear on the side of your leg, just below your knee? This is the location of a cricket's eardrum. No one knows why a cricket's ears are located in what seems to us to be such a strange place, but if a cricket had our intelligence and were writing this for other crickets to read, he might ask, "How would you like to have ears on your head?" And the crickets would marvel together about what strange creatures we are to have ears where we have them.

Where our ears are located is not nearly so important as what we are able to do with them. The female cricket, with ears on her knees, is listening for one thing only—the call of her mate. It is only the male who sings, and the female listens and seeks him out. If she happens to lose her front legs (where the ears are located) she will be deaf to her mate's call. But as long as she has ears she instinctively responds, because that is the way she is. She is possessed with a singleness of purpose.

What are you listening for in life? Do you have a singleness of purpose and give ear to the words of our heavenly Father, or do you let yourself be enchanted by the sounds of other influences? In the Bible Jesus referred to the church on this earth as His bride. We can certainly learn from the cricket's bride to listen closely with singleness of ear to the words of the King of heaven and to seek Him out with all of our heart. He says, "Incline your ear, and come unto me: hear, and your soul shall live" (Isa. 55:3). We also have the promise that our God "is a rewarder of them that diligently seek him" (Heb. 11:6).

It is interesting that when the female cricket finds her mate he then sings a new song to her. The Bible tells us that when we get to heaven with Jesus, we will all join in singing a new song.

224

HOT SPRINGS AND SEA WORMS

Hast thou entered into the springs of the sea? or hast thou walked in the search of the depth? Job 38:16.

Several years ago big news came from the Department of Invertebrate Zoology of the Smithsonian Institution. A completely new form of animal life, like none ever known before, had been discovered on the ocean floor near the Galapagos Islands. In the words of Dr. Meredith Jones, researcher in the department, these new creatures "are without precedent in the whole animal kingdom." What kind of animal could this be?

These new creatures live in tubes that are five feet long. The creatures construct the tubes themselves. They have no mouth, no eyes, and no intestines. Their anatomy is so different that all the biology books in the world will have to be rewritten to include a new basic form of living creature. Scientists don't know what to call the creature, but they have tentatively placed the new life form in the broad general category of marine worms. This is not a wriggly worm like those you see in your garden. These are more like the tube worms that are common in the sea; but tube worms eat, and these "worms" do not—or at least they don't have a digestive system. They seem to utilize symbiotic bacteria in their bodies as a food source.

The ten-foot worms were discovered by the operators of the deep-sea submarine *Alvin.* They are located about 8,000 feet below sea-level at the bottom of the Pacific Ocean near volcanic vents that heat the water of the ocean floor to high temperatures, supporting all sorts of new types of animal life. Finding these colonies of undersea life is one of the most exciting biological discoveries of the century. It is hard to say what else will be found down there.

It is so hard to imagine the living conditions that exist under 8,000 feet of water, where the pressure is exceedingly great and where no light from the sun has ever penetrated. Yet God's creative power to sustain life is there. Can we ever doubt His tender care for each of us?

THE MIRROR ORCHID

For many shall come in my name, saying, I am Christ; and shall deceive many. Mark 13:6.

If you want something very badly, but you aren't really sure what it is like, you could easily be deceived into taking something that is a fake. There are many such swindles taking place all the time in the business world. You have to know what the real thing is all about, and then you have to test all of the look-alikes to make sure that you aren't being deceived.

On the shores of the Mediterranean Sea lives a delicate flower called the mirror orchid. It is often true that orchids are closely linked together with a special type of insect that helps in the pollination process. The mirror orchid is no exception. There is a tiny wasp that has the right habits properly to enter the flower and transfer the pollen from the stamens to the stigma of another orchid flower, thus assisting in the production of seed so more orchids will grow. But the orchid gets the wasp to perform this task by deception. On the large liplike petal of the orchid is a perfect replica of the female wasp. But that is not all, the orchid also produces a chemical scent that duplicates the scent that the female wasp gives out to attract the male for mating. So first the male wasp is attracted to the scent of the orchid, and then he *thinks* that he sees her, so he alights on the orchid to get acquainted and gets covered with the pollen of the orchid. Then, realizing that he has been tricked, the male lifts off (covered with pollen, of course) and flies on. Soon he is attracted by the scent of another flower and again sees what he thinks is a female, so he lights on the second plant to investigate, and in the process pollinates the flower. Eventually, the male wasp may find a real female, but in the meantime the orchid has made a fool of him.

Hopefully, we are taking time to become acquainted with Jesus so that we don't get turned aside by one claim or another of a *false* messiah.

DREAM CLOUDS

Thy mercy, O Lord, is in the heavens; and thy faithfulness reacheth unto the clouds. Psalm 36:5.

My family raised cotton when I was very small, and after it was picked it would sometimes be piled in a great mound on my grandfather's porch. I remember how much fun it was to have my father or my uncle throw me into that pile. I would sink deliciously into all that softness and beg for someone to do it again. I guess that is why I used to like to lie on my back and look up at the fluffy clouds and think about how much fun it would be to jump around in them as if they were giant piles of fluffy cotton.

Now when I fly in an airplane and look down on those clouds I get the same urge. Wouldn't it be just super to jump out of the airplane and land right in the middle of one of those mounds of fluff? Well, it would be foolhardy for me to do that; I'm sure you would agree. But I have heard of a man who did just that and lived to tell about it. Oh, he didn't mean to jump, and he didn't really jump as I have always wanted to. He was a jet test pilot, and he had to bail out high above the clouds one day when something went wrong. He had a parachute but it was set to open automatically when he got down to a certain altitude. He was free falling to get down to that altitude when he happened to fall into one of those great big fluffy clouds called a thunderhead.

In case you didn't know it, inside a thunderhead is a very dangerous place to be. Airplanes can be ripped apart like toys in there. Pilots avoid thunderheads at all cost. The air is rising and falling at great speed, and lightning and thunder are almost constant. The test pilot fell right into the middle of all this. He was bounced around like a piece of popcorn in a popper for many minutes. Finally he fell through the roughest part to the altitude where his chute opened. He landed safely and wrote his story for all to read. That man should certainly know that the Lord's mercy and faithfulness reach even to the clouds.

Commit

GEESE AT PEACE

Blessed are the peacemakers: for they shall be called the children of God. Matthew 5:9.

Canada geese mate for life and often return year after year to the same location to raise their young. They fiercely defend their nest and young against all intruders.

Usually a pair of geese will build their nest and hatch the young in one location, then move the goslings on foot to a carefully chosen brood site, where they will stay until the young learn to fly. In nearly all cases, whether afloat or afoot, one of the parents leads the way and the other brings up the rear, with the young ones safely between.

A pair of Canada geese set up housekeeping on an island in a farm pond in New Jersey. Year after year these two returned to raise their young. One summer, only one of seven eggs hatched, and the hatchling died the next day. The parents moped for days only to be faced with a new problem.

From the woods by the lake another pair of Canada geese emerged with eight brand-new babies. For some reason, this new pair had chosen the farm pond—and woefully, the island itself—as their brood site. As they arrived on the scene they went straight to the island ready to do battle for the rights to the location. Of course the residents fought hard to keep what they thought was their own territory, but they could not drive the newcomers away.

As night approached, the resident pair still occupied the island—except for a corner where the new pair huddled with their young, having been granted sleeping privileges. The farmer and his wife went to bed that evening wondering what the outcome of the battle would be the next day.

Imagine the farmer's surprise the next morning when he looked out on the lake and saw eight baby geese swimming peacefully with not one but two parents in the lead and two bringing up the rear. By making peace, the adult geese had not only provided double protection for the goslings but had also provided the resident pair with babies to care for to replace the ones they had lost.

228

HAWAIIAN KANGAROO: "INSTANT EVOLUTION"

And God said, Let the earth bring forth the living creature after his kind, cattle, and creeping thing, and beast of the earth after his kind: and it was so. Genesis 1:24.

Recently we read an article in a science magazine entitled "Instant Evolution." The article told of a new species of miniature kangaroo that has developed on the island of Oahu in Hawaii. It has been named the Kalihi rock wallaby.

A pair of Australian wallabies escaped from a zoo in Hawaii in 1916. Since that time (just about 70 years) the descendants of that first pair have produced a population of several hundred members. But they don't look like their Australian ancestors, and therein lies a mystery that has somewhat baffled the zoologists studying these cute little fellows.

In less than 60 generations these small marsupials (pouched mammals) have managed to produce a type of wallaby that is smaller, lighter in color, and—most remarkable of all—has a different biochemical make-up, allowing it to eat plants in Hawaii that would have been inedible to its Australian forefathers. In human terms, it would be like producing a completely different type of people somewhere on earth in less than 1500 years—people who not only look different but are able to live in an environment that is radically different from that of their forefathers.

Given the length of time that most evolutionists believe it takes to do what these little wallabies did in such a short time, James Laxell, the zoologist who described them as a new species, said, "To evolve into an entirely new species in only sixty generations . . . that's pretty spectacular." Is this spectacular to those of us who believe that all of the creatures in the world have diversified to what they are today in only about 6,000 years? I don't think it is amazing at all. It is simply a testimony to the adaptability of the creatures that God created. Even after 6,000 years of sin, the breath of life is healthy.

229

Joe

M82

Thus saith the Lord, which giveth the sun for a light by day, and the ordinances of the moon and of the stars for a light by night, which divideth the sea when the waves thereof roar; The Lord of hosts is his name. Jeremiah 31:35.

One of the billions of mysteries in the universe is named M82. But don't let such a little name make you think that M82 is small, for you can't even *imagine* how large M82 is! Actually, no one really knows what it is, but there are some theories. M82 was first thought to be an exploding galaxy. A galaxy is a collection of millions of suns forming a sort of island in space; this is why galaxies are sometimes called island universes. But M82 has no stars—it is made up primarily of dust. And therein lies another part of the mystery: the dust is moving very slowly, and it ought to be moving at great speed if it were the result of the supposed explosion. This means that if there was an explosion, the dust was not the result—so, what exploded?

At the center of M82 is empty space, or that is what astronomers think is there. It is possible that there is a black hole at the center, because M82 gives many of the radiation messages that are associated with black holes. A black hole is hard to describe, but, simply put, it is an object that is so dense that the gravity is so great that nothing can escape it, not even light. So black holes are really objects that you can't see because they don't give off any light. Now the center of M82 gives off some of the radiation signals of a black hole, but the rest of the galaxy around it doesn't appear that it is being sucked into the center as it would be if there were a black hole there. So astronomers must assume that the center is empty. But why is the center empty? And if there was an explosion, as it appears there was, what blew up, and where are its remains?

These are only a few of the questions that await answers when we meet with Jesus, the greatest Astronomer in the universe, and the Creator of M82.

SOLITARY BOXCAR

And he said unto them, Come ye yourselves apart into a desert place, and rest a while: for there were many coming and going, and they had no leisure so much as to eat. Mark 6:31.

I have been thankful for this text many times. When you get busy working for Jesus, it sometimes seems that you should not take time to rest—there is so much to be done. But Jesus, who made you and me, knows that there is a limit to what a person can do, even when he or she is doing good things. So it is absolutely necessary to get away from the hustle and bustle of things on a regular basis and enjoy some peace and quiet.

If you live in the middle of the city you may be tempted to think that you can't get away into a quiet place, and you may be right. Not long ago I read of a man living in Houston, Texas, who found a way to find solitude within earshot of the city.

Mr. Lucian Smith wanted to get out of the city, and Houston is the fifth largest city in the United States, with all the noise and hurry that goes with it. But Mr. Smith couldn't afford to buy a nice house in the country—he couldn't afford to buy *any* house in the country. So guess what he did. Mr. Smith bought an acre of land in nearby Manvel, Texas (a Houston suburb). He then bought an old boxcar from the local railroad for $1,100. He moved the boxcar to his acre, moved in, and he has lived there ever since. He likes the boxcar, he said, because it needs little upkeep, is well insulated, and is easy to heat.

But Mr. Smith didn't stop there. He became concerned about some of the poor folks who had moved to the city in hopes of finding a job but found themselves out of money instead. So Mr. Smith ran an ad in the paper offering to provide free space for up to three families who want to live with him on his land. To qualify they must help with the garden and look for work. If Mr. Smith can find a solitary place in the Houston area, we can all find a place to go to take Jesus' advice.

ALL THE GOLD IN THE WORLD

I counsel thee to buy of me gold tried in the fire, that thou mayest be rich. Revelation 3:18.

If you had all the gold in the world, how large a building would you have to build to hold it? Before I tell you the answer, let me tell you that throughout recorded history man has been seeking gold. And it is quite certain that more than 99 percent of the gold ever found in the past 4,000 years or so is still around in one form or another, including the gold owned by the United States Government, which is stored in underground vaults at Ft. Knox, in Kentucky. A number of other countries have similar storing facilities and vast gold holdings. So you are going to have to find a building large enough to hold a *lot* of gold!

There is something else that you should know before determining how big your building is going to be. Only half of the gold in the world is owned by governments. The rest is owned by individuals and private companies everywhere. And then, of course, there is the gold in people's watches, in their teeth, and on the golden domes of temples and public buildings everywhere. Now, are you ready to figure the size of the warehouse that it would take to hold all the gold?

Would it all fit in the Superdome, or the Astrodome? Yes, it will all fit into one of those structures, but you don't need anything that large, because all the gold in the world, if it were made into one solid chunk of gold, would make a cubic block measuring only about 54 feet on each side. So if you were to build a warehouse to hold it and if you planned on having a 12-foot ceiling, the building would only have to be about 100 by 132 feet in area.

Before you begin dreaming about how wonderful it would be to have all that wealth, consider that if you did have it you wouldn't live long. The world's greed for gold is well known. And in terms of eternal benefits, even all the gold in the world would be worthless.

CHEE CHEE

And he arose, and came to his father. But when he was yet a
great way off, his father saw him, and had compassion, and ran,
and fell on his neck, and kissed him. Luke 15:20.

For 55 days Ethel Woolfenden nursed the American kestrel,
or sparrow hawk, from babyhood to adulthood. Chee Chee was a
bedraggled cripple when they brought her in—the lone survivor
of a nest of kestrels. The rest were killed when the nest was
destroyed. Ethel had been trained to care for orphan birds, so
she welcomed little Chee Chee.

Every day for nearly two months Ethel massaged the little
bird's leg. Chee Chee grew new feathers and seemed to relish the
cage that became his new nest. He would snuggle up to the side
of Ethel's head and chatter softly to her, as he pecked gently at
her hair.

The day came to release Chee Chee. He was a grown kestrel
and needed to be wild and free. Ethel, who has been nursing
injured birds and releasing them back to the wild for more than
40 years, says that she has often cried when the inexperienced
young birds leave her roost. It is so hard to see them go, but it is
better than keeping them in a cage for the rest of their lives.

Chee Chee looked at the open back door, which had always
been closed to him before, and then sailed through it into the big
outdoors. For two days Ethel would go out and call Chee Chee,
but he didn't come back. How was he? Was he eating? She had
hoped that he would return now and then until he became
accustomed to the wild. Several days later she heard a terrible
commotion in the yard. She rushed out to see Chee Chee on a
utility wire—he was being attacked from all sides by other
birds. He was losing tail feathers and getting severely pecked.
Ethel found the cage and blanket that used to cover Chee Chee's
cage at night. When she took them out to the porch, Chee Chee
dove straight into the cage under the blanket, grabbed a piece of
steak offered to him, and began to eat. Chee Chee was home. He
would fly again, but until he was used to the wild he would come
home often.

233

WHY ARE PINE CONES TILTED?

As for God, his way is perfect; the word of the Lord is tried: he is a buckler to all them that trust in him. 2 Samuel 22:31.

Who would think that the way a pine cone is situated on the tree is important? Karl Niklas, of Cornell University, wondered about pine cones, and many times when you wonder, wonderful things are learned.

What Dr. Niklas learned was that pine cones are built according to exact aerodynamic principles, which ensure that the greatest number of pollen grains will land inside the pine cone to pollinate the ovules and produce the seeds that make more pine trees.

Pine pollen is produced in the male cones and must be transported by the wind to the female cones. But the wind doesn't know where the pine cones are—it just blows the pollen around. So the female cones must be shaped in such a way as to encourage the reception of the pollen. What Dr. Niklas found was that the shape of the pine cone causes the passing wind to move in three specific patterns, each of which funnels the pollen into the waiting female cones. The three patterns are (1) tight spirals, (2) corkscrews, and (3) downwind eddies.

Dr. Niklas also found that each kind of pine tree has its own particular shape of pine cone. Therefore, each pine cone receives more of its own particular kind of pollen than it does the pollen of other pine trees that it doesn't need. But there is still more.

Pine cones normally sit up straight on the branch when they are at the stage of receiving pollen. In the laboratory Dr. Niklas found that the most efficient angle for the pine cones was a tilt of about 45 degrees. So he went back to the woods and observed and measured the trees again. Guess what he found. Yes, pine cones sit up straight when the wind is calm, but when the wind blows (and that is when the pollen is arriving, remember!) the pine branches twist, placing the cones at a 45-degree angle!

HARD WATER

But whosoever drinketh of the water that I shall give him shall never thirst; but the water that I shall give him shall be in him a well of water springing up into everlasting life. John 4:14.

Perhaps you have heard people talk about water as being hard or soft. Usually well water is called *hard* because it contains dissolved minerals from the ground. Rain water, on the other hand, is called *soft* because it doesn't have the minerals. There are all sorts of theories about which is more healthful—hard-water or soft water. A doctor at the University of Texas has been studying this question for many years and has found that in those areas of the world where the people drink hard water there is less heart disease. In one of his studies, Dr. Dawson found that hard-water drinkers had a 25 percent lower death rate owing to heart attack. Dr. Dawson has not yet found any special ingredient that helps the hard-water drinker, but his theory is that the body makes soap out of hard water, a process that actually cleans out the fats that would otherwise be taken into the body and would increase the chance of a heart attack.

Calcium and magnesium are minerals found in hard water. These two minerals combine easily with fat to make soap, and Dr. Dawson believes that this is exactly what happens inside the person who drinks hard water. The water provides the minerals, the food eaten provides the fats, and soap is the result. Since soap can't be digested and used by the body, it is eliminated, taking the unwanted fats along with it. So, if Dr. Dawson's theory is correct, hard water is like putting a special soap into your body to help clean your system of unhealthful materials there.

Our bodies are the temple of the Holy Spirit, and Jesus used water on a number of occasions as a symbol of His wonder-working power within us. Some of the things that Jesus tells us to do, however, are "hard sayings" (John 6:60), but, like the soap in hard water, they make us healthy Christians. Let's listen to Jesus and drink His water.

mamie

WAITING TICKS

Go ye therefore, and teach all nations, baptizing them in the name of the Father, and of the Son, and of the Holy Ghost. Matthew 28:19.

When I first read about how long ticks will wait for a warmblooded animal to walk by, I thought, "What lesson can that possibly teach us about the love of God?" A wood tick will wait many months for a feeling of warmth that tells it that it is time to drop down and get dinner! Well, I could say that the wood tick gives us a good example of patience, but I wouldn't want to go around telling people that they should be like the wood tick—those bloodthirsty little monsters who create so many problems for people.

Then I thought of how long the people of the world wait for the warmth of Jesus' love—the presentation of which can come only from His followers' living His life and spreading His warmth throughout the world. Before Jesus comes into our lives we are not much better than a wood tick. The Bible tells us that our self-righteousness is as filthy rags, so we don't have much to be proud of, do we?

What does a wood tick wait for, and how does it know when it is there? The tick climbs a shrub or tree, crawls out onto a branch, and waits until it feels a warmblooded animal approaching. The warmth is the signal to jump! The plan, of course, is to land on the origin of that warmth, which will normally be a mammal of some sort. But as a precaution, the tick tests the skin for butyric acid—a substance emitted from the skin of all mammals—and, if it is there, down will go the mouth drill and in no time the blood pump will be installed, filling the tick to capacity.

The tick is not the most welcome of visitors, and I don't mean that we will remain like wood ticks when we come to know the warm love of Jesus' character. What I do think is that there are millions of people in the world, some of them quite bloodthirsty, who have been waiting a very long time to feel the warmth of Jesus through you and me.

TREES HAVE A PLUMBING SYSTEM

I am the vine, ye are the branches: He that abideth in me, and I in him, the same bringeth forth much fruit: for without me ye can do nothing. John 15:5.

There are tiny tubes throughout plants that carry water from the roots to the topmost branches of even the tallest trees, which are several hundred feet high. There are a number of physical forces that cause the water to flow up that high, but there is an especially interesting thing about the internal plumbing system of plants.

Since water is piped up from the ground, you would think that the lower branches and leaves would receive more water than the upper branches do, but such is not the case. In many instances the upper branches, where growth is occurring at the greatest rate, receive the most water. This is especially true in times of drought. How can this be?

Well, there are thousands of tiny pipes called xylem cells (pronounced ZY-lem). These tiny pipes, which carry water from the roots to various parts of the plant, are not laid out to go straight up—not at all. Instead, they form a very complicated system of plumbing; some pipes carry water straight to the topmost branches, some carry water to the lower branches, and others carry water to the branches between. Furthermore, no one section of the roots supplies one section of the tree; that is, the pipes are interconnected as they go up the stem (or trunk) so that they form a network of vessels taking water from every part of the root system to every branch in the plant. With this system, though there may be a water shortage in one area of the ground under the tree, all the parts of the tree will still receive an equal amount of water. Also, if the stem of the plant is wounded, even severely, on one side, no one part of the tree will suffer more than another.

What a wonderful example of the way Jesus provides us with His Spirit—that living water that He has promised to everyone who asks. And He supplies special measures of His Spirit to those new Christians who are just developing.

corrnu

THE MIGHTY SMALL BEAST

But the tongue can no man tame; it is an unruly evil, full of deadly poison. James 3:8.

There is a beast of the forest that is probably the most ferocious of all the beasts of the earth. This beast thinks nothing of attacking, killing, and eating animals many times larger than itself. While occasionally seen in the daytime, this beast is most active at night, but it is rarely seen even then. One member of this family breathes more than 800 times a minute, and when it really becomes excited its heart beats 1,200 times per minute. The beast is so high-strung that a sudden loud noise can literally scare it to death. Have you guessed what the beast is?

Just in case you still don't know what we are talking about, here's a clue that will give the name of the animal away: this monster mammal is actually very tiny; it is as heavy as a quarter. In fact, a really small one, when fully grown, will weigh no more than a dime! Surely you know by now that we are describing the shrew. It is the world's smallest mammal, but also the most ferocious.

Shrews have to eat their weight in food every day just to stay alive. Some have been known to devour three times their body weight in a day and to attack and kill birds and mammals the size of large mice. Some shrews have poisonous saliva that aid them in doing away with their larger prey, but on the whole this mighty little beast just fights his way to dinner by attacking anything and everything that moves—if it isn't too big.

The shrew can't help being the way it is, but we can be sure not to act like one. We don't need to go through our days biting people's heads off, as it were, or being impatient and crabby. Maybe shrewish people feel unimportant and want others to notice them, so they try to get attention by being bullies. The trouble is that acting tough to appear important drives others away; when someone behaves like a shrew he is avoided and left alone, just as the shrew is.

238

THE RED-SEA REEFS

He brought them out, after that he had shewed wonders and signs in the land of Egypt, and in the Red sea, and in the wilderness forty years. Acts 7:36.

You all know about the wonders that took place when Moses and the children of Israel crossed the Red Sea, but there are some other wonders in the Red Sea that you might not know about.

Among the most beautiful coral reefs in the world are those of the Red Sea. These reefs have been growing on undersea cliffs for thousands of years—perhaps even when Moses crossed the sea. The Red Sea is 7,000 feet deep here, so it is unlikely that Moses crossed at this point, but it is interesting to imagine that some of Moses' friends, or perhaps even he himself, swam in the area. Maybe they saw the strange crocodile fish with its fat lips, or perhaps they saw the bright-yellow butterfly fish that always swim in pairs, or the venomous scorpion fish, camouflaged as coral and red seaweed. They could have seen the bright-red squirrel fish, the lionfish, or the trigger fish that change into spotted or striped pajama patterns for the night.

Living in the crystal clear waters of this coral jungle are schools of marine goldfish that have a very interesting ability. Each school is ruled by a headmaster—a dominant male. At his side is a ruling female—the queen of the school. When the headmaster dies the dominant female simply turns into a male and takes his place. Her color even changes from the pale yellow of a female to the bright orange of a male.

All of this wonder and splendor lives in the middle of one of the world's most war-torn regions—the coast of the Sinai Peninsula. Maybe if the selfish people of the world would take time to appreciate the beautiful creatures that inhabit the world and have learned to live in peace, they too would learn to tolerate the differences between individuals, races, and nationalities instead of making war—but that would be heaven, wouldn't it?

THE ESKIMO CURLEW

Ye have lived in pleasure on the earth, and been wanton; ye have nourished your hearts, as in a day of slaughter. James 5:5.

Jesus must have a special place in His heart for the Eskimo curlew. This beautiful bird once flew in such numbers that they were described as clouds. Tremendous flocks of Eskimo curlews would descend from their migratory flight to feed in a field, covering forty or fifty acres of ground. Flocks flying overhead were often as large as one-half mile in length and one hundred yards in width. Today you may not find one Eskimo curlew. There are rare reports, but there have been no positive sightings in more than twenty years.

Eskimo curlews nested along the Arctic Coast of North America and wintered in Argentina. To get from the Arctic to South America, these birds followed a route leading east to Labrador, south across Newfoundland and Nova Scotia, then across 2,000 miles of ocean to the West Indies, and on to South America. The return trip every spring took the birds up the west coast of South America, across the Gulf of Mexico, and north across the prairies from the Texas coast to their home in the Arctic.

But Eskimo curlews were doomed because they were good to eat. They brought a good price in the markets, so hunters were out in force when the curlews passed through. Before 1870, in Labrador, a group of hunters would go out in one day and bring back 2,000 curlews. In Kansas and Nebraska, hunters would fill wagons with the curlews that they had shot, and then they would sell them in Omaha, Kansas City, and St. Louis. It was an annual slaughter for the curlews. Some hunters just shot them for sport, leaving their bodies in heaps as high as haystacks on the prairie. By 1900 the Eskimo curlews were nearly gone; only *twelve* were found in Labrador that year. In 1912, eight birds were seen, and all but one were shot.

The selfishness and greed of man knows no bounds when his heart is not touched by the tenderness of Jesus.

THEY LAUGH AT DDT

There shall no evil befall thee, neither shall any plague come nigh thy dwelling. Psalm 91:10.

A few years ago DDT was the most effective insecticide known. It was used everywhere, and for a time bothersome insects seemed doomed. Before long, however, some of those insects began to become immune to the poison. Today DDT is not nearly so effective a pest killer as it used to be. Also, the poison played havoc with many insect- and fish-eating birds, since the effect of the poison builds, as greater and greater amounts of it are stored in the system. DDT was largely discontinued as an insecticide.

But DDT is still effective. For example, it takes only six micrograms of DDT to quickly eliminate a honey bee. With that in mind, the following story is certainly remarkable.

Several years ago, houses in the Amazonas state of Brazil were sprayed with DDT to eradicate the mosquitoes. Almost immediately swarms of local plant-pollinating bees invaded the houses. Only male bees came, for some reason. Thousands of the bees buzzed into each house, went straight to the DDT that was sticking to the walls, gathered the stuff into the pouches on their hind legs, and flew away with it. Nearly all the houses in the region were stripped of the DDT. The local people were unhappy about losing the insecticide, but they complained most about the terrible noise that the bees made in their numerous trips to collect the poison. There is no explanation for this incident. Each bee carried away as much as 2,000 micrograms of DDT without any apparent ill effects.

It is certainly true that in this world there is enough sin to eradicate all of us. Sin is the most potent "humanicide" in the universe. But, wonder of wonders, Jesus will come down and destroy it all, making it possible for us to live and feel none of the killing effects of even our own sins.

more

A FROG'S-EYE VIEW

Open thou mine eyes, that I may behold wondrous things out of thy law. Psalm 119:18.

You have been hearing a lot about computers these days. The first computers were very large, requiring large rooms to hold all of their units and wires. At that time someone wrote that a computer with the capacity of the human brain would have more wires and circuits than all the radio and TV stations in the world, would need a building as large as the Empire State Building to house it, and would require the whole Niagara River to cool it—and even then it couldn't decide whether to have waffles or pancakes for breakfast.

Scientists keep trying to produce the perfect electronic brain. One of the more recent breakthroughs has been the minicomputer—a very small unit, not much larger than a typewriter. A minicomputer can operate on its own or can be connected to a network computer to operate as a part of a giant computing system.

Scientists have been helped in developing better computers by studying various animals. Take a frog's eye, for example, it is connected to a minicomputer that can operate independently from the main computer in the frog's brain. If the frog's eye sees an insect flying too far away to reach, the eye computer simply screens out that information. This minicomputer calculates the size and distance of all insects flying by and sends a message to the mainbrain computer only when the fly is within range of the frog's sticky tongue. The brain then informs the tongue that there is a bug out there that is just so far away and flying just so fast. Out goes the tongue, and the frog has its dinner. The whole process takes only a split second.

We also are made up of systems similar to those of a frog, but ours are even more complicated. Not only do we have minicomputers that screen out what we see and hear, we also have systems that help us to understand God's word, in order to gain wonderful truths out of His law.

242

HELICONIUS AND THE PASSION VINE

Thy word have I hid in mine heart, that I might not sin against thee. Psalm 119:11.

You know that each butterfly, when it is still a caterpillar, feeds on a specific type of plant. Without that particular type of plant the caterpillar would starve. In most cases we don't yet know why each type of butterfly is restricted to the type of plant that it feeds upon, but in at least one case the secret has been discovered.

The heliconius butterfly is one of a number of related butterflies that inhabit the American tropics. An entomologist (one who studies insects) at the University of Texas has been studying the relationship between the heliconius caterpillar and the tropical passion vines that make up its entire diet. The caterpillar won't eat anything else—it cannot survive on anything else. How would you like to eat just one thing, say spinach, all of your young life? Well, we wouldn't like it a bit, but the heliconius caterpillar loves it. And there is a special reason.

The plant juices in the passion vine are poisonous to all insects but the heliconius caterpillar. But that fact in itself wouldn't be enough to explain why this particular caterpillar feeds on the passion vine exclusively. There is more. These plant juices contain chemicals that, when eaten by the caterpillar, make that caterpillar taste terrible to the birds and other predators that would like to eat it. So not only is the caterpillar dependent upon the passion vine for its food, it is also dependent upon the chemicals in that food to keep it safe from the animals and birds that would prey upon it.

What a wonderful illustration of our dependence on Jesus. The Bible says that Jesus is the "true vine" (John 15:1). Our daily spiritual food should be the words of Jesus. In His Word not only do we find the substance to help us grow up into mature Christians but also we find the special ingredients that keep us safe from temptation.

243

conver

SPIDERS FEED THE BIRDS

And they shall plant vineyards, and eat the fruit of them. . . .
They shall not plant and another eat. Isaiah 65:21, 22.

Have you ever worked hard to make something or to get something, only to have it given away or stolen? Laboring long and hard and then seeing the fruits of our efforts go to someone else can be very discouraging. A recent discovery about spiders has a lesson to teach us along these lines.

We all know that birds feed on spiders, but until recently it wasn't known that many birds eat the fruit of the spiders' labors—insects caught in their webs. Hummingbirds, because of their ability to hover, pick small insects from spider webs; however, because they use the webs as nesting material, as well, the feeding could be considered accidental rather than deliberate.

Ornithologists (scientists who study birds) have noticed birds other than hummingbirds picking insects from a spider's web, very much as you would pick fruit from a cherry tree. For example, a warbler was observed hovering in front of a web, plucking insects from its strands. A cedar waxwing sat on a branch next to a web and ate from it. Another kind of warbler was observed in Florida as it went to the large web of the golden-silk spider. On each visit to the web the warbler would pluck a stranded insect and take it to a distant perch, where the insect was eaten. Then the warbler would wipe its bill back and forth on the limb to clean off bits of sticky spider web. It could be said, of course, that the spiders catch more than they need, and that this is just one way that various animals have adapted to make the system more efficient.

I don't know whether there are spiders in heaven, but if there are, they will not catch unwary insects in their snares, nor will they catch and eat one another. Maybe they will spread their webs to catch seeds and small fruits that fall from trees and plants. We do know one thing: whether spider or human, each will enjoy the fruits of his own labor.

FIRE WALKING

When thou walkest through the fire, thou shalt not be burned; neither shall the flame kindle upon thee. Isaiah 43:2.

God never helps man defy His natural laws! To believe that He does is to believe the lie of Satan, who told Eve, in the Garden of Eden, that she would not die if she ate the forbidden fruit. In today's text the Lord is promising His people that He will watch over them and take care of them even in case of fire, but He doesn't intend that they *start* the fire to prove that they are His people! Such presumption is identical to the temptation that Satan presented to Jesus on the Temple pinnacle. In that instance Jesus said, "Thou shalt not tempt the Lord thy God" (Matt. 4:7). The devil is still luring people with such lies.

There are religious cults—some even claiming to be Christian—that practice pagan rituals, such as fire walking. Today's text cannot be used to justify this pagan practice. In fact, there is no support anywhere in God's Word for such a ritual.

A scientist took the temperature of the hot rocks that Fiji Islanders walked on during the making of a film. One fire walker even stood still on the rocks for up to seven seconds. The temperature was 600 degrees Fahrenheit, and the native man suffered not the slightest burn. Thinking that the feat was a trick, the filmmaker took a piece of calloused skin from the native's foot and dropped it on the rocks—it incinerated instantly into a charred black spot!

A tourist once walked boldly onto the fiery path and immediately screamed in pain—he was severely burned. On the other hand a believing American doctor joined in a fire walk in the South Pacific and wrote of the experience in the *Saturday Review*. "My legs and feet felt cold . . . I saw no one. I stepped off as if awakening from sleep." He then uttered the following blasphemous statement, "Bring me some water, and I'll turn it into wine!" There should be no doubt about the power that is behind such signs and wonders.

THE CREATOR OPERATES IN PICOSECONDS

Then shall thy light break forth as the morning, and thine health shall spring forth speedily: and thy righteousness shall go before thee; the glory of the Lord shall be thy rereward. Isaiah 58:8.

Isaiah presents here a promise to the followers of the Lord. To help us to get a better idea of just how speedily God can step into our lives and begin to work let's look at some of the processes in nature that we take for granted. For example, have you ever thought about the miracle that occurs in every green leaf on earth? The green color comes from the presence of a substance called chlorophyll, which helps the plant to convert sunlight energy into energy food for itself and animals that eat it, including humans. Just the fact that plants can do this is nothing short of amazing; let me tell you how fast it happens.

In order to describe the process properly, I will first have to tell you about a picosecond. One picosecond is a millionth of a millionth of a second, or one trillionth of one second. Did you get that? That means that there are one trillion picoseconds in one second!

Now, no matter how you look at it, a picosecond is not a very long time. Indeed, I can't even imagine anything happening that fast, but that is the speed with which the plant processes the incoming sunlight as it goes about its routine manufacture of energy food for you and me. Can you believe it? As the light arrives on the surface of the plant the photon passes from one molecule to another until it is received into the inner workings of the factory where the chlorophyll is located and where it is transformed into chemical fuel. Using laser light pulses lasting six picoseconds, it has been learned that the transfer from the first molecule to the next takes 34 picoseconds, and from that molecule to the next it takes 66 picoseconds.

Eventually scientists will time the entire process from light absorption to production of energy food, all measured in trillionths of a second. Yes, God can work speedily, don't you agree?

THE TREE THAT ATE
ROGER WILLIAMS

All flesh shall perish together, and man shall turn again unto dust. Job 34:15.

Roger Williams is unliving proof of that text. The famous champion of religious freedom who founded the State of Rhode Island died in 1683, and he was buried in the backyard of his home. Nearly 200 years later, Stephen Russell, one of Roger Williams' descendants, decided to move the remains of the founding father to a location that would be more appropriate.

When the workmen dug down to where the skeleton of Williams should have been, all that they found were some rusty nails and the remains of the wooden coffin. There were no bones. Had Roger Williams' bones been stolen by grave robbers? No! Something else they found showed that Roger Williams had not been stolen.

Near the Roger Williams gravesite was an old apple tree. In digging around where the bones should have been, the workmen discovered a root from the apple tree. The root appeared to be molded around something, but upon investigation, there was nothing there but dirt. Further investigation, however, revealed that the shape around which the root appeared to have been molded was the exact shape of a man, from head to heels. The root had apparently grown around the body of Roger Williams, taking his remains as dissolved minerals to feed the tree.

The root of that apple tree, shaped around the body of Roger Williams, was so remarkable that it was dug up and saved. If you want to verify this story, you can see the root at the Rhode Island Historical Society in Providence.

When Jesus comes and calls for the righteous to come forth, where do you suppose He will find Roger Williams? Will God have to reconstruct him from the shape in the root? Absolutely not! If God can give Roger Williams life in the first place, and if Roger Williams was ready to meet Jesus when he died, then his name is in God's book, and all of the specifications are there to bring him back—to re-create him—just as he was.

ma ml

FISH WITH SUNGLASSES

For now we see through a glass, darkly; but then face to face: now I know in part; but then shall I know even as also I am known. 1 Corinthians 13:12.

You have undoubtedly seen the type of sunglasses that change with the amount of light that is present. If you wear them inside, they look like clear glass, but if you go outside into the bright sunshine they become dark glasses. What seems like magic is actually a process controlled by the chemical reactions that occur in the specially produced glass used to make the lenses.

Our eyes are extremely sensitive to light, and too much sunlight can damage them—even blind us, if we aren't careful. Fortunately, the Creator gave us natural impulses that go a long way toward protecting our eyes from bright lights. We automatically squint, for example, when the light is very bright. The squint protects our eyes.

We don't naturally possess lenses that automatically darken when the sun shines bright around us. But a fish that lives in Southeast Asia had such glasses long before they were invented by optical scientists.

The fish with tinted lenses is a small fish, and is a member of the puffer family. At the edge of the cornea of the eyes on the puffer fish are tiny cells called chromatophores (pronounced cro-MAT-o-fors). When the light intensity increases, as when the sun comes from behind a cloud or as it gets higher in the sky, the chromatophores release tiny bits of yellow pigment, or color. The yellow pigment moves out over the fish's lens, shading its eyes from the intense rays of light. When the light diminishes, the pigment disappears, and the lens is unshaded again.

God is unable to give us a full-blown look at the things of heaven; in our sinful conditions we simply couldn't stand their brilliance. It is as though He has given us tinted lenses. But when Jesus comes and our eyes are opened, we will see Him and all of His wonders in all of their glory.

FIREFLY INTRIGUE

For such are false apostles, deceitful workers, transforming themselves into the apostles of Christ. And no marvel; for Satan himself is transformed into an angel of light. Therefore it is no great thing if his ministers also be transformed as the ministers of righteousness; whose end shall be according to their works. 2 Corinthians 11:13-15.

Where there are several kinds of fireflies each one has its own distinct signal flash. In spring and summer, when the fireflies are out and it is mating time for these "lightning bugs," the large females sit on a plant near the ground and wait for one of two things—food or a mate. The smaller males flying above can be either, depending on how they play the game of lights. The female is often more interested in food than in mating, however, because she emits the mating-signal flash of another species in an attempt to attract a male of that species to her table—so she can devour him! The small male is only looking for a mate, and he gives his signal flash in hopes that a female will respond. But he can't be sure whether the responding female below, is of his species or of another species trying to lure him to his death, so what can he do? You will be amazed at what takes place.

The male mimics the signal flash of other species in the neighborhood—not his own; this attracts the attention of a female below, who flashes back, "Come on down." Not knowing yet which species it is that is inviting him down there, but assuming that it is his lady love thinking that he is a meal of the other species, he lights nearby. Now that he has found the female, he has to figure out pretty quickly whether she is a friend or an enemy, so he begins to give the true light signal to entice the female into joining him for the marriage ceremony. Being a male lightning bug is risky business. He has to lie to counteract the lie that he assumes his desired mate is telling.

The behavior of fireflies is a good example of the way it is with lies. One lie leads to another until, before long, no one knows whether you are telling the truth or not.

PANDICULATION AND STERNUTATION

Know ye that the Lord he is God: it is he that hath made us, and not we ourselves; we are his people and the sheep of his pasture. Psalm 100:3.

If you aren't interested in this information you might pandiculate. You probably won't sternutate—that would be very strange. You say you don't know what I am talking about? Well, I can't imagine why, since both of those conditions are common everyday occurrences.

These two big words are the technical terms for stretching and sneezing. Don't ask me why anyone would need to use such words instead of the words that we normally use, but they are there if needed. (I have *never* heard them used.)

Pandiculation, or stretching out the limbs of the body, is a natural reaction of your body to slowing down because you are tired. It is often accompanied by a yawn, which is an attempt to get more oxygen into the lungs so that you can get back to being wide awake. It has nothing to do with being bored, except that when we are bored we are more likely to show the signs of tiredness. When we are interested in something, our adrenalin causes our heart to beat faster, which causes our blood to flow faster and get more oxygen to the brain, so there is less need of pandiculation.

Sneezing, or *sternutation,* is usually the result of an irritation to the lining of your nose. The sneeze is a violent expulsion of air through your mouth or nose. The purpose of the sneeze is to get rid of dust, dirt, and other things that have accumulated in your nose. You may also sneeze when your nose is stuffed up when you have a cold. Looking at a bright light is often helpful in bringing on a sneeze. Also, people often sneeze in certain numbers. I am a "two-sneezer." I have a friend who is a "three-sneezer." If I sneeze once and don't sneeze again, I feel as if something is missing. My body seems to need the second sternutation in order to feel that all is well again.

These are only two simple examples of the marvelous system that the Creator has given us to help us stay healthy.

THE WINDOW-TRAP PLANT

There is a way which seemeth right unto a man, but the end thereof are the ways of death. Proverbs 16:25.

There is a plant, sometimes called the window-trap plant, that eats insects. That's right, it is one of the plants that obtain necessary nutrients from capturing insects and digesting them. The window-trap plant catches its food by deception.

Plants that eat insects are called insectivorous (in-sek-TIV-or-us) or insect-eating. Insectivorous plants live in soil that is very acid and lacks such required elements as nitrogen. In order to obtain the nitrogen, they have adapted to deception to capture their insect prey. There are a number of insect-eating plants. Some are sticky like flypaper, so insects get stuck and digested; some are aquatic and have very sensitive trapdoors that spring open when an insect touches the trigger, which, in turn opens a chamber that literally sucks the insects into the death trap in the inrush of water; others have slippery and spiny inner walls that allow the insects in but not out. The famous Venus' flytrap has a tiny trigger mechanism between two hinged halves that clap shut, trapping the insect inside.

The window-trap plant has delicious nectar that is very attractive to the insects. But covering the nectar-lined lip of the entrance to the plant's insect trap is a canopy that has to be passed by the insects on their way in.

Once inside, the insects enjoy feeding on the delicious nectar until they are filled. When they are ready to leave they forget how they got in and are deceived by a patch of light shining through the back of the chamber. The light is coming through a window, but the insects think it is an exit and fly or crawl toward the light. On the way they lose their footing and plunge into a watery pit, where they end up as plant food.

Sometimes we just know that we are right but when the truth is revealed we find out that we were wrong. Let's pray that we will know the right way and go that way always.

ANTIMATTER

He that is not with me is against me; and he that gathereth not with me scattereth abroad. Matthew 12:30.

Matter is the stuff that the universe is made of; it is the stuff that everything is made of; it is what you are made of. When God said, Let there be this or that, what appeared was matter. But there are two forms of matter.

Let's review what we think we know about matter. Matter consists of atoms that are made up of tiny particles called protons, neutrons, electrons, and others. Protons have a positive charge and electrons have a negative charge. Because these two particles have opposite charges, they attract each other to hold matter together. Electrons on the loose are "electricity," and when channeled through a wire they are what make your electrical lights and appliances work. But when electrons are with protons in the atoms of matter they are said to be stable. This is a simple view of matter.

In 1932 a young researcher in California discovered an atomic particle, which he called a positron, that behaved like an electron but had the opposite electrical charge. Such a form of matter had not been found before. The most exciting discovery was yet to come. When a positron was introduced to a normal electron, instead of being attracted to it as a proton would have been, there was a very tiny microscopic explosion in which both of them disappeared into nothing, leaving all of their energy behind in the form of X-rays. As a result, the positron was called antimatter, and a whole new realm of science was born. Scientists are still trying to figure out what is going on in matter.

Jesus is a positive force. We are drawn to Him as electrons are drawn to protons, and we remain stable as long as we are with Him. But then there is Satan, who has established an antiforce that is seeking to destroy every one of us, knowing that he too will eventually be destroyed as the two forces collide in the end. But in Jesus there is the power and the energy to produce "new heavens and a new earth wherein dwelleth righteousness" (2 Peter 3:13).

THE WATCHDUCK

How excellent is thy lovingkindness, O God! therefore the children of men put their trust under the shadow of thy wings. Psalm 36:7.

Once a pet duck adopted a baby—not a duckling, but a baby girl—to protect. Every day the baby girl was placed in a carriage in the back yard, and the duck never left the side of the carriage. For some reason, known only to the loving Creator, that duck decided that it was her divinely appointed task to guard that small bundle. No person, dog, or cat could come through the gate without the duck's making him or her sorry he or she did. The baby was quite safe under the dedicated care of the watchduck.

One sunny day the baby was enjoying the back yard, and her mother was watching her from inside the house, doing her housework at the same time. The phone rang; a neighbor was calling to say that a mad dog had just turned into the driveway that led to the back yard where the baby girl was. The mother dropped the phone and raced for the door. Even before she got there she could hear a commotion—the mad dog was in the back yard. She raced through the door into the yard. There, a few feet from the carriage, was a huge dog with bloodshot eyes and dripping mouth. But between the dog and the baby was the duck, quacking, flapping, and attacking the dog with all her might. The mother scooped up the baby, ran into the house, and called the police.

The fight between dog and duck continued. Onlookers gathered before the police arrived. The back yard was in a shambles. The duck had the dog on the run, but the crazed dog didn't have enough sense to escape, and the duck's dedication to duty wouldn't allow her to sense the danger. She fought that dog back to the gate and with her last remaining breath she stationed her bloodstained body across the opening and died. The police shot the dog but said afterward that doing so was a sort of anticlimax. The duck had eliminated the danger to the child, but had given her all to do it.

Jesus did the same for you and me.

253

"FUZZ-BUSTER" MOTHS

But he turned, and said unto Peter, Get thee behind me, Satan: thou art an offence unto me: for thou savourest not the things that be of God, but those that be of men. Matthew 16:23.

You have undoubtedly seen or heard of the small instruments that some people have on the dashboard of their cars to detect radar ahead. The purpose, of course, is to keep from getting caught when you are speeding. Some of these devices are called Fuzz-busters, since they foil the attempts of the police (disrespectfully called "the fuzz" by some) to catch them. In some places it is even against the law to use such a radar detector. But there are moths that are equipped with what amounts to the same sort of device.

The noctuid moths have a special "ear" located below each wing, on the sides of their bodies. Like a radar detector, this special ear is equipped only to detect certain sounds of very high frequency that are made by a bat using sonar to locate its prey. Again, like the radar detector, the special ear is silent until there is a bat nearby sending out the sonar signals looking for a flying object, such as a moth, to catch and eat.

When the noctuid moth picks up the sonar of a bat on its special receiver, the moth immediately begins a set of aerial acrobatics that would make the greatest flying ace jealous. The moth is suddenly seen flying in all sorts of erratic and evasive patterns. It would take a *very* agile bat to capture a noctuid moth. The key, of course, for the moth, is to recognize the signals and to take action immediately. There is not a split second to lose.

One day the devil used Simon Peter to tempt Jesus. Now Jesus loved Peter, and it is quite probable that the devil thought that Jesus would not have His special sensors on when listening to one of His beloved disciples. But we can be so very thankful that Jesus never once let down His guard. He recognized the devil's signals in any form, and He took immediate action.

THE MEXICAN BUCKEYE

For there is hope of a tree, if it be cut down, that it will sprout again, and that the tender branch thereof will not cease. Job 14:7.

There is a small tree that grows in Texas, New Mexico, and in old Mexico that is very hardy. When the temperature soars well above 100 degrees the Mexican buckeye flourishes. In winter, when the temperature drops below zero, most of the tree freezes, and in spring the Mexican buckeye comes back strong. One of the most beautiful flowering trees of its range, this hardy tree holds many a hillside in place by keeping the heavy rains from washing away the soil. It grows in profusion in many areas, and its springtime blossoms turn the streamsides and hillsides into a cloud of pink that can last for three or four weeks.

The tree is named for its seed, a bean that is round, very dark, and as shiny as glass, giving it the appearance of the eyeball of a deer. A seed is about the size of a marble and makes wonderful ammunition for sling shots. Because of a favorite child's prank, the seeds are also called "hot beans." When the Mexican buckeye seed is rubbed quickly back and forth on the sidewalk, the bean becomes very hot. The bean is then tossed to any unsuspecting newcomer to the neighborhood, who catches it and immediately yelps with pain. No lasting damage is done, however, and the recipient of the prank usually looks for someone else to try it on.

Because of its many favorable qualities and because it is a favorite of kids, a Texas botanist has called the Mexican buckeye a "fun" tree; it can take all of the extremes of weather, only to come back healthy and beautiful, ready to provide fun and enjoyment for everyone.

Christians are like the Mexican buckeye. No matter what Satan and this world presents in the way of adversity, Christians come back strong—as beautiful people who are fun to be around.

WHAT DO YOU DO AT NIGHT?

And God saw the light, that it was good: and God divided the light from the darkness. And God called the light Day, and the darkness he called Night. And the evening and the morning were the first day. Genesis 1:4, 5.

There are at least two nerve clocks inside our bodies according to Dr. Martin Moore-Ede, of the Harvard Medical School. We are biologically built to go to sleep when it gets dark and to wake up when it begins to get light. Now that isn't very funny when you think of all the efforts that are being put forth in the world today to keep us up so late that we are groggy every morning.

Dr. Moore-Ede says that when we go against the natural timekeepers of our body we pay a price in health deterioration. In support of this, he tells of research done with mice that had their day-and-night schedule reversed every few days. Their life span was shortened by up to 20 percent as a result. No such research has been tried on humans, of course, but there is evidence that the stress that results from trying to reverse or override the body's natural clocks produces stress, which makes us more susceptible to disease and more difficult to get along with.

One time clock that we know about consists of a pair of tiny nerve centers less than one millimeter in diameter but containing at least ten thousand nerve cells each. These tiny pacemakers are located in the hypothalamus of the brain and operate on a 25-hour-day cycle, which is reset every day by about one hour, depending on when the sun rises and sets. The day-night regulator is not a clock, but is the resetting mechanism, and it is a specialized bundle of nerves connecting the eye to the hypothalamus. Another clock regulates the internal body functions in accordance with the daily cycle. Not much is known about this clock, but it is known to exist.

We must be careful about how we use our nighttime hours. The Creator gave us wonderful bodies that must be taken care of in order to function properly.

A 14-FOOT PET PYTHON

And the Lord God said unto the serpent, . . . I will put enmity between thee and the woman, and between thy seed and her seed; it shall bruise thy head, and thou shalt bruise his heel. Genesis 3:14, 15.

Our text for today has often been called the first promise of a Saviour. After Adam and Eve sinned, God spoke to them and to the serpent, representing the devil, who had tempted Eve to sin in the first place. God said that there would be a struggle between the serpent, or the devil, and the woman. But God's promise was that while the devil would nip at the heel of the Saviour, the Saviour would bruise Satan's head. This meant that even though there would be trouble for God's people, in the end that old serpent called the devil (Rev. 20:2) would be overcome and destroyed.

This fact was brought forcibly to my attention by a story that I read several years ago. It seems that a man living in Gainesville, Florida, had a rather unusual pet—a 14-foot python. The snake seemed like a harmless pet.

One day the python's owner was taking a nap in his living room. He was rudely awakened when the snake began to strike at his head. Before the man could collect his thoughts and escape, the python wrapped itself quickly around his body, unhinged its jaw, and began to swallow him, starting with his head.

The man finally let out a terrifying scream, and a friend in the next room came running in to see what was the matter. Another friend was nearby and also hurried in to help. It took both of them, one grabbing the snake's jaws and the other jabbing at the snake's eyes and mouth, to make the python let go of the man. It was very fortunate indeed that his two friends were around.

That old serpent the devil is just as intent on doing away with each of us, but fortunately we have a friend in Jesus, who has promised us since the beginning of this world that He would deliver us from the devil.

THE PASSION VINE STRIKES BACK

Lord, how are they increased that trouble me! many are they that rise up against me. . . . But thou, O Lord, art a shield for me; my glory, and the lifter up of mine head. . . . Salvation belongeth unto the Lord: thy blessing is upon thy people. Psalm 3:1-8.

Throughout the American tropics there is a very large group of butterflies known as the heliconians. There are many different kinds, and they are very colorful. Some heliconians feed exclusively on passion vines, and there is an ongoing battle between the passion vine and the heliconians.

If the heliconians had their way, they would lay eggs on every single passion vine leaf, and the caterpillars would soon consume all the passion vines. The passion vines need to avoid this fate, and the Creator has built into them a means to dissuade the heliconians from laying even one egg on their leaves.

But before we tell you what the passion vines do, let us first tell you that the female heliconian, in looking for the best place to lay her eggs, places as few of them as possible on each leaf. If she laid too many eggs on one leaf there would not be enough food there for all the tiny caterpillars to get started. So, the female heliconian examines the passion leaves very closely. When she sees that several eggs have been laid on one leaf she goes on to another. Here is where the passion vine throws its punch.

The passion vine grows fake eggs on its leaves! That's right, and they are often randomly spaced just the way those of the heliconians would be. The heliconians have to search for quite a while before they find a suitable leaf on which to lay their eggs. This, of course, limits the population of heliconians, so that there aren't so many caterpillars that they would eat all the passion vines.

The Lord is our Salvation, and He has promised to see to it that we survive in our Christian battle with sin. He has promised that we will not have to suffer more temptation than we are able to bear with His help.

THE JABIRU VISIT

Ye men of Galilee, why stand ye gazing up into heaven? This same Jesus, which is taken up from you into heaven, shall so come in like manner as ye have seen him go into heaven. Acts 1:11.

Early on the morning of September 7, 1981, our telephone rang. It was our friend Benton calling from Tennessee.

"There's a jabiru in Corpus Christi!" he said.

We were very excited. A jabiru (pronounced JAB-u-roo) is not only an extremely rare bird from Central America, but it is also the tallest bird in North America. And none of us had ever seen one. So travel arrangements were made. We would pick up Benton at the airport and drive to Corpus Christi. Hopefully, the jabiru would still be there.

Birders have a national network of people who keep track of the very rare birds, and when a bird like the jabiru is spotted the word goes out. By the end of that day birders were flying in from all over the continent.

When we arrived at Oso Bay, where the bird had been most recently seen, we looked out onto the bay with great anticipation. There it was—a jabiru! What a bird! It is a stork—black-and-white with a maroon chest-band. A jabiru's bill is a foot long—on a five-foot bird, that is quite a beak! It was a magnificent sight.

A few days later, while a small group of birders were watching, the bird spread its great wings, lifted off, and began to ascend with the rising air currents. Soon it was only a speck in the sky above, and then it was out of sight. The birders stood there gazing into the sky where it was last seen, hoping for another glimpse—hoping it would return. But it did not come back.

The jabiru was here for such a short time, and there were many who missed seeing it. How we hoped that it would stay longer. Thinking of the jabiru's visit we remembered Jesus' visit. He too stayed only a short time. We don't know whether the jabiru will come back, but we know that Jesus will return. And this time "every eye shall see him" (Rev. 1:7). Put out the word! He's coming back!

LIVING FOSSILS

All in whose nostrils was the breath of life, of all that was in the dry land, died. Genesis 7:22.

Every living thing that was on land before the Flood died in the Flood, except those creatures that were aboard the ark. However, the Bible does not indicate that every creature in the sea died. The Bible teaches that God created every kind of creature in the seven days of Creation and that these creatures have continued to reproduce after their kind from that day to this, with a dramatic interruption during the Flood. Those who believe in long eons of evolutionary time hold that even sea creatures have passed through endless changes, going from simple cells to complex creatures, and that all land creatures evolved from the sea creatures at one time or another and in one form or another. There are elaborate charts showing the supposed relationships between the different forms of life, from the simple one-celled plants and animals to man.

One idea that evolutionists hold dear is the succession of life forms as they are found in various layers of dirt and rock. To believe in such a theory, however, one must discount the Flood, and the evolutionists do. Thus it was with a good deal of surprise that a paleobiologist named Edward Petuch recently found areas in the tropical sea where species of shells thought to be extinct for millions of years are still alive and well. Petuch said, "It's almost like finding a living dinosaur." There are whole communities of these living fossils, adding up to more than 200 species, all of which were previously thought to be extinct. Petuch calls these tiny areas of the sea "relict pockets." These pockets aren't particularly deep; they vary from about ten or fifteen feet up to perhaps one hundred feet. All the relict pockets found so far have been in the Caribbean Sea. It appears that these creatures have been living in the same environment since the Flood. The Flood was so devastating that most of them were crushed and buried under the earth, but in pockets here and there, they remain as living testimonies to the Creator and His word.

MOSQUITO MONSTERS

There is that speaketh like the piercings of a sword: but the tongue of the wise is health. Proverbs 12:18.

Perhaps the greatest hurt on earth is when words are spoken that cut deep into the feelings of someone else. Usually, we hurt people with what we say because we are selfish. We want something for ourselves, and we don't care what hurt is caused by our words. Consider the mosquito in this regard.

A mosquito is incredibly well equipped to hurt you. I am not talking about all the diseases that are carried by the mosquito. I am talking only of the formidable surgical package that the mosquito carries with her at all times in her search for blood. Male mosquitoes feed primarily on plant juices, and not all female mosquitoes bite humans, but those that do, cause all sorts of pain and itching, because the tiny bloodthirsty monster often sneaks up on you and gets away before you know what has happened.

Contained in the snout of every hunting female mosquito are six surgical instruments: two tubes, two lancets, and two serrated knives. First the mosquito swabs the skin with an anesthetic that deadens the nerves of the skin. Then she sets to work with the lancets and serrated knives, literally sawing and stabbing her way into your skin. But you don't feel a thing. With one of the tubes the mosquito bathes the wound with an anticoagulant (her saliva) to keep the blood flowing freely. With the other tube, madame mosquito pumps your blood into her fuel tanks as fast as she can. The whole procedure takes only a minute if she is lucky enough to hit a capillary.

Once the mosquito's tummy is full, she leaves, but she takes the anesthetic with her, and your body fluids start a violent reaction to the mosquito's saliva. Very soon a welt appears, and the bite begins to itch.

Someone who has a sharp tongue may get what he wants, and he may do it deftly, but when he is gone he leaves hurt behind. It is so much nicer when people use their words to help and to bring happiness.

261

THE PELICANESIAN WAR

I say unto you, that likewise joy shall be in heaven over one sinner that repenteth. Luke 15:7.

One day in September, 1955, a pelican, tired and exhausted from its migration journey, made an unscheduled stop on the Greek island of Mykonos in the Aegean Sea. The visit changed the recent history of that tiny island.

The great white bird was unable to fish for itself, so the local fishermen, taking pity on it, took the bird to Theodoros. Now Theodoros was a giant of a man, a hero of World War II, and he loved wild creatures of all kinds. The pelican was added to the menagerie of Theodoros, which included several other birds and a baby seal. Theodoros named the pelican Peter, after another Mykonian war hero. (I think Peter is a good name for a fisherman like the pelican, don't you?)

Soon Peter became the island's mascot. Everyone petted him and gave him fish, or turned on the faucet for him to get a drink. The Mykonians began to say that maybe Peter was a good omen sent to bring them prosperity. Peter grew strong and had the run of the island.

One spring day Peter vanished. The islanders immediately went into mourning. Then word came that Peter had been found on the nearby island of Tenos. There was instant jubilation. But the men of Tenos would not give Peter back to Mykonos. There was instant indignation.

"How dare they claim our pelican," stormed the Mykonians.

"Peter has deserted Mykonos and selected our island now," retorted the men of Tenos.

The affair was called the Pelicanesian War. Finally the regional governor settled the question by ordering that Peter be returned to Mykonos. All 3,600 Mykonians were at the dock to meet the pelican's return. The church bells rang as Peter walked solemnly down the gangplank.

When we give our hearts to Jesus all heaven rejoices. I can just imagine the celebration, can't you?

DUCK-BILLED DINOSAURS

And, behold, I, even I, do bring a flood of waters upon the earth, to destroy all flesh, wherein is the breath of life, from under heaven; and every thing that is in the earth shall die. Genesis 6:17.

The Bible says that the ark held animals of every kind that God had created. While there were many kinds of dinosaurs, it seems that none were taken into the ark; the only record that we have of them is their fossil remains buried under the rocks and dirt piled up by the Flood. There have been rumors of extinct monsters, or dinosaurs, living in deep lakes and in the ocean depths, but so far there is little evidence that they are there. Even if such do exist, they are probably descendants of sea creatures that survived the Flood.

The very first dinosaur fossils discovered in North America were those of the duck-billed dinosaur. So many fossil bones of the duck-billed dinosaur have been found that it appears that they were quite common before the Flood. Back in 1858, when the first duck-bill fossils were uncovered, it was believed that these dinosaurs had lived in swamps, eating aquatic plants. Recent finds indicate differently. A duck-bill fossil was found with fossilized pine needles inside it, hardly indicating a diet of aquatic plants. Every kind of duck-bill also had a horny crest filled with large air cavities. No one knows what purpose these cavities served. It has been suggested that they were a type of snorkle device, but that would make sense only if the duck-bills had been water-dwelling creatures. They may have been amphibious.

There are many puzzles locked in the earthly remains of that great Flood, but one thing is sure: the hand of God brought the Flood, and He set the rainbow aloft as a promise that He would never again destroy the world by water. And while there are many aspects of nature that we don't understand, we can understand one thing: when God has to destroy a wicked world He gives plenty of warning, and all who follow His direction will not be lost.

263

PARASOL ANTS

Go to the ant, thou sluggard; consider her ways, and be wise: Which having no guide, overseer, or ruler, provideth her meat in the summer, and gathereth her food in the harvest. Proverbs 6:6-8.

It is well known that ants work hard. That is undoubtedly why Solomon advised the sluggard, a lazy do-nothing, to go watch them. If you want to get tired just thinking about something, find an ant colony and watch it; think about working that hard yourself, with no rest, no recess, no play, no break—nothing but endless work. How would you like that?

Take the leaf-cutting ants, for instance. These tiny creatures, which are abundant in the warmer climates of the world, grow their own food down inside their subterranean tunnels. You might not like their diet, but they think that nothing tastes better than mold, a form of fungus. And to grow the mold, they need fresh leaves. So endless hours of the day and night are spent going back and forth between their underground home and the tops of various trees nearby where they carefully cut out sections of the leaves with their pincers. They then carry their precious piece of leaf down the tree and into their tunnels. Sometimes the pieces of leaf are much larger than the ant and look like green umbrellas. This is why they are often called parasol ants.

Just think about how long that journey is for the ant. Let's say the ant is a quarter of an inch long and that the trip one way is 30 feet. That means that each ant travels 1,440 ant-lengths. If we think of the trip in terms of boy- or girl-lengths, we are talking about a walk of more than a mile, one way. You would then have to pick up a very large green umbrella and carry it back to grow mold for you and your family to eat, and as soon as you set one down, you would turn right around and go after another one. That would be your job from dawn to dark, every day.

If you ever feel lazy and don't want to do your chores just remember the leaf-cutting ants—and be thankful.

HECTOR, THE PRODIGAL DOG

For this my son was dead, and is alive again; he was lost, and is found. And they began to be merry. Luke 15:24.

Hector was a terrier belonging to a ship's officer stationed in the Pacific. One day in 1922, before the ship sailed from Vancouver, British Columbia, with lumber bound for Yokohama, Japan, Hector went for one last run. But instead of coming right back, the dog went exploring.

When Hector finally decided to return to the docks the ship was gone. What was Hector to do? There were five ships at the dock. Hector went up the gangplank of each one and sniffed the cargo. An officer of one of the ships, which was also carrying lumber to Yokohama, watched the dog, but had no idea to whom he belonged. The dog sniffed the cargo of lumber. He then went to the next ship and sniffed the cargo of fruit, flour, and fir timbers bound for England. Next he boarded the third ship, which was loading pulp headed for the Atlantic Ocean, and sniffed its cargo. He checked the cargoes of the remaining two ships, as well.

Making his choice, Hector returned to the ship bound for Yokohama. How did he know which ship to choose? Did the smell of the lumber help him decide, or was it something else? No one will ever know, but Hector stowed away and did not emerge until the ship was well out to sea.

For eighteen days Hector explored the ship, stopping now and then to sniff the air. When the ship arrived in Yokohama it happened to pull alongside Hector's home ship. Hector suddenly sniffed the air, barked, and began to jump up and down. Several men from the other ship saw Hector and called his master, who came to the rail. Hector became so excited that he jumped overboard and started toward his master's ship. He was fished aboard for a very happy reunion.

Do you ever feel that you've missed the boat? We all do. There are many ships, but only one will take us to Jesus. If we are on the right ship we too will be reunited with our Master. That day will be a very happy reunion.

THE GROUSE IN HER LAP

Fear thou not; for I am with thee: be not dismayed; for I am thy God: I will strengthen thee; yea, I will help thee; yea, I will uphold thee with the right hand of my righteousness. Isaiah 41:10.

Once in a while I hear of experiences where wild creatures forget or overcome the natural fear that they have for mankind. Perhaps the Lord provides such experiences to let us know what it will be like in the earth made new.

One mid-September day Jacque went for a walk in the woods behind her home in Minnesota. She spied a male ruffed grouse crouched not more than two feet away from her. After staring at the grouse for a few moments, Jacque decided to sit down. Soon the grouse rose slowly and began to walk along the edge of some brush, but he never took his eyes off Jacque. As time passed, the grouse seemed to become more accustomed to the presence of this human.

Eventually the grouse began making soft clucking sounds, which Jacque answered with her own clucking notes. Upon hearing these sounds the ruffed grouse seemed to respond and come closer. He just kept walking around the young lady until he actually walked under the arm on which she had propped herself. And then, as the grouse went on around, he hopped up onto her leg, stood there a few moments, hopped down, and then went around her again. This time when he came around the grouse hopped onto her lap. That grouse kept that up for a long time. When Jacque stood up and started to leave, the grouse would follow her, so she sat back down and let the grouse climb back up on her lap again. It was when the grouse pecked Jacque's hand and startled her that she decided it was time to leave. As she left, the grouse hopped up on a log and watched her go as if to say, "I had such a good time. Please come again."

Won't it be wonderful when the natural fear that is in animals for man will be gone, and we can enjoy their company as friends—as Adam and Eve did in the Garden of Eden?

CUBIC LIGHT-YEARS

O the depth of the riches both of the wisdom and knowledge of God! how unsearchable are his judgments, and his ways past finding out! Romans 11:33.

In trying to figure out the universe, astronomers have to use measurements different from those that we use in everyday life. Instead of using a ruler with inches or centimeters, the scientists measure distance in light-years, and they measure the volume of space in cubic light-years. A light-year is the number of miles that light travels in a year. Some of you probably already know that light travels at a speed of 186,000 miles per second. To find out how far light travels in a minute, you would multiply 186,000 by 60; it's 11,160,000 miles. If you want to know how far light travels in an hour, you multiply 11,160,000 by 60 again, and you get 669,600,000 miles. Would you like to know how far light travels in a day? Multiply the last number by 24, and the answer is 16,070,400,000 miles.

But that is just a "light-day," and distances are too great in space to use such a short ruler, and a "light-week" or a "light-month" would still be too short. So astronomers use the "light-year" as their ruler. It is 5,865,696,000,000 miles long—that's five trillion, 865 billion, 696 million miles. You can see why the astronomers don't use miles—they would get lost in the zeros! But that is only the length of their ruler; having this measurement doesn't tell them much about the universe. So there are more measurements that have to be devised, measures such as a "square light-year" and even a "cubic light-year."

Would you like to know how many cubic feet are in a cubic light-year? This would be an absurd measure but if you want to figure it out, multiply the number of miles in a light-year, times the number of miles in a light-year, times the number of miles in a light-year again, times 5,280 cubed. The number is so large that it is past our comprehension. But think of it! The number of cubic light-years in the universe is much more than that! Our God is a really great God!

LIVING DUST

And they took ashes of the furnace, and stood before Pharaoh; and Moses sprinkled it up toward heaven; and it became a boil breaking forth with blains upon man, and upon beast. Exodus 9:10.

Perhaps you have noticed as part of the weather report on TV that there is often a "pollen count" presented to help those who suffer from such allergies as hay fever and asthma to know when it is safe to go out. This count is the number of pollen grains and other particles in a cubic foot of air. These tiny grains of pollen, carried by the wind, are only part of the living "dust" particles that are present by the untold millions in the air all about us. Without the aid of a strong magnifying glass they look like dust, but besides pollen, there are the spores of such plants as algae and fungi, as well as even some one-celled animals.

Taking such counts from the air 82 feet above the ground in Texas one April and May, botanists from the University of Texas found that the spores of algae outnumbered pollen grains, but that fungal spores greatly outnumbered the other two types combined. When only the algae spores from these living dust samples were studied the scientists found that there were 52 different kinds of algae.

Fewer and fewer forms of living dust occur in samples taken from respectively higher points in the air. At 11,000 feet only 5 or 6 microbes can be found, and between 30 and 40 thousand feet the number is down to one microbe per 400 cubic feet of air. But spores have been found at even higher altitudes. For example, living spores of *Penicillium* mold have been found between 125,000 and 135,000 feet above the earth.

The air is full of tiny living things, and the air currents are constantly carrying these living dust particles to all parts of the planet. If it were not for the health-keeping qualities that the Creator has also provided, no one would be able to survive the possible hazards carried by the wind throughout the world.

SUNBEANS

For this is the covenant that I will make with the house of Israel after those days, saith the Lord; I will put my laws into their mind, and write them in their hearts: and I will be to them a God, and they shall be to me a people. Hebrews 8:10.

Plant scientists are now learning how to take a desirable trait from one plant and add it to the traits of another plant, creating a stronger plant. Just how to do this presents some real challenges. For instance, a plant develops into a certain type (such as a rose bush, a grapevine, or an oak tree) because of a tiny microscopic code called DNA. The coded DNA is made of about 10,000 even tinier bits of coded information called genes, and no one knows what sort of codes are still locked within the genes.

But let's say that in a dandelion one of those genes makes the plant immune to some deadly plant disease that also attacks a valuable food-crop plant such as the soybean. It would be great if we could give the soybeans a shot that would make them immune, as we can do with humans, but we can't. Besides, it would be difficult to treat all soybean seeds. So the scientist wants to somehow get that gene from the dandelion, transfer it to the soybean, and grow a whole bunch of soybeans that have the new trait.

Amazingly, scientists are figuring out how to transfer the desirable traits of one plant to another. For example, one experiment has worked out quite well between the sunflower and a type of bean. The result, a "sunbean," has positive qualities from the sunflower and the bean.

Like the plants, we are in need of being strengthened by desirable traits. And the greatest Scientist, Jesus, has promised to give us His character traits so that we can be protected from the disease called sin. "The Sun of righteousness [shall] arise with healing in his wings" (Mal. 4:2), and by a means as marvelous as the genes, which Jesus also created, He will write the coded language of heaven on our hearts and in our minds.

PEPTIDES

But the Comforter, which is the Holy Ghost, whom the Father will send in my name, he shall teach you all things, and bring all things to your remembrance, whatsoever I have said unto you. John 14:26.

This text is one of the most reassuring in the Bible. There is just no way that I can remember all the things that I need to know in order to represent Jesus on this earth. But we have this promise, that if we study the words of Jesus and store them in our hearts, then His Spirit will bring them to our memory when we need them. That's wonderful!

Of course I don't know how the Holy Spirit brings things to our remembrance, but I do believe that God works His wonders through natural laws that He authored. To Him nothing is impossible, and I think I understand a little better today how we remember than I did yesterday—because today I read about peptides.

Peptides represent a family of chemicals in our bodies. Recently they have been found in great abundance in our brains. Why? Well, apparently peptides are messengers between the billions of nerve cells in the brain. Peptides are combinations of amino acids, which are the building blocks of proteins. You could think of the amino acids as letters in the alphabet that can be put together to make words, sentences, and even paragraphs that have meaning and communicate information. Somehow your brain stores vast amounts of information that you have learned, and you can recall only a small portion of what you really have stored up there. The theory is that maybe the information that you have stored in your brain is stored in the form of chemical codes, those codes being the peptides made of amino acids.

So all that the Holy Spirit has to do is to stimulate the right peptides, and you remember what you need to know to meet temptation or to give an answer for what you believe that the Bible teaches. But remember, the Holy Spirit can't stimulate peptides you haven't stored with information.

THE SEA ROACH

In his hand are the deep places of the earth: the strength of the hills is his also. The sea is his, and he made it: and his hands formed the dry land. Psalm 95:4, 5.

The sea roach was given its name because it looks like a cockroach, but it is not really a roach. You can be glad that this creature isn't a roach that lives in or near your house, for it grows to a length of 14 inches and would present quite a formidable sight if you found one prowling around in your basement. But there is absolutely no chance of that happening, because the sea roach lives in the depths of the sea; its routine living quarters are some 4,000 feet below the ocean waves.

The sea roach is related to the crab and other crustaceans, but the relationship is probably very distant. It is covered by a hard shell and has copper-based blood, which causes it to bleed blue when its blood is exposed to oxygen. The creature has what appears to be two triangular eyes, which give the sea roach's head the look of a spaceship. But its eyes seem to be of no use; there is no response to light whatsoever. But what good would sight be at 4,000 feet, where there is absolutely no light except that which is made by a few light-producing creatures?

The creature has been known for nearly one hundred years only from dead specimens dredged from the ocean depths. Recently, however, several specimens were brought up alive, and they now live in the New York Aquarium, where they are being eagerly studied for the first time as living creatures. This denizen of the deep has five sections to its digestive system, which is unusual. The scientists studying it do not know what its food might be, although its powerful jaws are capable of tearing flesh.

The sea roach is a mysterious creature about which so little is known that there are more questions than answers. I wonder how Jesus feels about sea roaches. They are at least descendants of a creature that He created, and His creative power continues to sustain them as it does us.

FIRE ANTS

Deliver me from mine enemies, O my God: defend me from them that rise up against me. Psalm 59:1.

The fire ant arrived on the North American continent in 1918 as a stowaway on a South American freighter that docked in Alabama. Since then this vicious insect has been steadily gaining ground until it has now infested more than 200 million acres in nine of the Southern United States. It has become one of the most harmful pests in North America, mainly because it has no natural predators to keep it under control. Agricultural chemicals have helped to control the insect, but they have been relatively unsuccessful when you consider that there are billions and billions of fire ants.

The bite of this imported fire ant is extremely severe. If you happen to step on its nest or come too close, the fire ant will attack in defense of its colony. The ant first bites its victim's skin to steady itself; then it stings its victim, injecting a poisonous venom that causes great pain. The sting can be extremely dangerous if the person stung is allergic to this particular venom; it can even cause death in the same way that bee stings can for those who are allergic to them.

Perhaps the most interesting aspect of the fire ant's habits is its ability to communicate information about an attack to its fellow colonists. If one or more begin to bite you in defense of their colony, they emit into the air a chemical message that is carried through the air almost immediately to the other members of the colony. Every member of the colony that gets a whiff of this chemical message drops what it is doing and rushes to the attack. Before you know it there aren't just one or two, there can be a quarter of a million fire ants coming to bite and sting the victim. It is time to act!

Sometimes, when everything in my day seems to go wrong, I think that the old devil has got his imps, like fire ants, coming at me from everywhere to do me in for sure. But I just lift my heart to Jesus as David did when he was faced with his enemies, and Jesus delivers me. It is wonderful!

LICHENS AREN'T WHAT WE THOUGHT

Now unto him that is able to do exceeding abundantly above all that we ask or think, according to the power that worketh in us. Ephesians 3:20.

You have all seen lichens (pronounced LIE-kens). They grow just about everywhere and have even been found growing on rocks in the frigid cold of the Antarctic.

A lichen is a combination of a fungus and an alga, both being types of plants. Until recently it was believed that the alga provided the fungus with food from photosynthesis and that the fungus provided a home for the algae. This relationship was once among the best examples of a condition known as symbiosis, where two organisms grow together in cooperation for the benefit of each other.

However, recent scientific studies show that every lichen is an example of controlled parasitism. That is, the various kinds of fungi that make up lichens are actually invading the algae plants and are trying to destroy them much as they do other types of plants—both living and decaying. So, instead of being a part of a cooperating partnership, the fungus part of a lichen is a good example of superselfishness.

In some instances, however, the algae plants have internal defenses that keep the fungi from killing them. While the algae cannot get rid of the fungus, it can control its growth. Under this condition we have what we sometimes call a standoff, where neither side can win. Every species of lichen is an example of such a standoff. Both the algae and the invading fungus go on living, but their situation is greatly changed, producing what we call lichens.

Satan, like a fungus, has forced himself onto our world in an attempt to destroy it and all of us, as well, and he is successful with all but those of us who have that special ingredient—Jesus. We may not be able to get Satan out of our world, but with Jesus there is no standoff—the tempter's power is broken.

273

CITY HAWKS

Abram dwelled in the land of Canaan, and Lot dwelled in the cities of the plain, and pitched his tent toward Sodom. Genesis 13:12.

In recent years the peregrine falcon has been sharply declining in numbers to a point where ornithologists fear that unless something drastic is done this type of hawk will become extinct. The reason for the falcon's decline has been primarily the interference of man in its natural habitats, which are mountain peaks and sea cliffs. One of the drastic measures that have been taken to restore the world's population of peregrine falcons is placing these birds in large cities where it is hoped that they will see the similarity between the skyscrapers and the peaks, canyons, and cliffs of their natural habitat.

Tom Cade, of Cornell University, and David Bird, of McGill University, have released nearly one hundred of these remarkable birds of prey in several of the large cities in the northeastern United States and in Canada. For the adult falcons, this arrangement seems to be working very well. There are plenty of sparrows, starlings, and pigeons to eat, and the peregrine's mortal enemy, the great horned owl, is virtually absent from the big cities. But there are some serious problems. While the adults can handle the problems of the city, the chicks are not so well equipped.

In the wild, when a peregrine falcon toddler leaves the nest it usually spends a few days on the ground nearby; but in the city, when a young falcon goes for a stroll on the sidewalk it may be clubbed to death by a frightened pedestrian or eaten by a dog. In spite of the problems with the young, Drs. Cade and Bird believe that this program is still the best chance to save the peregrine falcon from extinction. Cornell University alone has spent more than $2.5 million dollars on the project.

Since the days of antiquity, the cities have been places unsafe to live in. Cities are certainly not the place to try out new wings as young Christians.

SINGING FROGS AND KILLER BATS

Be sober, be vigilant; because your adversary the devil, as a roaring lion, walketh about, seeking whom he may devour. 1 Peter 5:8.

Will you permit me to paraphrase the text above so that it reads in terms of the Central American frogs I want to tell you about? It would read "Be sober, be vigilant; because your adversary the devil, as a silent bat, flieth overhead, seeking whom he may devour."

Merlin Tuttle is one of the world's leading authorities on bats. As a boy, Merlin, with his father's help, began to study these night-flying mammals, and by the time we studied biology together in college he was already known and respected by the world's "batmen." Dr. Tuttle is now with the Milwaukee Public Museum. Not long ago Merlin, along with a fellow who studies frogs, spent many nights at a pond in Panama watching fringe-lipped bats swoop down and carry away singing male frogs.

The male frogs would pick a prominent place in the midst of the pond and begin "singing" to attract a mate. Meanwhile, the females were out of sight on the bank waiting for the songs they liked best. The fringe-lipped bats, flying silently overhead in the darkness, were also listening for the songs that they liked best. Based on the pitch, loudness, and speed of the whining and chucking notes of the frogs, the bats were able to determine accurately which frogs were just the right size to make a good meal. Then they had only to swoop down and pick up the frog.

There are also poisonous frogs in this area, and they too sing for their mates, but the bats somehow know that they are poisonous and rarely bother them. How do they know which frogs will make a good meal and which ones are too big, or too small, or are poisonous? Tuttle doesn't know.

Sometimes we get so carried away with the things around us that we forget to watch out for the devil, and he snatches us away before we know it. But we have a Saviour who has already beaten the devil and can get us back.

TERMITES WITH BUILT-IN BAZOOKAS

For the weapons of our warfare are not carnal, but mighty through God to the pulling down of strong holds. 2 Corinthians 10:4.

The world seems to be obsessed with war. On all sides we hear of preparations for armed conflict. Paul tells the Corinthians that as Christians we too are to be armed with weapons, but our warfare is not of this world; it is against the prince of the power of darkness. Sometimes the devil tries to make us think that we are powerless and have no defense against his arms.

Consider the lowly termite—seemingly a defenseless insect, but much better equipped to take care of itself than it appears to be.

Several species of termites have a modified soldier caste called "nasute." One species living in the South American country of Guyana has a special weapon for defense. Like most termites, this one eats wood and digests it by using the services of tiny microbes that live in its stomach.

Sometimes a tree falls or gets torn open, exposing the termites to the dangers of insects and birds that would like very much to feast on termite steaks. But in the termite colony there are bazooka-headed soldiers, each with a powerful though very tiny squirt gun in the center of its face. The nasute soldiers line up in defense of their colony. As the enemy, usually ants, arrives, it is met by shots of long-lasting, strong-smelling, sticky glue that sticks even to oily surfaces. Any ant that is shot by this substance forgets all about attacking and eating termites; it will be occupied for a long time merely getting itself unstuck.

While we don't fight against flesh and blood but against powers that rule the spiritual wickedness of this world (Eph. 6:12), we still need as effective a weapon against Satan as God gave the nasute termite. Our primary weapon is the Word of God, which the Bible says is sharper than any sword (Heb. 4:12).

276

CRICKET

But he was wounded for our transgressions, he was bruised for our iniquities: the chastisement of our peace was upon him; and with his stripes we are healed. Isaiah 53:5.

Cricket was a horse. Steven was a boy. An old Indian had selected Cricket for Steven, but no one understood why, because Cricket had been abused and was terrified of a rope. Steven had fallen from a horse and broken his leg. Now he was afraid of horses. This pair did not seem suited for each other at all. Steven would bring clover and sugar lumps to Cricket, but the fence was always between them. Their mutual fear was very much alive.

One day Steven's father and a ranch hand were trying to catch Cricket to trim her hoofs. She bolted toward the corral fence and tried to jump it but her legs caught in the barbed wire, and she fell heavily to the ground, with her hind legs and feet cruelly entangled in the wire. Cricket raised herself and lunged, tearing out one of the posts and snapping another strand of barbed wire, which whipped around and cut savagely into her sides and haunches.

"Get the wire cutters!" yelled Steven's dad, as he ran toward the horse, fearing for its life.

But suddenly Steven was between them, limping toward the terrified horse. He placed his hand on her face and gently began to speak to her while he stroked her. Cricket froze for a desperate instant and then slowly exhaled, uttered a great moan, and lay down quietly on the ground.

Reaching behind him, Steven quietly called for the rope and slipped it over Cricket's head without meeting any resistance. Slowly, he tugged, and she raised herself until she was standing. Then, after freeing her from the entangling wire, boy and horse limped through the gate to a place where Steven could treat her wounds, feed and water her, and rub her down. In no time Steven was riding Cricket. The fear had left both of them as they learned in that terrible instant to trust each other.

Jesus understands your hurts. Let Him lead you.

LAND TIDE

No man can come to me, except the Father which hath sent me draw him: and I will raise him up at the last day. John 6:44.

Did you know that twice every day you are quite a bit taller than you are the rest of the day? Well, that isn't exactly true, but it would be true if you measured your height in feet and inches above sea level. For example, the Empire State Building, in New York City, is as much as 20 inches higher above sea level on these two occasions each day than it is the rest of the day. No, the building doesn't grow and shrink in height, and neither do you. Actually, the entire city of New York, including the Empire State Building, rises nearly two feet higher above sea level and then falls again, twice in every 24 hours. This action caused by the pull of the moon is called "land tide."

Land tide is a worldwide occurrence. The moment when the earth's land surface is highest is precisely the same moment when the moon is at its highest point in its path through the sky.

Land tide is not exactly the same as water tide, even though the moon is responsible for both. High-water tide occurs *after* the moon passes its high point in the sky, and water tide rises quite a bit higher than the land tide.

Both types of tide are caused by a pull that the moon exerts on the earth. The moon is tied to the earth by gravity like an invisible string. If you tied one end of a string to a small weight and the other end to your finger, and then twirled the string around and around, the weight would stay out at the end of the string by a power called centrifugal force. You would also feel the tug on your finger as the weight went around. That tug is similar to the pull on the earth by the moon that produces the tides.

Like the moon above, God looks down on a dark earth and loves us all with a love that draws us unto Him. He loved us so much that He gave us His Son. Our response to God can be a tidal wave of praise and thanksgiving.

SMILE RESEARCH

A merry heart doeth good like a medicine: but a broken spirit drieth the bones. Proverbs 17:22.

Do you want to make a difference in your world today? One simple action—smiling—will do it. You might think that a smile isn't really that important, but let me tell you about some simple experiments performed by a psychologist in New York City that may change your mind.

A young woman who was doing smile research would stand waiting for an elevator in a department store. When another woman came to ride the elevator also, the researcher would simply smile at her but would say nothing. Once in the elevator, the researcher asked the other woman for directions. The interesting finding was that when smiled at by the researcher the other person would provide the requested assistance much more often than if she had not first been given a smile before boarding the elevator. There may be a number of explanations as to why the experiment worked the way it did, but the only planned difference in the two situations was whether or not a smile was used.

A smile is so easy to produce. You all know how to do it. In fact, smiling comes naturally to babies, not because they see other people smile, but because they come "programmed" to smile—babies who are blind from birth smile at the same age as those who can see. People can create ugly smiles, but those are sneers and leers. When you give the world the real smiles that you are born with, you make those around you feel better; and, since it is hard for you to be grumpy when you are smiling, you feel better too!

With all that we as Christians have to be thankful for, we should never stop smiling in our hearts. And those heart smiles will often erupt onto our faces, giving us a special radiance resulting from feeling the joy of Jesus deep in our heart. Do you know the song, "Sing and Smile and Pray . . ."? Those three things go together. When you have talked to Jesus about things He keeps you singing; and when you have a song in your heart your face will surely show it.

279

FRESH PRAYER

Pray without ceasing. 1 Thessalonians 5:17.

If you think of prayer as something you say several times a day before you eat and just before you go to bed, you aren't going to understand that text at all. One of the most famous quotations of Ellen White is this: "Prayer is the breath of the soul."—*Messages to Young People,* p. 249. If you think of prayer in this way, then you know that you have to pray without ceasing, just as you know that you can't stop breathing and continue to live.

These days we hear a lot about pollution. The air that we breathe is said to be growing more and more polluted; it is becoming harder and harder to find fresh air to breathe. I wonder whether the same thing could be said for the prayer that our souls breathe.

One area of particular concern regarding fresh air is the air in our homes. In the old days, before all of the concern over conservation of energy, there were always enough cracks in the walls, around the windows and doors, to let fresh air into the house. Also, before air conditioning, houses were open day and night except in the cold winters. But now, winter and summer, most homes are not only shut tight but sealed to make them as airtight as possible. This practice may save energy but it also produces polluted air in our homes. Without the free circulation of air through the house, such pollutants as oxides of nitrogen, carbon dioxide, and even carbon monoxide can build up to levels that, while not immediately seen as deadly, can cause an increase in breathing disorders and respiratory diseases. This problem is a growing concern of government energy agencies and health agencies. We must have fresh air in our houses day and night. To quote a well-known phrase, "It's a matter of life and breath."

I can't help wondering whether we have sometimes also sealed the fresh air of God's Spirit out of our lives—out of our homes—by neglecting the breath of the soul.

"I HAVE KILLED A LION IN YOUR HONOR"

These things I have spoken unto you, that in me ye might have peace. In the world ye shall have tribulation: but be of good cheer; I have overcome the world. John 16:33.

Several years ago I heard a wonderful story about an American journalist and an African Masai warrior. The journalist was in Morocco on an assignment, and he happened to be in the police station when the Masai warrior was brought in. The warrior had set out from his village some 4,000 miles southeast to "measure the sky" and to "count the children of God." His trek had led him through the great forests of the gorilla, across mighty rivers, and across the vast desert where nothing lived. And his journey had been almost entirely on foot—a feat worthy of the proud Masai.

But in the city of Casablanca, in Morocco, the Masai chief did not understand how things were to be done. When his honor was insulted he responded as he would at home in Tanzania—he challenged the man to fight. He was arrested and taken to the police station. There he was ordered to pay 400 francs or serve time in jail. He had no money and was being led away to the jail cell when the American intervened. The journalist paid the fine, and the Masai warrior was released. The American offered to pay his way home, but the Masai declined, saying that he must return the way he had come. Before he left, however, the warrior asked for the journalist's name and address, and with raised spear he saluted the American and said, "Lord, I will honor your name at this time of each of the years left me," and he was gone.

The American receives a message every year that reads simply, "Lord, I have killed a lion in your honor." The journalist was mildly impressed at first, knowing how common lions are and how easy it is to shoot one. Then he learned from a friend of the Masai whom he chanced to meet that the warrior went out each year with only his knife and killed the lion by hand to honor the great American chief who had saved him from the dishonor of prison.

281

BEES AREN'T DUMB!

Now all these things happened unto them for ensamples: and they are written for our admonition, upon whom the ends of the world are come. 1 Corinthians 10:11.

Smart people learn from experience. If they make the same mistake once or twice, they don't usually make it again. Also, smart people learn to anticipate what is going to happen because of what they have experienced or what has been told to them in the past. We know, for example, what happens to people when they break the laws of good health, because we have seen the results in our own lives, the lives of our loved ones and friends, and others.

The Bible was given as a guidebook to show us what to expect in all sorts of situations that are important to our salvation. If we heed the lessons from the many examples in the Bible we are wise. If we ignore them we are foolish.

Every scientist who studies honeybees knows that they have intelligence that seems to go beyond merely performing instinctive habits. Perhaps the best example is what happens when we study the bees' ability to locate alternate food sources. To test this ability, scientists first placed a dish of sugar-water near the opening to the hive. Once the bees had discovered the food and began coming to the source the dish was moved—just a short distance at first, but each time a little farther. Before long each move was several hundred feet or more. At this point you would think that a simple creature like a bee would begin to have trouble finding the new location, but nothing could be further from the truth.

At some point in the experiment the bees suddenly seemed to "catch on" and began anticipating where the food was going to be next. When the dish was moved, there were the bees, waiting to pick up where they had left off!

Would that we were as smart as the bees appear to be. Then we would realize what God has been telling us about the future: we would be ready and waiting for each new development and ready to do our part in the finishing of the Lord's work on earth.

SPARROWS THAT SING LIKE CANARIES

And they sung as it were a new song before the throne, and before the four beasts, and the elders: and no man could learn that song but the hundred and forty and four thousand, which were redeemed from the earth. Revelation 14:3.

Perhaps I am too hard on house sparrows, but they don't have very many redeeming qualities. They are mean, they aren't very attractive, and about the only sound that they make is an unmusical chirp, which gets on my nerves. They build very untidy nests almost anywhere that they can cram a bit of grass together. Sparrows evict other, more gentle birds from their nests; they murder not only the young and even the parents of other species, but on occasion they also attack and kill their own kind. There just doesn't seem to be much good that you can say about the ever-present house sparrows. They are pests at bird feeders, where they hog all the food and scatter what's left all over the place, all the while filling the air with noisy gossip.

You know, my description of the sparrows sounds very much like a description of people, doesn't it? When you think about it, people are pretty terrible. The Bible says that even our own righteousness is like filthy rags. And if you read the newspaper or watch TV you will see that people are the meanest and most ornery of all creatures on earth. I wonder why God isn't as irritated by us as I am with house sparrows? Probably because He loves us and sees what we can become when we love Him in return.

On several occasions sparrow eggs have been placed in the nests of canaries. When the young sparrows hatched they believed they were canaries—so they learned to "sing" somewhat like canaries! That seems like a miracle to me, and perhaps it is, but it is no greater miracle than the one Jesus has promised to work in me when I accept Him. He takes me into His nest as though I am born again like Him. His Spirit begins to teach me how to live like Him. My life becomes beautiful like the song of a canary instead of like the mean and monotonous chirp of the sparrow.

THEY LIVE WHO RESIST THE WOLF

Submit yourselves therefore to God. Resist the devil, and he will flee from you. James 4:7.

We usually picture a pack of wolves attacking a defenseless beast that has no hope of survival. What you may not know is that there are important behaviors that come before the attack—behaviors on the part of the wolves and behaviors on the part of the prey.

To begin with, wolves tend to go after the weak, the sick, and the old animals in a herd. This practice is to the wolves' credit, of course, because it serves to keep the herd strong and healthy by weeding out the culls. But there are subtle behaviors on the part of the prey that aid the wolves in the kill—behaviors that if changed, often cause the wolves to ignore the prey and look elsewhere.

Once, a pack of wolves was observed stalking three buffaloes in Alberta, Canada. Two of the buffaloes were healthy; the third was sick. All three were lying peacefully on the grass, chewing their cuds. When the wolves' presence was sensed by the buffaloes, the two healthy ones stayed where they were and ignored the pack, but the sickly one became nervous, stood up, and met his doom. The healthy two were not bothered.

Another signal that the prey animal gives is to run. For example, if a wolf pack approaches a moose, the moose's best chance for survival is to hold its ground, refuse to run, and perhaps even walk toward the wolves. This is apparently a sign that the intended prey is too healthy to kill. Also, it seems that the wolves prefer to attack when their prey is on the run. If the moose runs, it will almost certainly be chased and killed.

Satan likes nothing better than to scare us into thinking that we haven't got a chance. And if our relationship with Jesus isn't as healthy as it could be, then we become perfect targets for him. But when we depend on Jesus and keep our relationship with Him secure, we can look the devil in the eye and watch him flee in fear.

THE BUBBLE NET

And Simon answering said unto him, Master, we have toiled all the night, and have taken nothing: nevertheless at thy word I will let down the net. Luke 5:5.

As unbelievable as it was, Simon Peter was ready to do as Jesus said. What faith! There is an animal at sea that uses an almost unbelievable method of feeding that involves a type of fishnet called a bubble net. We think of a fishnet as being made of string or thread that is interwoven to produce a mesh through which fish cannot swim. The bubble net serves the same purpose—but is made entirely of bubbles.

The animals that make bubble nets are humpback whales, which can reach fifty feet in length but on the average are about forty feet long as adults. These great whales live in groups and use various methods of obtaining the great amounts of food that are necessary to sustain them. The bubble net is one of these methods. Use of the bubble net is difficult to describe, but let's try.

When a school of small fish is located, the whales dive to get beneath the fish. One or two humpbacks begin swimming in circles under the fish. As they do so, they begin to blow a constant stream of bubbles—little bubbles for little fish and bigger bubbles for bigger ones. So many bubbles are produced and drift upward that they form a curtain that rises to the surface. The whales continue to swim in circles, spiraling upward in smaller and smaller circles, constantly blowing the curtain of bubbles. Soon the net of bubbles completely surrounds the school of fish, and the circle becomes smaller and smaller. Fish, by instinct, flee from anything flashing in the water, so they swim away from the bubble net and concentrate in the center of the net; the whales have only to lunge upward to fill their mouths with food.

The same Jesus who told His disciples to let down their net on the other side of the boat has given one of His creatures a net that never wears out or needs mending.

THE WINGED BEAN

He causeth the grass to grow for the cattle, and herb for the service of man: that he may bring forth food out of the earth. Psalm 104:14.

"Hey, Mom, what are we having for dinner?"

"Winged beans."

"Winged beans! What are they?"

This promising plant is presently found only in Papua New Guinea and in Southeast Asia, where the natives grow the plant as a source of food. Since these areas are typical of the tropics of the world around, it is hoped that the winged bean may served as a food source in the poorer tropical areas where protein deficiency is high.

The winged bean has qualities similar to the soybean, but unlike the soybean, the entire winged bean plant can be eaten—seeds, leaves, flowers, shoots, and roots. The young pods, eaten like green beans, are very tasty and can be eaten raw. The seeds provide oil that is high in polyunsaturated fats essential to health.

The roots are somewhat like sweet potatoes, but they contain ten times as much protein. Like all beans, the winged bean has the ability to take nitrogen from the air so it can grow in soils poor in this essential element. The plant can also be used to increase the amount of nitrogen in the soil.

Isn't it amazing that this plant, with all of its valuable properties, has existed for centuries tucked away in the tropics of the South Pacific, unknown to the rest of the world?

The Lord has given us much to be thankful for. There are many natural plants that have medicines that help make us well, and there are undoubtedly still many more plants just waiting to be discovered that contain not only medicines but food value, as well. Even though sin has depleted some of the original value of the plants, we can still thank the Lord for giving us "every herb bearing seed, which is upon the face of all the earth . . .; to you it shall be for meat" (Gen. 1:29).

YOU ARE A BLOOD FACTORY

There hath no temptation taken you but such as is common to man: but God is faithful, who will not suffer you to be tempted above that ye are able; but will with the temptation also make a way to escape, that ye may be able to bear it. 1 Corinthians 10:13.

Right now your body is producing blood at an incredible rate. By this time tomorrow your blood factory will have made about 15 million new red blood cells! And besides that, your factory will make millions and millions of white blood cells, platelets, and other odds and ends necessary to keep your system in order.

The main production line is in the middle of your bones—in what is called the marrow. But the marrow doesn't make blood cells without instructions. There is a watchman in your kidneys, where your blood is strained to check for impurities, oxygen level, and other properties. When the watchman notices a drop in the oxygen level in your blood, he sends a telegram to the bone marrow, where production is speeded up immediately.

Other watchmen notify the marrow to produce white cells to fight disease. Still other watchmen give the message to make platelets. A reserve force of white cells and platelets is maintained in the marrow in case your body needs more than can be produced all at once.

Each blood cell you produce may last for about four months. Worn-out blood cells are taken out of circulation by your spleen, which is the trash disposal in your blood factory. You have an extremely efficient factory that is ready for any emergency. The watchmen never take a break or a vacation or become lazy, except under conditions of overwhelming disease—a condition that is usually brought on because we don't take proper care of our bodies.

Your bodies were created to be ready to meet invading alien forces and to resist and eliminate them. We should be just as ready in our spiritual life to dispel the invading forces of Satan. Jesus has promised to help!

BOMBSHINE OR SUNSHINE?

That ye may be blameless and harmless, the sons of God, without rebuke, in the midst of a crooked and perverse nation, among whom ye shine as lights in the world. Philippians 2:15.

You have, no doubt, sung the song "This little light of mine; I'm going to let it shine." You have also probably heard the saying "Let your light shine." All true Christians glow with a light from the Sun of Righteousness, Jesus, and they can do nothing but let that light shine. It shines out in everything that we do.

Sometimes, in our zeal to let the world and its sinners know just how much Jesus loves them, we get a bit overzealous and attempt to let too much light shine. Too much light is damaging. For example, too much sunlight can scorch the grass and the crops in the fields. So, too much light is not what we want to share; we want to let Jesus, the Light of the world, shine through us in just the right amount.

You have probably read about the atomic-bomb blasts that virtually eliminated the city of Hiroshima at the end of World War II. I was very young at the time, so I don't remember it, but I do remember the atomic-bomb tests that took place thereafter. I have seen moving pictures of those gigantic blasts and the terrible havoc that they wrought.

Now, let me surprise you—the same amount of energy that was released by those atomic bombs is received every day by every one and one-half square miles of the earth's surface! When the energy is released in a split second, it sends forth a killing shock wave, but when it is received gently over a period of a day of sunlight, it can work the wonders that give us food, a suntan, and just the right amount of light for our work.

Sometimes we need to ask ourselves whether the light we wish to share with someone will be like the gentle sun or more like the blast of an atomic bomb. "Let your light so shine before men, that they may see your good works, and glorify your Father which is in heaven" (Matt. 5:16).

DEEP HAWK

He will turn again, he will have compassion upon us; he will subdue our iniquities; and thou wilt cast all their sins into the depths of the sea. Micah 7:19.

The last places left on earth that man has not explored are the depths of the sea. To illustrate just how difficult it is to get there and live to tell about it, let me tell you about *Deep Hawk.*

An undersea engineer by the name of Graham Hawkes has designed and is building a one-person, deep-sea explorer craft called *Deep Hawk.* It is designed to operate initially at a depth of five thousand feet. At that depth the pressure is two thousand pounds per square inch. The pressure on the entire surface of *Deep Hawk* is 5.5 million pounds.

Eventually, Hawkes hopes to perfect his craft to descend to the deepest part of the ocean—the Marianas Trench, which is 36,198 feet below the surface of the Pacific Ocean south of Guam. The problems of operating at these depths are incredible. The *Deep Hawk* cannot have any cracks or even any wires penetrating the glass shell. All of its mechanical action must be controlled from within by remote radio signals, which will pass through the thick hull to the motors and electronic gear that move the vehicle along the bottom and through the water.

Small winglike flaps on either side of the bubble-shaped craft will assist in the descent of the *Deep Hawk,* allowing it to glide at an angle or settle slowly. Enough oxygen for one hundred hours will be stored inside the craft, but if anything should go wrong, the *Deep Hawk* will automatically dump its weights and rise swiftly to the surface.

It was no accident that Jesus used the depths of the sea as an example of where He will place our sins when we ask Him to forgive them. Once we have given our past sins to Jesus, He has promised not only to cast them into the depths of the sea but to remember them no more. Isn't Jesus wonderful?

WHEN THE GRINDERS ARE GONE

In the day when the keepers of the house shall tremble, and the strong men shall bow themselves, and the grinders cease because they are few, and those that look out of the windows be darkened. Ecclesiastes 12:3.

It is generally believed that the author of Ecclesiastes was writing about old age when he wrote the words of chapter 12. The "strong men" are the muscles. The "grinders" are the teeth that are few because many have been lost in growing old. "Those who look out of the windows" are the eyes. You can read other texts and figure out what the other phrases mean.

Let us consider the grinders. You know that you are supposed to brush your teeth every day. You know that you are not supposed to eat many sweets or chew sugary gum, because such things damage your teeth. But we don't usually want to remember these things until we begin losing our teeth. Then suddenly we wish we had paid attention to our mothers and fathers when they told us to brush often.

Elephants, on the other hand, have another problem. They eat small tree limbs, a diet that is rough on teeth, and before long their teeth fall out. But these animals have the ability to grow more replacement teeth than do man and the general run of animals. You might think that would be a great plan, but there is a limit. The elephant can produce only six sets of grinders. Once the beast has used up the last set, it will die of starvation. This is the natural end of the noble elephant—the grinders cease.

Besides our physical food and the need for teeth to help us eat and stay healthy, we also need spiritual food. It is fun to bite into a tough idea and chew on it until we have it ready to digest. That was what "The Preacher" was doing when he wrote the book Ecclesiastes. And when all of his grinding was finished, he came to a final conclusion, found just ten verses later: "Let us hear the conclusion of the whole matter: Fear God, and keep his commandments: for this is the whole duty of man."

EVERY PLANT INTO JUDGMENT

For God shall bring every work into judgment, with every secret thing, whether it be good, or whether it be evil. Ecclesiastes 12:14.

Sometimes I am completely amazed at what scientists have done. When I think of the wonders that science has been able to perform, I have no trouble believing that God can do what He says He will do. Take, for example, trying to keep track of everything I do. I used to think that would be a very hard task, even for God, but with the invention of computers it now seems almost easy. And think how puny our best computers are compared to God's ability!

A scientist in Arizona has hooked up wires to cotton plants growing thirty-five miles away from his air-conditioned office. With the help of very sensitive listening devices, this scientist can listen in on the action of the plants as they develop a crop. Electrical impulses are produced in a plant when water, minerals, and oxygen combine with sunlight in the presence of chlorophyll to make sugar. This process is called photosynthesis, and it involves electrical energy, which makes tiny little noises in the plants.

By monitoring these sounds of photosynthesis, the scientist is already able to get the plant's reaction to being irrigated, and he says that he will soon be ready to tell the farmer when the cotton is ready to pick. When the system has been perfected it will be possible for a central office in, let's say, St. Louis to call up the apple trees in Washington and find out how they are coming along; to call up the tomatoes in southern Florida and ask them whether they have been getting enough vitamins and minerals; and to call up the wheat crops in Manitoba, or the bananas in Honduras, or the macadamia nuts in Hawaii and ask them how they are doing. And one central computer will be able to monitor all the crops in the world to determine where the shortages will be and to make allowances for them.

See what I mean? It is amazing! And we wonder how God can keep track of how we are getting along. He's far more wonderful than our most sophisticated computers.

THE SINGING SUN

Where wast thou when I laid the foundations of the earth? . . . When the morning stars sang together, and all the sons of God shouted for joy? Job 38:4-7.

The sun is a star. It is the nearest star to our planet. We are dependent on the sun's light and its warmth to sustain life on earth. It's no wonder that throughout history pagan tribes of the earth have worshiped the sun. Since they didn't know the Creator of the sun, they instead revered this life-sustaining ball of fire.

It is amazing how little we know about the sun. We know that it is 93 million miles away, we know that the sun is a constantly exploding hydrogen bomb, and we know that there are sunspots on the sun that seem to have some effect on this earth—but we don't know much about why these things are so or how the sun works.

Sunspots, for example, begin their life about halfway between the sun's equator and the sun's poles, and then they migrate slowly toward the equator. It takes them eleven years to complete the trip. Why?

Our earth rotates once every twenty-four hours, and all of the earth rotates at this same speed. But parts of the sun rotate at different speeds. For example, if you lived at the equator on the sun, you would make a full revolution once very twenty-five of our days, but if you lived near the poles it would take you thirty-three of our days to get all the way around. There also seem to be alternating bands around the sun—fast tracks with slow tracks between. Every eleven years a new band emerges—first a slow one and then a fast one. This phenomenon is very hard to describe.

Now some astronomers have detected gigantic vibrations in the sun. It seems that the whole star is vibrating like a gigantic bell in the sky—vibrating at the rate of about twenty beats per hour. Now that is a real bass note! This discovery has led solar scientists to talk about our "singing sun." There is much more to learn about our universe than any of us can ever imagine.

A PET ALLIGATOR

But if ye bite and devour one another, take heed that ye be not consumed one of another. Galatians 5:15.

A physician whom we know in south Texas has a pet alligator in his back yard. The alligator has lived there for many years and is quite large by now. We once spent the night in this man's house, but he did not tell us about the alligator on the other side of the window over our bed. (And we are glad that we didn't know!) The alligator will not hurt anyone as long as it stays in the back yard and as long as the doctor is careful, but it seems to us that the man is flirting with danger.

The alligator eats meat, of course, and to supplement its regular diet, the doctor picks up road kills and takes them home to his alligator. Another friend of ours was taking the doctor for a ride one day when the doctor yelled, "Stop the car!"

Our friend slammed on the brakes, wondering what could possibly be wrong.

"Back up," commanded the doctor.

Again, our friend dutifully obeyed, backing up until the car came to the place where a large dead dog was lying beside the road. The doctor opened the door, jumped out, and ran to the carcass. He picked up the dog, carried it back to the car, opened the back door, and heaved it onto the floorboard of the back seat. He then dusted himself off, seemingly oblivious to the smell, jumped back into the front seat, and casually exclaimed, "That will make a great meal for my alligator!"

You see, the doctor has become so used to living with an alligator in his back yard, and so used to picking up dead and decaying animals by the road, that he is no longer aware that such action is rotten behavior.

People who love to gossip get to a point where they no longer realize that their behavior is rotten; their habit—like the alligator—must be fed with decaying matter.

CB-CARRYING MOURNING DOVE

Call unto me, and I will answer thee, and shew thee great and mighty things, which thou knowest not. Jer. 33:3.

Have you ever wondered whether God really hears your prayers? After all, there are billions of other people, and He is billions of miles away.

A nest of baby mourning doves in Alabama were outfitted with their own individual radio transmitters. Each young dove was given its own special signal so that when the young left the nest, the whereabouts of each bird was always known.

One evening one of the researchers monitoring the doves noticed that one of the young birds had not returned to the usual roost tree. A thunderstorm kept the observer from checking on the dove until the next morning. When he returned, he heard the dove's special transmission coming from a clump of trees. But the bird could not be located. Later the signal was found to be coming from a pile of debris on the ground near the clump of trees. This was very strange indeed, because it would have been unusual for the dove to be in such a location. When the pile was carefully removed, a gray rat snake nearly six feet long was found. The snake had a conspicuous bulge in its body—from that bulge was coming the steady signal from the transmitter that had been placed on the baby mourning dove.

I wish that I could report that the snake was prevailed upon to give up its dinner and that the dove was recovered alive. Unfortunately, the dove was a good-sized meal for the snake, who has to eat too in a world where such predation is a way of life and death.

I learned from the story anyway: if man can keep track of a bird even when it has been eaten by a snake, I have no doubt that the great God of heaven can keep track of me. He can hear me when I call to Him, and He can save me from that old serpent, the devil—even when I have been captured. He heard Jonah in the belly of a whale, and He has promised to hear me when I call.

GERRY, THE SNORKELING ELEPHANT

Then the waters had overwhelmed us, the stream had gone over our soul: then the proud waters had gone over our soul. Blessed be the Lord, who hath not given us as a prey to their teeth. Psalm 124:4-6.

It was Tuesday the thirteenth that was unlucky for many of the animals at the Frank Buck Zoo, in Gainesville, Texas. On the night of October 13, 1981, there came a rip-roaring rain. In the terms of some of my childhood friends, it was a "frog-strangler." The rain fell in torrents, in sheets, and in buckets, and the creeks rose too fast to allow zoo personnel to clear the animals from the area. In some places thirty feet of water surged over the cages and pens. Many animals were reported drowned, including Gerry, the zoo's only elephant—a favorite of all the children.

Park officials and volunteers worked until late in the night rescuing stranded animals. At about 1:00 A.M. someone spotted the floating body of Gerry. In the light of several flashlights they could see that Gerry's back and the top of her head were floating above the waterline; her eyes were just above the waterline and still gleaming with the light of life; the tip of her trunk was poked up into the air. She was breathing just fine. But her mouth was under water, and she was caught in a tangle of trees. It was four hours before the crew could get back to Gerry. In the meantime the water had gone down somewhat and she freed herself from the tangle and was standing at the water's edge.

Only one animal was lost in that flood. All the rest of them were found or rescued, thanks to quick thinking zookeepers, who cut the fences just in time to free the animals before they would have been overcome by the flood.

But for more than four hours Gerry had been stranded under the floodwaters that surged over and around her. Thanks to her trunk, which she was able to put up onto the air, she had no trouble surviving the ordeal. Would you be as calm and trusting as was Gerry if you were in the same situation? Our God has promised to take care of us, also.

THE HUGE VOID

And the earth was without form, and void; and darkness was upon the face of the deep. And the Spirit of God moved upon the face of the waters. Genesis 1:2.

Many have argued about what the word "void" means in this text. Our dictionary defines it as meaning "without contents; an empty space." According to that definition, and the way I have always been taught, there was nothing here at all before Creation week. Others believe that the basic earth was created earlier as a ball of rock and water, void of any life until Jesus arrived and said, "Let there be light" (Gen. 1:3). The question will probably not be resolved until Jesus returns—then we can ask Him.

Astronomers have recently discovered a section of the universe that has been called a "huge void," where there is apparently nothing at all—no sun, no moon, no stars. Nothing. In one direction the huge void is 300 million light years across. How far is that? It is 1 sextillion, 759 quintillion, 708 quadrillion, 800 trillion miles. Expressed another way, it is about 1,760 billion billion miles, or 176 with nineteen zeros after it. That is a lot of nothing—a long way to travel through a space desert without so much as a single celestial cactus.

The discovery of this huge void means that theories about the universe will have to be revised again. Astronomers have theories to explain the universe without a Genesis creation. One of these theories, the "Big Bang" theory, holds that the entire universe happened as the result of a giant explosion, with billions and billions of bits and pieces being flung outward to become the stars and other heavenly bodies that we see. The "huge void" has poked a gigantic hole in that theory, because if there had been a big bang, all the stars would be more or less evenly distributed throughout the universe, and there could not be a huge empty space anywhere.

We have a wonderful Creator who "hangeth the earth upon nothing" (Job 26:7).

"KILLER SQUIRREL"

For all the law is fulfilled in one word, even in this; Thou shalt love thy neighbour as thyself. But if ye bite and devour one another, take heed that ye be not consumed one of another. Galatians 5:14, 15.

Seventy-five-year-old Mrs. Frisbie was walking along the sidewalk near her son's home in Austin, Texas, when she was attacked from behind by a vicious animal. The savage attack was being mounted by nothing less than a fat resident gray squirrel. Mrs. Frisbie was naturally frightened when the rodent began biting her legs. She tried to run but the animal chased her. It grabbed hold of her and climbed up her coat, biting his way up to her shoulders. She pulled the coat over her head and ran for protection to a house on the street.

A State health-department veterinarian was called to the scene. He took his gun, since he wanted to dispatch the squirrel and check it for rabies as quickly as possible. Soon a party of people were roaming about the neighborhood, looking for the "killer squirrel." They learned that the small beast had bitten others. Two motorcycle police officers joined the search, and soon one of them yelled, "Hey, I think I have him!" And, sure enough, there was the squirrel—but it wasn't clear just who had whom. The squirrel was attacking the officer, biting right through his boots, according to observers.

Needless to say, the squirrel didn't live long, and the remains were taken to the lab for the rabies check. No disease was found. The only explanation offered was that the mating season had arrived and that this was one extremely territorial squirrel, attacking anything or anybody who moved into its area.

One could say that the squirrel was only doing what it believed to be right, but that didn't make its actions any more desirable. There is sometimes a limit to what one can do in the name of what is right. We have to use common sense in defending even right causes. We can often hurt by not having tact or by coming on too strong.

DOLPHIN STRESS

We are troubled on every side, yet not distressed; we are perplexed, but not in despair. 2 Corinthians 4:8.

We are told that the dolphins are among the most intelligent of animals, that they even have a language that they use to communicate under water, and that they seem to express a form of affection that may be similar to that of humans. With all of this intelligence and ability, there is a problem that the dolphins demonstrate, which is also a human problem. They suffer from ulcers caused by stress.

Mimi, Kibby, and Aphrodite were three dolphins at the National Aquarium in Baltimore, Maryland. They lived in a noisy and poorly lit tank that did not allow enough room for them to "get away from it all." There was no place for the dolphins to escape from the constant stream of people who enjoyed watching them, and there was no place for them to get away from each other just to relax. So Mimi, Kibby, and Aphrodite developed ulcers from the stress.

"To watch them feeding and frolicking, you'd assume they're fine," said a director of the aquarium. But the constant pressure of such a cramped and public place was more than the three dolphins could bear. Even daily doses of Maalox failed to ease the tension on their systems. So they were sent to the Flipper Sea School in Grassey Key, Florida, aboard a chartered plane. There they would receive much-needed rest and relaxation. Back home in Baltimore, their home tank was renovated for better dolphin health.

Isn't it amazing that other creatures that God has made are no more able to avoid the effects of stress than we are? As a loving heavenly Father, God has given us instruction on how to live healthfully. Living under stress is not healthful. When we disobey the rules, we suffer the consequences. Sometimes it takes a playful and enjoyable animal like the dolphin to teach us the results of unhealthful living. By trusting in Jesus to take care of the daily problems, our stress is reduced, and we don't suffer the consequences of living under pressure.

MONARCHS FLY PILOT'S CLASS

Then we which are alive and remain shall be caught up together with them in the clouds, to meet the Lord in the air: and so shall we ever be with the Lord. 1 Thessalonians 4:17.

One October day in Rhode Island a kindergarten teacher found two monarch butterfly caterpillars feeding on milkweed plants. The caterpillars had hatched out too late in the season to develop before winter, and they would undoubtedly freeze to death. The teacher picked enough leaves to provide food for the caterpillars for several days, and she took them to her schoolroom, where they ate and ate and were warm and safe. Soon they spun their light-green chrysalides. In each chrysalis, the miracle of transformation was taking place, and the following month, long after winter had arrived, the two monarchs emerged from their sleeping cases and spread their beautiful wings to dry.

Monarchs migrate south for the winter, and it was long past the last flight. The two butterflies would never make it if released in the frigid November air.

But the teacher had an idea. She prepared a tiny cage and placed the two monarchs inside. She took the precious parcel to the airport, where she went to the United Airlines ticket counter and asked for the customer-service supervisor. The supervisor listened patiently while the teacher told him that she needed to purchase tickets for two butterflies. Without batting an eye, the supervisor arranged for the monarchs to be flown south. Those two monarchs flew south as no other monarchs have ever made the journey—with the pilot in the cockpit of a United Airlines jet. When released, they flitted into the warm air, as if this were all part of their usual trip south.

As long as time lasts, it is not too late to get ready for Jesus to come. But time is running out, and we need special help from the Master Teacher to help us prepare for the trip so that when He comes we will be prepared to go home with Him. We too will be traveling with the Pilot.

WHEREIN WERE SCORPIONS

Behold, I give unto you power to tread on serpents and scorpions, and over all the power of the enemy: and nothing shall by any means hurt you. Luke 10:19.

Perhaps you have never lived where there are scorpions, but one of the major menaces where my family lives are these tiny dragons with stingers in their tails. There is nothing good that I can say about scorpions. They are poisonous, belligerent, sneaky, ugly, and first cousins of the devil. I don't know anyone who likes scorpions. They are terrible! In the first month that we lived in our house in the country, we found three of them scurrying around the house and two more, with babies, in a pan. Needless to say, we did away with the little beasts before they could hurt us.

Speaking of hurt, the scorpion is a pain machine. It is literally a walking promise of excruciating pain. The stinger at the end of the long, jointed tail is curved like a scimitar, and it is connected to two large venom glands that contain a nerve poison. The poison is more powerful than that of some of the world's most deadly snakes. When you are stung by a scorpion, the pain is immediate and intense. My one experience was enough to convince me of this for life. I was stung on the finger as I was picking up some old newspapers (scorpions love to hide out in old papers, clothes, and such). No pain that I have ever suffered was so severe.

Death from a scorpion sting is uncommon, but it does occur. The lethal effects of the sting are similar to strychnine poisoning. First there is vomiting, sweating, shivering, and speech difficulties, then the victim begins to froth at the mouth and nose, and finally, the victim goes into convulsions and dies.

To me the scorpion is a perfect example of the true nature of the devil. He is terrible! I don't apologize for calling sin by its right name. "The sting of death is sin. . . . But thanks be to God, which giveth us the victory through our Lord Jesus Christ" (1 Cor. 15:56, 57).

THE MINKS COME BACK

Lift up thine eyes round about, and see: all they gather themselves together, they come to thee: thy sons shall come from far, and thy daughters shall be nursed at thy side. Isaiah 60:4.

Minks are raised for their fur on mink farms. In order to obtain the best fur, it is important that the mink farmers take very good care of their animals. They are fed well, their pens and cages are kept clean, and they are generally as happy as minks can be.

There are those who feel that raising wild animals and keeping them penned up when they should be wild and free is terrible. A band of such sympathetic folk invaded a mink farm in Essex, England, several years ago. Masked raiders arrived and tore down the fences, letting all the minks go free. These people believed that they were doing the minks a favor by giving them their freedom.

Well, as it happened, almost all the minks came home the next day at mealtime; they lined up at their feeding troughs, and waited to be fed as usual! They weren't upset at all when they were herded back into the pens and the fences were repaired.

You see, a wild mink has to work a lot harder for its meals, and it has to locate its own sleeping quarters, which may not be warm and dry. A wild mink may go for days without eating before it finds a meal. Being wild and free isn't all that it is cracked up to be.

Sometimes people want to be wild and free, and they think that being a Christian is like being caged—they aren't free to do the things that they want to do. So they tear down the fences and walls that the Lord has built around us to protect us from danger, and they become wild and free. Today's text is a promise to mothers and fathers that even though their children might want to be on their own for a time, Jesus is calling them still, and they will come home to Jesus when they are lonely and hungry for love.

THE SPARROW THAT FELL IN CHURCH

Are not five sparrows sold for two farthings, and not one of them is forgotten before God? ... Fear not therefore: ye are of more value than many sparrows. Luke 12:6, 7.

One afternoon my telephone rang. The voice on the other end said, "This is CBS News in New York. We are calling for Roger Mudd, and we need to know how much a sparrow weighs." They didn't say why, but they were obviously in a great hurry for the information. I didn't learn until later that the information was to be used on the CBS Evening News that was to be aired in less than 10 minutes.

I did not know the weight of a sparrow, so I told the woman that I would call her back very quickly. I hung up, looked up the weight, and learned that it was about an ounce. So I placed the call and gave the information to the man who answered. He thanked me, and that was that.

Later I learned that a world-famous guitarist was being recorded as he performed in a church in a small village in England. The recording was to be broadcast by the BBC, so the church authorities were quite eager that nothing interfere with the performance. They thought that they had taken care of everything, but a sparrow in the rafters apparently liked the music and joined in with its own song.

Pastor Robin Clark was angered by the interruption. He ordered the audience to leave and then called in someone to shoot the sparrow. The concert then went on without another hitch. But when the news got out about what had happened, that shot was heard round the world. The London *Daily Telegraph* carried the following headline on the front page: "Rev. Robin orders death of a sparrow."

Roger Mudd simply told the story and then ended the nightly news by making the observation that it was certainly a large fuss over something that weighs only about an ounce.

A large fuss indeed! A woman in the audience had cried when the sparrow fell, and I suspect the Ruler of the universe may have shed a tear, as well.

THE YELLOW-FRONTED GARDENER BOWERBIRD

In my Father's house are many mansions: if it were not so, I would have told you. I go to prepare a place for you. And if I go and prepare a place for you, I will come again, and receive you unto myself; that where I am, there ye may be also. John 14:2, 3.

Some years ago a number of self-styled theologians proposed the idea that maybe God was extinct. It was a time when you heard people everywhere discussing whether or not "God is dead." When I read about the recent rediscovery in New Guinea of the yellow-fronted gardener bowerbird, I remembered these discussions.

Until 1980 the only evidence anyone in the Western world had that the yellow-fronted gardener bowerbird had ever lived were three skins and a few feathers from the bird. These had been brought to England in 1895. A number of expeditions to New Guinea had failed to find any trace of this "mystery bird." It was assumed that the bird was extinct. Then in 1980, on a trip to help the government set up a national park in the largely unexplored Gauttier Mountains, explorers found the bird. Not only is it there, but there are quite a number of them.

Male bowerbirds build special creations, called bowers, for their ladyloves. The yellow-fronted gardener bowerbird builds a four-foot-high tower of sticks against a small tree trunk or tree fern. The sticks are crisscrossed in maypole style, and the base of the bower is a round, moss-covered platform about three feet across—a mansion, if there ever was one, for Mrs. Yellow-fronted Gardener Bowerbird. On the platform, the male places colored fruit. The male calls to the female and holds fruit in his beak, offering it to her as a gift if she will only come and be where he is and accept the mansion that he has prepared for her.

God is not extinct! Jesus died, that is true enough, but He arose again and has gone to prepare mansions for His people, who are called His "bride" in the Bible. He is calling and offers the fruit of the tree of life—we need only accept.

HYSSOP

Purge me with hyssop, and I shall be clean: wash me, and I shall be whiter than snow. Psalm 51:7.

Hyssop is a plant that we first hear about in connection with the first Passover supper when the Israelites were ready to leave Egypt. Bunches of it were used to splash blood from the Passover lamb over the door and on both doorposts of every house in the Israelite camp. The blood was the signal to the destroying angel that those in that house believed God and that they were willing to follow Him completely.

It is believed that hyssop was the plant that botanists today call the gray-green marjoram. It is a small plant that grows throughout Palestine even today. It has hairy stems and a mass of white flowers at the end of each stem. The plant is very fragrant, and it tastes very much like peppermint. We don't know much about its use in Bible times except that it was used as a symbol for cleansing, but in modern times hyssop has been used as a spice or condiment, and it is said to have medicinal value.

Solomon, one of the Bible's greatest naturalists, studied the hyssop plant. In 1 Kings 4:33 we are told that "he spake of trees, from the cedar tree that is in Lebanon even unto the hyssop that springeth out of the wall." And sure enough, it is characteristic for the hyssop to spring up among the rocks and in the walls of the Holy Land.

God told Israel to use hyssop not only as a means of sprinkling the blood on their doorposts but also as a part of a number of other purifying rituals: it was used in the cleansing of a leper, or a house in which someone had been sick with a plague, and it was used in the purification of those items or persons who were declared unclean through contact with the dead.

Perhaps the most beautiful reference to hyssop in the Bible is the one David uses in Psalm 51 to entreat the Lord to cleanse him from sin. We can certainly pray that prayer with David; we all need the blood of Jesus to make us clean.

THE NOSE KNOWS

Thou lovest righteousness, and hatest wickedness: therefore God, thy God, hath anointed thee with the oil of gladness above thy fellows. All thy garments smell of myrrh, and aloes, and cassia, out of the ivory palaces, whereby they have made thee glad. Psalm 45:7, 8.

The psalmist is describing the great qualities of God's kingdom. In the days when this was written, people would often pack their clothes with substances that gave them an attractive scent. Myrrh, aloes, and wood from the cassia tree were among those items that made clothes smell so fragrant that you were made glad by either wearing them or having someone nearby who was wearing them.

God made man with the ability to smell and to appreciate the wonderful fragrances that are present throughout nature. He also provided man with the ability to read certain things from the scents and odors that are given off. There is another type of scent to which we all respond but which is not so obvious.

Physiologists tell us that the usual nasal abilities of man are not involved in the reception and mental processing of many types of scents. Besides the ability to smell wonderful things such as perfume, fragrant flowers, new-mown hay, and the like, we also have the ability to smell scents that we don't even know we are smelling. It is like being able to hear sounds too high for our ears to perceive. There is a special organ in the general vicinity of the lower floor of the nasal cavity of every mammal except the porpoise. It is called the Jacobson's organ, and for many years it was thought to have no purpose at all, but now it is believed to be the receptor of special scents that affect the way we act and the way we feel. The Jacobson's organ is connected by nerves to a different part of the brain—the part that controls hormonal production. To find such a sense is like discovering a sixth sense that we didn't even know we had. As the psalmist who said, we are fearfully and wonderfully made!

SHADES OF JADE

Every word of God is pure: he is a shield unto them that put their trust in him. Proverbs 30:5.

If you were to ask a mineralogist what jade is, he or she would have to say that no one knows. This is not to say that a mineralogist couldn't tell you what a piece of jade is made of; this simply means that one piece of jade is composed of one group of minerals, while another piece of jade may be composed of quite a different group of minerals. The controversy over what jade is and is not has been going on for centuries, and it has to be resolved as a problem with the language rather than a problem for the mineralogist.

The truth is that a number of different minerals are called jade. What is called jade may be *jadeite,* which is sodium-aluminum silicate, or it may be *nephrite,* which is calcium-iron-magnesium silicate. Jadeite can be pink, blue, gray, white, red, orange, yellow, black, or green. The most highly prized color is a bright-green, caused by small amounts of chromium. Nephrite occurs in yellow, brown, gray, white, green, and, rarely, blue or black.

These two minerals are so similar that there is no simple way to tell them apart. The composition of jade isn't important to the jade carver, since both minerals work equally well in the production of fine artwork.

To make jade matters more difficult, there are many ways to copy jade carvings, and the world is full of counterfeit jade. Only an expert could distinguish true jade from figures carved in serpentine, which is a beautiful green mineral that looks like jade. "Jade" figures are also produced in glass that is made to look like the real thing. If you want to be sure that you have a jade figure, you must have it tested by experts, who can tell you only the mineral composition. Whether or not you can call it true jade is up to you.

Like jade, there are many people with different personalities who claim to be Christians. When it comes down to who is and who is not a Christian, only Jesus can analyze our true characters.

306

LEFT-BRAINED CANARIES

Sing unto the Lord a new song, and his praise from the end of the earth, ye that go down to the sea, and all that is therein; the isles, and the inhabitants thereof. Isaiah 42:10.

There is a wonderful relationship between the two halves of our brain. We usually use the left side of our brain to learn to talk and listen to others speak. With the right side of our brain we normally see pictures, work arithmetic problems, and listen to music without words. The left side of the brain is usually the logical side, while the right side is the more creative side. But there are always exceptions to the way things usually work. In some people the functions of these two sides are reversed. Also if a portion of the brain becomes damaged on either the left or the right side, the unhurt side can learn to do what formerly was taken care of by the injured side. Well, so much for *our* brains—what about bird brains?

It was recently discovered that in birds too each side of the brain controls different functions. For example, experiments show that canaries use the left side of their brain to learn to sing—just as we do. And the older a canary is, the more different songs it knows—which is also true of most people. The canaries, as well as most other songbirds, learn much of the songs they sing, but they are also born with the ability to recognize the songs of their own kind.

Science has still not figured out why birds sing. If the primary purpose of birdsong is to stake out a territory, birds wouldn't continue to learn new songs and add new parts to their old ones. Birds seem to like to learn, and they seem to love to sing.

Isn't it wonderful that God gave us brains that we can use to learn new songs? Isn't it fun to sing? Listen to the birds as they sing praises to the Creator, and lift your own voice in a song of thanks to Jesus, who gave you and the birds such wonderful brains.

THE WOLF LADY

Ask now the beasts, and they shall teach thee; and the fowls of the air, and they shall tell thee. Job 12:7.

She comes every week—two or three times a week, in fact—to sit on a concrete bench in front of the wolf pen at the Philadelphia Zoo. She is Janet Lidle, a graduate of Columbia, South Carolina, Bible College, who now lives in Philadelphia. She is partially blind, but she can see the wolves, and through watching them she says that she has found a peace that she was lacking before. She has discovered the joy that comes from being "able to appreciate something for what it is, not what you can gain from it."

When asked why she keeps coming to the wolf pen in snow, rain, or shine, Miss Lidle says, "I'm not sure, but something is calling. God calls people to different things.... And the animals are as much a creation of God as you are." She says that each of God's creatures displays some unique quality of God's character.

"Take the dodo," the wolf lady explains. "He was an expression of God's character as a creature. And because the dodo became extinct, there is some aspect of God's character that is now invisible, that we'll never be able to learn about."

Miss Lidle has taken thousands of pictures of the wolves, and she plans to write a book about her observations and feelings since coming to watch the wolves. She doesn't try to interfere with the wolves' activities; she doesn't try to pet them or get close to them. Her favorite wolf is called Shy Boy, but she won't talk about him at all. She says that her book will be primarily about Shy Boy and what she has learned from watching him.

Haven't you ever wished that you could talk to animals—to the squirrels, the birds, the toads, and the butterflies? Well, in one sense you can: Jesus, who made them all, speaks to you by His Spirit as you observe these wild things, and you can talk back to them by telling Jesus what you learned about Him from them.

THE CROSS SPIDER

Whose hope shall be cut off, and whose trust shall be a spider's web. Job 8:14.

Some years ago I asked a friend why he was not a Christian. His response was "Because I watched those who claimed to be Christians, and their lives were not worth copying." While we should not look at other people for our examples, a true follower of Jesus grows in His likeness. There are many who claim the cross but don't let that cross have any effect on their daily lives. They may lie, cheat, steal, or do worse, but come church time, they are there. How can this be?

The cross spider is named for the sign of the cross that appears prominently on her beautifully decorated back. She is one of the orb-weaving spiders and weaves one of the most beautiful webs in the world. What looks to the naked eye like a number of beautifully organized single strands carefully placed and tied to make the spider's net is actually much more. Each thread that comes from the cross spider's abdomen is not just a single strand, but can contain up to forty thousand strands of spider silk. And each of these strands is from one thousandth to two thousandths of a millimeter in diameter. The finest thread that man has ever produced is made of fiberglass or tungsten and is five thousandths of an inch in diameter. The cross spider's spinner is like a loom with forty thousand individual, incredibly small nozzles, from which come the strands. Each nozzle is hooked up to a nerve that can be switched on and off by the spider's central nervous system, depending on the size of thread needed.

Once the threads are strung and the spider's web is in place, the beautiful and talented cross spider waits for the first insect to come along and be trapped by her talent. Even a mate who might be attracted by her beauty will have to watch out. She will try to eat *him* for dinner, too.

Many talented and otherwise wonderful people operate under the sign of the cross, but that doesn't make them Christians. A Christian is continuously becoming like Jesus.

309

BUG VERSUS PLANT VERSUS BUG VERSUS PLANT VERSUS BUG

Wherefore take unto you the whole armour of God, that ye may be able to withstand in the evil day, and having done all to stand. Ephesians 6:13.

What has been called "an arms race" has been going on between plants and insects for a long time. At some point when insects begin to attack plants in great numbers, the plant has the ability to begin production of chemicals that are distasteful and even poisonous to insects. Eventually the insects will go hungry unless they can come up with a way to handle the new weapon of the plants.

Well, insects have a way—their *own* mixture of different chemicals, called mixed function oxidases, or MFO. MFO can take the harmful chemical and transform it into a substance that is no longer distasteful and at first is not as harmful to the insect. Now it is the plant's turn again, and, sure enough, it has another weapon in its arsenal. Now it begins production of chemicals that the insect will change to a delectable chemical, but one that will be poisonous to the insect. So the insect, using its best defenses, takes what it has come to believe is a harmful chemical and changes it into what it thinks is a safe chemical—only to have what it thought was a safe chemical turn out to be poisonous.

At this point in the research, it appears that the war is being won by the plants. They have the last word. But the insects have mobility, so when overcome by the plants, the insects simply move on to other unsuspecting plants and start the process all over again.

Our lives are much like those of the plants. Satan comes along like an invading insect with all sorts of tricks. We must have the whole armor of God, because we never know which weapon will be needed. We need the belt of truth, the breastplate of righteousness, the boots of the gospel of peace, the shield of faith, "the helmet of salvation, and the sword of the Spirit, which is the word of God" (Eph. 6:17).

310

FISH SCALES

These shall ye eat of all that are in the waters: whatsoever hath fins and scales in the waters, in the seas, and in the rivers, them shall ye eat. Leviticus 11:9.

In His mercy, God presented the children of Israel with a set of health principles. And God's rules were very simple and very practical. When He told them which fish were acceptable food and which ones were not, He made the difference very clear so that there could not be any question. God's rules are always clear, but we become confused by trying to bend them to mean what we want them to say.

A few facts about scales might help us to know why they are on a "clean" fish. In the first place, scales provide an armor against disease. Second, they are also found primarily on fish that inhabit the clearest water, the reason being that scales have special light reflecting abilities, which offer protection to the fish from predators above and below. Finally, it may be that scales tend to slow down the fish that wear them. That would make them less likely to become carnivorous, because they would not be able to swim fast enough to catch other fish. So fish with scales and fins would also tend to be the vegetarians of the water world.

Fish without scales and fins are more likely to be carnivorous or scavengers. The closer an animal is to the vegetable diet that God gave us originally, the more likely that it is to be healthy. So, while God may have known that the diet that He permitted was not best, it was the best that He could recommend under the circumstances.

There is a lot of discussion about whether these rules still apply today. Generally speaking, the rules are health principles and, as such, are just as true today as they were in the time of Moses. We should also consider any additional recent information about the deteriorating condition of all flesh meats. Today it is hard to find a disease-free environment, even in the midst of the sea or in the most crystal-clear mountain stream.

311

PLANTS THAT GROW IN THE DARK

His lord said unto him, Well done, thou good and faithful servant: thou hast been faithful over a few things, I will make thee ruler over many things: enter thou into the joy of thy lord." Matthew 25:21.

Growing profusely in almost total darkness at the bottom of several Antarctic lakes, below an eighteen-foot-thick layer of solid ice that never melts, are large quantities of algae plants. These algae plants were discovered when scientists used a special steam generator to melt through the solid ice that has covered these lakes for untold hundreds of years. To their surprise, the scientists found tons of pinkish-orange algae growing on the bottom of the lakes, in patches three to four inches deep.

How could these plants, which require light to live, survive under such conditions? At first the scientists thought that the plants had the ability to generate food by what is called chemosynthesis. Such a condition is to be found at the bottom of the sea in one other situation, but as the algae in these frigid lakes were studied more intensely, it was found that there is another explanation for their healthy, flourishing condition.

The pink-orange color of the plants gives them the greatest amount of light-absorption capability possible. And for eight months out of the year there is an infinitesimal amount of light that gets to these algae plants. The amount of light that they have to use is one one thousandth of the amount that is available above the ice covering. With that tiny amount of light the plants are able to grow great quantities of foliage in the darkness.

When we have only a little of something to work with, we must make the best of the situation. There is always something that can be done when conditions seem poor. We can live up to what little light we have, and as we develop our Christian lives we will find that we have more light to use and to share with others.

"SPOOK LIGHTS" EXPLAINED

For the living know that they shall die: but the dead know not any thing. Ecclesiastes 9:5.

At night at various points on the earth's surface there appears a phenomenon that has intrigued people for centuries: what appear to be mysterious ghostly balls of light seem to arise from the ground, sway to and fro, and move about as if they know where they are going. Many people have believed these lights to be the ghosts of the departed dead, while others call them UFOs. Some Christians who had no other explanation said that the lights were evil spirits and that to go near was to get onto the devil's ground.

These "spook lights" have been studied recently by scientists who believe that the lights represent a natural phenomenon associated with cracks in the earth's crust, or fault lines. As it turns out, almost every "spook light" area is right over a geological fault zone. As the stress increases along such fault lines, the threat of an earthquake increases. However, before an earthquake can occur, other things can happen, and in some areas these other things include "spook lights."

What causes the lights? Apparently the lights occur only above areas where there are large quantities of quartz at the fault line. As the stress increases, pressures up to two tons per square inch are exerted on the quartz crystal rock far below the earth's surface. When quartz is pressed or twisted with such force, it gives off an electrical charge. From underground, the charge from crushed quartz leaks upward and "bleeds" into the air, where it heats up and begins to glow. The resulting ball of soft light can be from two inches to three feet in diameter.

There are spirits, good and evil, but the good spirits are angels who don't play such tricks, and the evil spirits don't congregate in an isolated spot in the woods unless there are people there who worship them instead of God. There are certainly no ghosts of the dead; the Bible is clear on that point, so another myth has been dispelled.

THE HYPOTHALAMUS DECIDES WHETHER I SWEAT OR SHIVER

They shall have linen bonnets upon their heads, and shall have linen breeches upon their loins; they shall not gird themselves with any thing that causeth sweat. Ezekiel 44:l8.

We have a very practical God—a God who is concerned about our physical comfort, as well as our spiritual well-being. In today's text the Lord is presenting the regulations for the priests as they work in the Temple. Among all the ordinances is a rule that priests shall not tie themselves with anything that would make them unduly hot, and therefore sweat. If God didn't tell them this, the priests might be tempted to abuse themselves physically, to make themselves uncomfortable in order to serve the Lord "properly." God wants our worship and our love, but He doesn't require us to do penance to please Him.

If God had intended for us to suffer all the time, then He wouldn't have formed a thermostat in the part of our brain called the hypothalamus, located right in the center of our head beneath the major portion of the brain. In the hypothalamus is an automatic thermostat. The blood flows through this instrument in the hypothalamus. If the temperature is 98.6 degrees Fahrenheit nothing changes, but if the temperature is a tiny fraction higher or lower than that, then the automatic thermostat flashes a number of chemical messages throughout the body to correct the temperature.

As I am writing this I have just taken a break to mow the grass. It is 100 degrees Fahrenheit outside, and before I was through I was wet with sweat. Now I am back in the air-conditioned house, and I feel cold. I have "goose bumps." Both the sweat and the goose bumps were ordered by my hypothalamus. The work of the hypothalamus is far more complicated than merely causing me to sweat or shiver, but that action alone is enough to cause me to thank my Creator for thinking of my comfort.

BEETLE HORNS USED IN BEETLE BATTLES

All the horns of the wicked also will I cut off; but the horns of the righteous shall be exalted. Psalm 75:10.

Throughout the Bible horns are used as symbols of power and strength, both physical and political. When a horn or horns are broken or cut off, the power and strength of the beast that they represent is also broken, or ended.

For years entomologists wondered about the purpose of the horns that beetles often have on their heads. Are they weapons; or are they intended to attract mates, since the males have the horns? A young British scientist named Timothy Palmer decided to find out. He placed a male horned beetle into an observation cage with two females. The beetles went about doing their chores as usual, but the male never used his horn. These beetles live in burrows, so the observation cage was constructed in such a way that Timothy could view the beetles in their burrows, where they carried on their routine activities.

The scientist then placed a second male, also with horns, of course, into the cage. Battle erupted immediately. For more than an hour these two beetles battled, primarily using their horns as the means of tormenting each other. They could not do much physical damage with the horns, but they certainly used them to push each other around and to turn each other over. Sooner or later, one beetle would give up and leave the burrow, with the victor pushing from behind.

All of Timothy Palmer's observations failed to find any purpose for the beetle horns except to assist them in their beetle battles. Furthermore, any male beetle without horns that showed up for battle was automatically a loser. Apparently, the beetles are also subject to the rule that the psalmist is setting forth. Without the power of God, we are helpless against the "beetles" of the world. But He has promised to cut off their horns and to provide us with His power unto salvation through Jesus.

315

STUMBLING-BIRDS

Let us not therefore judge one another any more: but judge this rather, that no man put a stumbling block or an occasion to fall in his brother's way. Romans 14:13.

In this text Paul is telling the Romans to be careful about the way they live with their new freedom in Jesus. They were to avoid doing things that, although not wrong in themselves, would cause others to sin.

On the morning of September 8, 1981, Lt. Col. David Smith, the commander of the U.S. Air Force's flying team called the Thunderbirds, took off from the Cleveland airport. One of Smith's team companions, Staff Sgt. Dwight Roberts, was right behind him. The team had just spent three days of precision flying at the Cleveland National Air Show. It was a routine takeoff; the planes were running perfectly.

Birds, probably gulls resting on the runway, took to the air as the jets thundered toward them. But the gulls' aerial ability was no match for the jets, and many of them were literally sucked into the intake vents and ingested into the engines, causing what is called flameout, which simply stops all thrust. The jets were dead in the air. Both pilots ejected, and their jets crashed. Staff Sgt. Roberts' parachute opened, and he landed safely; Commander Smith was not so fortunate. He took the time to aim his plane at Lake Erie instead of crashing on the runway, so he lost valuable altitude, and his parachute did not have time to open. He died on the rocks at the edge of the lake.

Those birds didn't mean to get in the way, and they were certainly not doing anything wrong, but they caused several million dollars' damage and the loss of a life. You would be correct in saying that they didn't know any better. Sometimes when we are told that what we do might hurt someone else, we say, "Well, I'm just minding my own business; I can't help what they think or do." But if we can make a difference in someone else's life by what we do or say, then don't you think we should behave accordingly?

316

HE PETTED AN EIGHT-POINT BUCK

Thou shalt not kill. Exodus 20:13.

Sometimes you hear about something that is almost unbelievable. Such is the story told by Mr. Kulik, who used to be a deer hunter. One snowy day during deer-hunting season Mr. Kulik went out with his rifle, three sandwiches, and a thermos. He tramped through the woods until he came upon a well-used deer trail. The hunter looked around for a hiding place where he could keep a sharp lookout for deer. He found a sheltered nook in some rocks and settled in to wait. After an hour he became hungry and decided to have lunch. He had just finished two sandwiches and enjoyed a drink from his thermos when he saw the buck.

Less than twenty feet away was a magnificent eight-point buck. The closest cover for the deer was thirty yards away. There was no way that Mr. Kulik could miss. He had been hunting for many years and had shot many deer, but he had never had a chance like this. But Mr. Kulik didn't move. He just sat there waiting for the buck to realize that he was there and break for cover. If the deer had done that, then Mr. Kulik would probably have felled him with one or two shots. But the deer did not run.

That eight-point buck, who must surely have had to flee from any number of hunters, didn't even offer to run when he became aware of the hunter. Instead, the deer began to slowly walk toward Mr. Kulik. Carefully, step by step, he moved closer, curious perhaps, until he was right in front of Mr. Kulik, looking steadily into his eyes.

What would you do if this happened to you? Mr. Kulik didn't know what to do, so he just reached out and scratched the buck's head, between his antlers. The deer didn't even flinch, so Mr. Kulik ran his hand over the buck's side and flanks—he was petting a wild deer! The hunter proceeded to give his last sandwich to the deer, and the deer ate it. Soon the buck moved away and slowly continued down the path.

Mr. Kulik never shot another deer. After such an Edenic experience, he just couldn't.

317

DEOXYRIBONUCLEIC ACID

I will praise thee; for I am fearfully and wonderfully made: marvellous are thy works; and that my soul knoweth right well. Psalm 139:14.

Don't feel bad if you can't pronounce the title above. Most people never learn to say that long word the right way (it goes something like dee-OX-ee-rye-bo-new-CLAY-ik acid!), so scientists have given the whole term an easy code word—DNA. But what *is* DNA? Well, it is just about the absolutely most important stuff in the whole world, that's what. It is what made you what you are, and it is what made me what I am.

When you were first conceived in your mother's womb, you inherited traits from ancestors through your parents—the color of your eyes, the shape of your nose, the length of your fingers, and other characteristics. These traits are all packaged as coded messages in the genes. They are called genes, spelled g-e-n-e-s, which is a word that comes from the same root word as the word *genesis,* meaning "creation." Genes from your mother and father created you. Perhaps the most wonderful thing about Creation is that Jesus gave our first parents the ability to create by having children. And the secret is in the DNA.

No one knows yet how DNA works, but we do know that all the traits that you inherit, all the traits that your cat or dog inherits, all the traits that the plants inherit, all the traits that all living things inherit, are carried as coded messages in the DNA, which is what genes are made of. Now if you think that is wonderful, which it is, then wait until you hear about how big these coded messages are. If you take every person in all of the world today—more than 4 billion—and if you were to take all the DNA that was needed to produce all these people, you would have enough DNA to make a pill about the size of an aspirin tablet! Can you imagine that! Isn't it wonderful!

EL NIÑO

"But when the fulness of the time was come, God sent forth his Son." Galatians 4:4.

About every seven years, at Christmas time, on the west coast of South America a natural phenomenon occurs that the local residents call El Niño, for the Christ child. It is anything but a welcome occurrence. It signals a halt to the primary businesses of the coastal areas. The whole region is plunged into economic depression.

Normally the western coast of South America is washed from the south by the Humboldt Current, which is clear, cold water teeming with sea life. It is this expansive amount of sea life that serves as the basis for the economy for most of the coastal areas of Peru and Chile.

But once in every few years the warm waters from near Panama push down the coast and overflow the natural waters of the area. The arrival of the warm water from the north spells doom for the sea life. The fish descend to the cooler depths and are not available to the fishermen. Onshore winds blowing over the unusually warm water drop torrential rains on the land, which causes muddy runoffs that cloud the ocean so that it cannot receive enough light to support the incredibly large amount of plant life that is normal. The plants die, followed by the death of the fish that eat the plants. Decay is everywhere. Microscopic organisms known as dinoflagellates suddenly begin to multiply in epidemic proportions, turning the waters blood-red as in "red tide." And in such numbers, the dinoflagellates are poisonous to what little marine life is left, including the sea turtles. It is a calamity of major proportions that takes many months to clear away before conditions are normal again.

It is interesting that the local people call this time El Niño. When Jesus came to earth it was in time of darkness, too—spiritual darkness. But He did not cause the darkness. Instead He came to remedy it. The world was blessed with the Christ child, and His life and sacrifice gave hope for the entire world.

319

AN UNDERGROUND ORCHID

And this is the condemnation, that light is come into the world, and men loved darkness rather than light, because their deeds were evil. John 3:19.

Some people just don't want to hear about Jesus because He, being the Light of the world, reveals the darkness of their sins, and they love those sins so much that they don't want the light of Jesus' love in their lives. Such people are like the underground orchid of Australia.

The scientific name of this strange flower is *Rhizenthella gardneri* (pronounced rye-ZEN-thel-la GARD-ner-i). *Rhizenthella* lives its entire life underground. It has a stem, bears a single flower consisting of a cluster of red and purple blossoms in a cup of white and purple petals, and has tiny scalelike leaves—but it has no roots whatsoever. A fellow by the name of John Trott first discovered the flower when he was clearing trees and brush on his farm in Australia. He was clearing out a type of tree called broom honey-myrtle when he noticed the peculiar violet plantlike material underground around the stump.

As it turns out, *Rhizenthella* is completely dependent upon two other oganisms for its existence—the honey-myrtle and a fungus. The fungus sends threads through the soil, looking for the decaying stumps of honey-myrtle trees. The fungus then takes nourishment in the form of sugar and minerals from the dead wood and transports the food to the *Rhizenthella* by sending other threads into the orchid's stem. (Since it is fed this way, the *Rhizenthella* needs no roots.) But the fungus plant doesn't keep any food for itself. *Rhizenthella* takes all the food, and the fungus dies.

These two strange plants, feeding on dead wood, are destined to die from the beginning; the fungus commits suicide by catering to the *Rhizenthella,* and the orchid kills its only food source by taking all its food.

Such a fate also awaits the people of this world who prefer to live in darkness rather than enjoy the Light of the world—Jesus.

Jose

RAILS

_For in the time of trouble he shall hide me in his pavilion: in
the secret of his tabernacle shall he hide me. Psalm 27:5._

It is always a thrill to see a rail. Among the most secretive of
all birds, the rails hide themselves away so well in the grasses,
reeds, and water plants that it takes a lot of patience and some
"luck" to see the smaller ones. Larger rails often emerge from
the marsh grass to walk along the edges of streams and
mudflats, but the small rails, or crakes, just don't come out
except on rare occasions. Rails range in size from four inches
long to hen-size.

One day in southern Mexico we wanted very much to see the
tiny red rail. We could hear the whinnying calls of many of them
in the tall grass of a marsh, but we couldn't catch even a glimpse
of their deep-rufous-colored plumage. No larger than a sparrow,
they made almost as much racket as a yardful of chickens. We
even tried to lure them into the open by using a tape recorder.
We would record their call and then play it back to them, hoping
that they would come close enough for us to see them. They came
close, all right—we could immediately hear their answering
calls, and we could see the grass move as they moved toward us.
One of them actually came up to my boots! He was that close. I
could see the grass moving, and I could hear him calling—but I
could not see him. I didn't get even the slightest glimpse of a
single red rail, and they were all around us in broad daylight. In
three trips to Mexico and several visits to the same marsh, I
have never seen a red rail. It is a mystery to me how those birds
can hide like that.

In the United States we have the black rail, which is about
the same size as the red rail. In thirty years of searching, I _think_
I saw one once.

If God can provide a pavilion of grasses that can hide the rails
so well, surely He can hide us in times of trouble.

THE HYENA BORDER PATROL

For he hath strengthened the bars of thy gates; he hath blessed thy children within thee. He maketh peace in thy borders, and filleth thee with the finest of the wheat. Psalm 147:13, 14.

The hyena is not as bad an animal as most of us have been led to believe. In many respects it fills the place on the African plains that the wolf fills across the plains of the western hemisphere, and it appears to be every bit as intelligent and as well organized in its habits as the wolf.

Hans Kruuk spent three and one-half years observing hyenas in Africa and has written a book entitled *The Spotted Hyena* (1972), telling of what he observed. The most remarkable departure from the hyena's reputation was the finding that a pack of hyenas prefer to bring down their own prey, and they do so swiftly and in a more merciful manner than do lions. They are not given exclusively to stealing their food, as we have been led to believe, although they are not above it.

Hyenas have a highly developed social system, and they maintain strictly laid-out territories, which are patrolled regularly. A group of eight or ten hyenas will gather at a regular spot for border-patrol duty. After much sniffing and friendly nuzzling, the dominant female leads the border patrol to the portion of the border to be patrolled on this day. The hyenas not only have scent glands under their tails as do other carnivores, but they also have scent glands on the bottoms of their feet. As a result, they spend a good deal of time along the border scratching and pawing the ground to make sure that the scent is well planted in the soil. After they have covered about a mile or so of their boundary, the patrol will quit for the day, only to reassemble the next day and continue the patrol.

In this manner the hyenas maintain a very well-respected territory where other packs of hyenas are very unlikely to bother them, and vice versa. Thus, even some of the more unlovely of God's creatures are provided with a means of maintaining their borders.

man?

WHEN THERE IS LIGHT
THERE IS LIFE

In him was life; and the life was the light of men. John 1:4.

One day, while reading a book about caves, I came upon a section that had this title: "When there is light, there is life." I thought this was a strange heading in a book about caves, but I quickly learned what the authors meant. Even though there are living things in the cave—some of them are even blind and colorless from living in the dark for so many hundreds of generations—they are still dependent on the light outside to provide them with life.

Life on earth is dependent on the light of the sun, and the creatures that live in the darkness of caves receive that life after it has passed through several forms of life and decayed into nutrients that the scavenging cave creatures can eat. Cave creatures receive their food primarily from the leavings of other creatures who go outside the cave to feed and return to hide in the shelter of the cavern. In the cave these creatures often die, leaving their carcasses for food also.

Even plants that grow in the darkness of a cave or in the darkness under your house, such as bacteria, mold, or fungus, receive their nutrients from the decay of things that were once alive in the sunlight, such as wood from trees, tree and other plant roots, dead insects and other types of animal life, and even other fungi, bacteria, or molds.

No life originates in the darkness; it must all depend on some source of life that lives under the light. "When there is light, there is life."

This truth is also a fact in our own lives. We cannot exist without Jesus to sustain us. He is the Light of the world. Some people are able to live as parasites from the light that others receive from Jesus, but our salvation depends on the light that *we* receive directly from Jesus, not on what we glean from others.

323

DOCTOR ANTS

Because that which may be known of God is manifest in them; for God hath shewed it unto them. For the invisible things of him from the creation of the world are clearly seen, being understood by the things that are made, even his eternal power and Godhead; so that they are without excuse. Romans 1:19, 20.

Sometimes we think that the heathen people of the world who have never heard about Jesus have had no way of knowing about God. In this text Paul is telling the Romans that these people are without excuse because they have had God's created wonders all around them at all times.

The native peoples of even the most primitive tribes in the jungles and deserts of the world have learned to use the things of nature to take care of them. There are natural medicines and remedies that have been used for thousands of years, and many of them have been adopted by the learned doctors of the world. Some of these remedies are very primitive, but they do work in the absence of anything better. The doctor ants are a good example.

In the jungles and forests of Brazil there is a fairly large type of leaf-cutting ant that the Indians have put to a very special use—the world's first sutures. These ants have large, very sharp, vicelike jaws. When one of the Indians gets a cut, a fresh supply of doctor ants is obtained. The wound is cared for, and then the edges of the skin are pressed together. Then the doctor ants are taken, one at a time, and allowed to bite the skin so that its sharp jaws pierce the skin on either side of the cut. Once the ant has bitten the wound closed in this manner, the ant's body is snapped off, and the jaws hold tight until the wound is healed. Those Indians have learned to use ants just as your doctor uses thread to sew up cuts that need stitches.

One of the wonderful things that Christian missionaries can tell the primitive peoples of the world is that Jesus loves them and wants to be their Great Physician.

CHARMED QUARKS

*Canst thou by searching find out God? canst thou find out the
Almighty unto perfection? Job 11:7.*

All matter is composed of quarks, which are probably held
together with gluons! When I first read a more complex version
of that sentence, I was flying on a plane, and the thought struck
me so funny that I started laughing out loud. People stared at
me and then smiled, probably thinking that I was reading a
joke. Well, quarks and gluons are not jokes, but I kept on
laughing, because the article went on to say that no one had ever
seen a quark—and that some of them had not even been
discovered yet! Quarks are hard to find because some of them
last only about (note that "about") two millionths of a second!
You have to really be on your toes to catch a glimpse of one of
those.

Yet the equipment and research of science these days is so
accurate and wonderful that such things can be studied. Not too
long ago, mankind thought that the smallest particle of matter
was the atom. The discovery that atoms were made up of even
smaller particles, known by such names as protons, electrons,
and neutrons, originally came as a shock. Now new machines
bombard the atom harder and harder, and other particles have
started to show up: muons, neutrinos, and the like. Soon there
were so many of these particles that there had to be names for
families of them. So particles such as protons and neutrons were
called hadrons, while such particles as muons, electrons, and
neutrinos were called leptons. Maybe you are laughing
too—from the funny names and from the frustration of trying
even to imagine things that are so small that no one has ever
seen them, even through the most powerful electron microscope.

So when I read that protons are composed of even smaller
particles called quarks, I was ready to give up. So far physicists
claim to have found "up quarks," "down quarks," "strange
quarks," and the "charmed quark"! I have only one question left:
What are quarks made of?

MONKEY HEAVEN

The earth is the Lord's, and the fulness thereof; the world, and they that dwell therein. Psalm 24:1.

Visiting a zoo has always been somewhat depressing to me. I like seeing the animals, but even the best zoos can't provide animals with the freedom that they enjoy in the wild. Small roadside zoos with big signs to attract the tourists are such jails for wildlife that I wouldn't think of ever visiting another one. On the other hand, there *are* a few instances in which people have provided a close-to-natural setting for wildlife, so that it is delightful to visit or read about.

Scott Lindbergh, one of the three sons of Charles Lindbergh, has established a country home in France for various types of monkeys. Scott has a degree in animal psychology, and he is studying the habits of the various primates that share his estate. There, with his wife, he has prepared a virtual heaven for monkeys. Howler monkeys, wooley monkeys, saki monkeys, cotton-top tamarins, marmosets, and squirrel monkeys live in relative peace with one another except for territorial squabbles between dominant males. One monkey even decided he wanted to run away from home and live in the woods—so he did. Mr. Lindbergh would go out into the woods every once in a while to check on him, but otherwise he let the monkey fend for himself.

The rest of the monkeys have free range of the yard and can go to the woods if they wish, but they seem to love it at the Lindbergh manor. The monkeys are learning to get along and are doing quite well at it, probably because all of their needs are taken care of by the Lindberghs. In most cases there is no need to cage them, because they rarely leave the premises.

We aren't monkeys, but we often act like them when we make war in the jungles or fight for food and land. In Jesus we have all that we need. There is no need to struggle for more. When will we learn to trust our Lord and live at peace? If the monkeys can, surely we can too!

Jose

LADY LUCK OR LADY BUGS

And I will rebuke the devourer for your sakes, and he shall not destroy the fruits of your ground; neither shall your vine cast her fruit before the time in the field, saith the Lord of hosts. Malachi 3:11.

She comes in many forms and is known by many names, but she is still one of the most valuable natural pest-killers known to man. Farmers of the Middle Ages believed that the ladybug could work miracles for their crops, so they named the beetle Our Lady, after the Virgin Mary, who was supposed to have sent the beetle to help the farmers. Other names for the ladybug include ladybird, lady beetle, and ladyfly. There are more than four thousand different kinds of ladybugs in the world. Besides the familiar red with black spots, they also come in brown, yellow, and black. A particularly beautiful color is black with red spots—exactly the opposite of the familiar type.

Myths abound about this fascinating beetle. In olden times it was believed that the ladybug brought good weather and good luck. It was even believed, in some areas, that ladybugs could cure a toothache—the beetle was crushed and placed into the hurting tooth. But it was no myth that the ladybugs brought the farmers good crops. The ladybug is one of the most beneficial of all insects, eating billions and billions of aphids, scale insects, and mealybugs. You can even buy ladybugs and place them in your garden to eat the pests that are there. Ladybugs are very hardy beetles. They are able to live for weeks without eating, and they can switch from eating insects to eating pollen. Ladybugs taste terrible to birds and other predators that would eat them, so they survive quite well. In winter ladybugs get together in huge groups where they hibernate under sticks, leaves, bark, and even stones. In one such wintering group in California, 750 million ladybugs were found.

With all the insect pests in the world, it is wonderful to know that God has provided the farmer with beneficial insects. The Creator has to allow sin to run its course, but He has promised to bless those who trust in Him.

WHEN THE LIGHTNING STRIKES

For as the lightning cometh out of the east, and shineth even unto the west; so shall also the coming of the Son of man be. Matthew 24:27.

Do you know where to go when lightning begins striking all around? Perhaps more important, do you know where you should *not* be when lightning strikes? Did you know that more people are killed by lightning each year than are killed by hurricanes, tornadoes, and floods combined? And, contrary to popular myth, lightning often strikes twice in the same place. It is very important that you know what to do and *not do* in a lightning storm.

One thousand lightning-caused deaths were studied to determine where people are the safest in a lightning storm. The following spots are places where you should *not* be: in an open space, under a tree, in or near water, near tall objects and metal objects, inside small sheds or small barns, near large appliances and electrical fixtures, in front of a fireplace, in front of an open door or window, talking on the telephone.

To be safe, you should be in a large building, especially one that is protected with lightning rods. The larger the building or house, the better. An enclosed automobile (not a convertible) is also good.

If you happen to be out in the open when a lightning storm overtakes you, get quickly into a gully or ditch that is lower than ground level but that isn't filling with water. If the ground is dry, no rain is falling, and no gully is available, lie flat on the ground; if the ground is wet, or if it begins raining, squat down on your feet and tuck your head between your knees. If you are in the woods, find a clump of the smallest trees or low bushes you can get to quickly and take cover in the clump, but don't lean against even a small tree.

Now when the lightning of Christ's coming shines throughout the world, are there places where you should not be found? Where *should* you be when Jesus comes?

THE PRAYING FLOWER

And for this cause God shall send them strong delusion, that they should believe a lie. 2 Thessalonians 2:11.

Most of you are probably familiar with a common insect that is a member of a large family that occurs worldwide. In North America the insect is called the praying mantis, named for the way it holds it front legs in a position that resembles hands folded in prayer. However, the mantids are not likely to be good examples of a healthy prayer life. Rather, they make excellent examples of a life of deceit and bloodshed. In spite of its name, the praying mantis is no exception—it is, in fact, an aggressive and relentless hunter.

In Southeast Asia there are many different kinds of mantidae. Some of them mimic the appearance of diseased leaves, complete with the leaf veins, bruise spots, and other blemishes; others mimic dead leaves. But perhaps the most interesting mantid of all is the one that appears as a beautiful orchid.

The flower mantis starts life with one form of deceit and then changes to another. At first the young mantis is bright red with black spots; it looks almost exactly like a plant bug that predators don't bother because it tastes so bad. After its first molt, however, the flower mantis takes on the appearance of a flower, and the resemblance is so close that people have examined what they thought was a flower, never realizing that they were even touching the body of the flower mantis hiding camouflaged among the flowers. One of these flower mantids is a delicate pink, exactly the color of the orchids on which it lives; its upper legs are expanded and look like flower petals, and its finely striped abdomen looks like the flower's center. When unsuspecting insects come to feed at what they believe is a flower, they instead end up as food for the flower mantis.

Satan's deceptions are every bit as well hidden as is the flower mantis. Only Jesus, living in us, can sense the danger in time to save us from the devil's lies.

THE GOOSE AND THE GOLFER

Great peace have they which love thy law: and nothing shall offend them. Psalm 119:165.

Did you ever do something that you wished you hadn't done? And then did you ever tell a lie to try to avoid the consequences of doing wrong? According to reports at the golf course in Baltimore a few years back, that is what one of the players did.

We will call the man Dr. Smith (that's not his real name, but it will do). According to the story, Dr. Smith lined up his putt on the seventeenth green, and as is often the case, he was tense as he made the final approach to the ball with his putter. That's when the goose honked. Dr. Smith missed the putt, blamed the goose, took after the goose with his putter, and clubbed the goose to death.

You know, I doubt that Dr. Smith felt any better after killing the goose, but when the bloody deed was done he had to face the fact that he had not only lost his temper but also broken several laws. In an attempt to cover up the evidence, Dr. Smith stuffed the dead goose into his golf bag and carried it away. But witnesses to the incident reported Dr. Smith to the authorities, who arrested him. He was charged with killing a goose out of season and with illegally possessing a Canada goose, a bird that is protected under the Migratory Bird Treaty Act.

In an effort to clear himself, Dr. Smith told a different story from that of the witnesses. According to him, the goose had accidentally been hit by his golf ball on the approach shot, and the goose was injured so badly that he had to put the goose out of its misery. He apparently found friendly witnesses to testify in his behalf, and since the goose had disappeared, there was little to go on but the opposing stories of those claiming to be witnesses.

If the witnesses to his act are right, Dr. Smith was easily offended and provoked to do wrong. He did not respect the laws protecting the goose, and he certainly did not respect the goose. What does it mean to love the law?

330

BEES THAT MAKE POLYESTER BAGS

I will say of the Lord, He is my refuge and my fortress: my God; in him will I trust. Psalm 91:2.

If we believe that God created all things, and that He provided for the protection of His creations, we should have no trouble at all believing that the same Creator, our Lord and Master, Jesus Christ, will certainly be able to protect us and keep us from the dangers about us.

Take, for instance, the bees of the genus *Colletes* (pronounced co-LET-eez). From extensive chemical tests it has been learned that these bees actually produce polyester bags for their young. These bags are made from essentially the same material as are the plastic sandwich bags that we buy at the grocery store. It is absolutely amazing that these tiny creatures have been producing this complex substance all along.

While it has long been known that the plastic bags were produced, little was known about how they were made until an entomologist (a person who studies insects) named Suzanne Batra began her studies of the *Colletes* bees. It had been previously thought that the plastic bags were made from a secretion of the bee's mouth. However, Dr. Batra learned that the substance is actually produced in the stinger, then is licked off in tiny drops and spread as clear plastic on the soil where the bag is being produced.

The final product is about the size of a thimble, with an open flap at one end. When this container has been filled with a mixture of pollen and nectar, an egg is laid, and the bag is sealed shut. The process takes several hours from start to finish, but when it is completed, the plastic bag is virtually impervious to any liquid. The egg and future food of the hatched larva is kept dry in the soil even when the ground is constantly soaked by heavy rain. The baby *Colletes* bees will be dry and protected from a number of animal and fungus predators.

If Jesus so protects the tiny baby bees, will He not so much more protect you and me?

SUPEROXIDE DISMUTASE

The angel of the Lord encampeth round about them that fear him, and delivereth them." Psalm 34:7.

There is a potentially dangerous situation that exists in every single living cell of all life—plant or animal. It is the presence of oxygen. Now, you say, oxygen is not dangerous! We must have it! That is true, but the physical makeup of oxygen provides for the possibility that the oxygen atom can pick up a stray electron very easily. In fact, it would happen if it weren't for a special protecting agent in all the cells of living things.

In the routine operation of living cells, oxygen can pick up any electron that happens by. And throughout nature such electrons are abundant.When an electron is added to the structure of oxygen, it suddenly becomes a deadly force in the cell, destroying the DNA, which is the life-giving substance in the cell. So why doesn't it happen?

There is a hunter of stray electrons in every cell that goes about like a vacuum cleaner, grabbing every electron that happens along and attaching it to something else so it won't be available to the oxygen atoms. The name of this marvelous hunter is superoxide dismutase—SOD, for short. SOD is found in every living cell on earth.

It is interesting that the only place that you find SOD is in the cell, just where it is needed to take care of the possible danger. When God made us, He gave us all the protection that we need. As long as we take care of our bodies and remember the rules of good health, these bodies will work well.

It is also true that the same Creator who gave us protection in every cell of our body has given us protection from sin and danger in this world, which is no more than a cell in the vast universe. He has given His angels charge over us, to keep us in all our ways (Ps. 91:11). We are as essential to God's program as oxygen is in nature, and He has given us all the protection that we need.

ALMONDS AREN'T NUTS

And it came to pass, that on the morrow Moses went into the tabernacle of witness; and, behold, the rod of Aaron for the house of Levi was budded, and brought forth buds, and bloomed blossoms, and yielded almonds. Numbers 17:8.

Perhaps it is a picky point, but almonds are actually fruit kernels, not nuts. The almond is closely related to the peach. In the early stages of the developing fruit it is hard to tell the difference between an almond and a peach. If you have ever taken a peach seed and cracked it open to examine the kernel inside, you will recognize the relationship between these two trees; the kernel inside the peach seed looks like a miniature almond. But when the two fruits mature the peach becomes the juicy fruit that we all love, while the almond's fruit becomes a leathery hull that contains the seed and the almond inside.

California grows the best almonds in the world and has the greatest yield per acre. The only other places in the world that can grow almonds commercially are a few countries around the Mediterranean Sea. Almonds are very nutritious; they are rich in minerals such as magnesium and phosphorus, they are low in cholesterol, and they are high in linoleic acid, which is necessary for healthy skin. Around the world almonds are considered wonderful food, but they are usually rare and expensive. One of the special gifts that Jacob sent to Pharaoh was almonds.

Throughout the Bible, the Lord uses the almond tree to symbolize His special favor and watchcare over His people. When it was to be decided which tribe would serve as the spiritual leaders of the children of Israel, God asked Moses to have a representative of each tribe bring his rod to the tabernacle. The tribal representatives were to leave their rods there overnight, and the rod representing the chosen tribe would blossom. On the following day, Aaron's rod not only blossomed—it also yielded almonds.

THE SPITTING COBRA

But he that hateth his brother is in darkness, and walketh in darkness, and knoweth not whither he goeth, because that darkness hath blinded his eyes. 1 John 2:11.

Not all cobras spit; some simply strike. But in Africa, at least, cobras normally spit rather than strike, preferring, it seems, to debilitate their victims by blinding them before catching and eating them.

The British naturalist R. C. H. Sweeney tells of his first encounter with a black-necked, or spitting, cobra in Africa. He had not had any previous experience with spitting cobras, so he was not aware of the deadly accuracy with which they can project their venom into the eyes of their foes. Sweeney's next-door neighbor, Tommy, called on him one day and said that there was a snake in a box in his garage. Sweeney went to have a look. He cautiously opened the lid to the box, but, when no snake came forth, he leaned over and peered into the box. The last thing that he saw that day was part of the dark body of a snake. Suddenly, there was liquid all over his face and extreme pain in both eyes. He groped for Tommy's arm and shouted, "Get me to the house! Get milk for my eyes! It's a spitting cobra!"

The only thing that saved Sweeney from blindness was getting his eyes rinsed immediately with an alkaline solution to neutralize the acid of the venom. Even then it was three days before his eyes were normal again.

The spitting cobra does its spitting through two fangs on either side of the upper jaw—the action is very much like that of a water pistol. The accuracy is amazing, and it always spits at the eyes, which it recognizes by the reflected light. (Goggles and mirrors also induce spitting.) A four-foot cobra can make a direct hit up to four and one-half feet away.

It is quite fitting that John likened hate to that which causes blindness. Hate is the devil's venom, and the only antidote is the love of Jesus.

THE GREEN POSSUM

Deliver me, O Lord, from mine enemies: I flee unto thee to hide me. Psalm 143:9.

To those of us who live in North America, the word *possum* conjures up the picture of a rather ugly grayish-white animal with a ratlike tail. The two kinds of possums in North America are the Virginia opossum and the Mexican opossum, and they look very much alike. But in Australia there are more than twenty different kinds, and they are among the most beautiful animals of the world. Like our possums, those from "down under" are primarily night creatures. The list of possums includes such intriguing names as Queensland long-tailed pigmy possum, common ringtail possum, feathertail glider, fluffy glider, and green possum. It is the green possum that we will discuss, although the rest are equally fascinating.

The green possum is actually lime-green in color, a condition caused by a combination of black, white, and yellow pigments in its fur. The green possum is an absolutely beautiful fluffy mammal, about twenty-five inches long from its nose to the tip of its tail. About half its length is tail. The green possum's long, thick fur lies in beautiful waves, and the animal spends much time in an elaborate grooming procedure. At one point in its grooming, the green possum performs a remarkable contortionist act: it doubles back to get at the fur of its hindquarters, and it actually looks as if the animal has been taken apart in the middle with both ends now facing the same direction.

The green-looking coat conceals the green possum when it sleeps, curled up in a thicket of trees surrounded by green leaves. Protected in this manner, the green possum is one of only a few possums that do not need a den or a hollow tree to hide in during the day.

If you ever find yourself afraid, just think of the green possum. It is able to hide in broad daylight. Jesus, who gave the green possum its protection, can certainly protect you and me.

SAVED FROM KILLER BEES

They compassed me about like bees; they are quenched as the fire of thorns: for in the name of the Lord I will destroy them. Psalm 118:12.

The people of Bible times knew about killer bees. In Deuteronomy 1:44, Moses tells how the Amorites chased the children of Israel "as bees do" and destroyed them. In recent years we have heard that African killer bees have been brought to South America. According to reports, they are moving northward and may reach the United States before many years. If the reports are correct, we may one day be able to relate to Psalm 118:12 very directly.

A naturalist was traveling by Land Rover through a deserted portion of northeastern Africa. One morning, as he and his native assistants were sitting down to breakfast, a swarm of bees attacked. It happened so fast that there was no time to escape to the Land Rover. The three men fled on foot, with black swarms of bees right behind each of them. The naturalist escaped into tall grass and fell flat on his face. Bees don't like grass, so he was safe. The native assistants were badly stung before they escaped.

Unfortunately, their camp, with all their water and the Land Rover, their only means of escape, was being guarded by the swarms of killer bees. After several hours and many attempts to reach their equipment, and after scores of very painful stings as their only rewards, the men were concerned for their lives. If they could not get to their water, they could die in the desert heat, and if the bees continued to sting them, they could die from the poison.

On a hunch, the naturalist and one of his assistants cut two branches of a highly fragrant verbena plant and held them over their heads as they made yet another attempt to get to their vehicle. The plan worked. The bees were temporarily confused by the fragrance, and the two men were able to get to the Land Rover with only a few more stings.

The fragrance of Jesus, the Rose of Sharon, has confused the enemy for us, too, and we will be saved.

336

OOPARTS

Hast thou marked the old way which wicked men have trodden? Which were cut down out of time, whose foundation was overflown with a flood? Job 22:15, 16.

In his book *Secrets of the Lost Races* Rene Noorbergen provides evidence that suggests that people who lived before the Flood had many, if not all, of the scientific inventions that we have today. Much of the evidence comes from archeological findings that don't fit the standard ideas concerning the history of the world. If you don't believe in the Bible, then you are left with the problem of explaining certain items that have been found. Since these items don't fall into place with the theories of man, they are referred to as out-of-place artifacts, or "ooparts."

One oopart was found in 1961, when several rockhounds were searching for specimens in California near the top of a 4,300-foot peak in the Coso Mountains. What these people found looked at first like a geode—a rather round, plain-looking rock, usually hollow and lined with crystals. The next day, one of the members of the group cut the "geode" in two and found inside an item that has baffled all scientists who have attempted to explain it.

Inside the geode-looking rock was a ceramic cylinder about three fourths of an inch in diameter. In the center of the cylinder was a strand of magnetic wire, and surrounding the cylinder were rings of copper. After all efforts to identify the item, all that could be determined is that it appeared to be some kind of spark plug, but not like any spark plug known today. When the rock was given to geologists to determine how old they thought it was, they said it was at least 500,000 years old.

There is every reason to believe that people before the Flood knew about electricity, and had engines and even more fantastic inventions. The "old way" that Job describes was complete with wonderful things, but wickedness ruled to a point where all the wonderful inventions were used for the glory and degradation of man instead of to the glory of God.

DO FLOWERS TALK?

But seek ye first the kingdom of God, and his righteousness; and all these things shall be added unto you. Matthew 6:33.

If you were to ask me whether flowers talk, I would ask you what you mean by "talk." If you mean do they communicate in some human language, the answer is No, of course not. But I do believe that the flowers speak to us if we know how to listen. In fact, I believe that every living thing that God created was given to us to tell us about Him.

But to learn how to hear what God has to say to us through nature requires that we learn an entirely new language, one that is inside and is felt more than spoken or heard. We hear the voice of God as a still small voice. Adam and Eve went to school to learn how to read, but they did not have any books or desks as we know them. How would you like their school? They learned from the Master Teacher and the angels how to read the love, mercy, and greatness of God by listening to the things about them in the Garden and by watching all the beautiful sights that were portrayed before them. Can we learn as they learned? I think so, but maybe not quite as easily.

We can't talk directly to Jesus, but He speaks to us. We can hear Him as we look at the flowers and think about Him. For example, today's text reveals something that the flowers teach us. Jesus has just invited His listeners to consider the lilies of the field. He was using the flowers to tell them, and us, that he will take care of all our needs and that all we have to worry about is being like Him. Here is another example: We all know that flowers fade. In his first book Peter tells us something that the flowers told him, that of ourselves we are like fading flowers, but "the word of the Lord endureth for ever" (1 Peter 1:25).

Flowers tell us things that Jesus wants us to learn about Him and about ourselves. Can you think of some things that flowers have told you? Practice letting the flowers talk to you. You will be surprised by what they say.

338

HARDY, HEALTHY, AND HAPPY

He that handleth a matter shall find good, and whoso trusteth in the Lord, happy is he. Proverbs 16:20.

Not long ago Dr. Kobasa, of the University of Chicago, studied the relationship between health and happiness. She found that when people don't know how to take care of a situation that comes up, they are more likely to get sick.

Dr. Kobasa analyzed the lives of 350 businessmen, for example, and learned that when the businessman didn't mind the problems that confronted him each day, he was also more likely to be well—he would rarely stay home from work because of sickness. But for the man who was made miserable every time something different came up unexpectedly, sickness was a way of life—he coped with stress by becoming sick.

Healthy people, says Dr. Kobasa, are those who not only handle problems well but almost relish them. Healthy people welcome the challenge that comes from life; for them, problems are more like adventures rather than discouraging events. Do you look forward to problems?

The Bible tells us that for a healthy Christian, the temptations that come every day are welcomed as ways of showing that the power of God is at work in you (James 1:2, 3; 1 Peter 1:6, 7). When Moses tried in his own strength to handle the problems of life, he was a miserable failure, but when he let God take over in his life, he *chose* "to suffer affliction with the people of God, than to enjoy the pleasures of sin for a season" (Heb. 11:25).

As an experiment, try every morning to say, "Lord, You can have this day. If I do my own thing, I'm sure to fail, but I trust You not to lead me into any temptation that is too great for me to handle, and I will look forward to the adventures that You will bring my way." Then go about the day's activities looking forward to what the Lord will bring your way. You will find that you have far more strength to meet the problems of the day than you otherwise would have had, and you will be happier and healthier.

BLACKBIRD FEEDING ROTATION

It is he that sitteth upon the circle of the earth . . . ; that stretcheth out the heavens as a curtain, and spreadeth them out as a tent to dwell in. Isaiah 40:22.

Blackbird roosts are a common thing in the Southern United States. The size of these roosts vary, but they can be made up of millions of various kinds of blackbirds that come together each night. While the roosts are common enough, little is known about how the birds behave in the roost or how they come to select the location for it. However, two ornithologists happened to observe the beginnings of one of these roosts, and their report is remarkable.

Steve Fretwell and Elmer Finck observed a roost of about 300,000 blackbirds. It was apparently the first morning of the roost. The birds departed, flying just south of due east. The next morning the birds all flew out due east. On the third morning the birds flew just north of east. Each morning thereafter, the birds would shift the direction of flight by about twenty-five or thirty degrees counterclockwise on the compass. Furthermore, when the birds returned each evening, they would be flying in a long continuous stream from a direction about fifteen degrees conterclockwise from the direction in which they had left that morning. The birds continued this rotation each day until they had completed the circle and were ready, or so the watchers thought, to begin the circle again. But on the morning after the blackbirds had completed their rotation, they broke into different flocks and flew in no apparent pattern to all points of the compass. It appeared that they had scouted all the country round about and were each now on their own to find what they could in the area. As Fretwell tells it: "It was a mob scene, with waves of birds heading out in all directions."

The Lord, who sitteth upon the circle of the earth, has placed a knowledge of that circle within the blackbirds and helps them to find their winter food.

MONKEY OUT OF A CAGE

And be not conformed to this world: but be ye transformed by the renewing of your mind, that ye may prove what is that good, and acceptable, and perfect, will of God. Romans 12:2.

Several years ago a new exhibit was built at the Brookfield Zoo in Chicago. The $9 million project is called the Tropical World Building. It is a natural setting, bigger than a football field, complete with trees, cliffs, vines, a waterfall, and pools of water. It is a magnificent exhibit depicting the tropical regions of the world.

When the exhibit opened, a number of small monkeys were released into the new, wonderful environment. Everyone assumed that the monkeys would be right at home in what was their native setting. But the monkeys had spent most of their lives in cages, behind bars, and this new place was so unfamiliar to them that they did not know what to do.

The little monkeys fell out of the trees—something that no self-respecting monkey would ever do. One monkey saw a gorilla and was so frightened that it fell into a pool of water and would have drowned if a zoo worker hadn't rescued it in time.

You see, the monkeys had had no experience with trees, vines, and the like. But they were given a little time in the new environment, and before long they were able to adapt to all of the wonders of the jungle that they had never before experienced. Their understanding of the world underwent a complete transformation in just a few hours.

Being a Christian after being a sinner is very much like the experience that those monkeys had. We have been slaves to sin, and when Jesus releases us into our new life with Him, it takes a while to adjust to this new and wonderful life. If those monkeys had not been given a little time to adjust, they might have preferred their old lives in the cages. It is the same with us. When we become Christians, we stumble and we fall, but Jesus gives us time, and He rescues us when we get into trouble.

GOLD DIGGERS

But without faith it is impossible to please him: for he that cometh to God must believe that he is, and that he is a rewarder of them that diligently seek him. Hebrews 11:6.

Prospectors in Africa are using termites to help them find gold. It is believed that there are huge deposits of gold under the sands of the vast Kalahari Desert. The problem that the prospectors have, however, is knowing where to dig. Not only are there thousands of square miles in the desert, but the gold veins are probably some three hundred feet below the surface. It would be far too expensive to drill millions of test holes in hopes of striking gold.

But termites live throughout the region and have been burrowing as deep as five hundred feet to find water. These termites grow fungus in their earthen castles for food, and humidity is needed to grow this fungus. So the tunnels that the termites make down to the water table aren't so much for the water to drink as they are to allow the water, which evaporates upward, to flow in vapor form to their fungus-growing chambers.

The dirt that the termites get from these tunnels is deposited on the surface as part of their homes. These termite castles may be six feet tall. All that the prospectors have to do is to take nine-ounce samples of the dirt from hundreds of termite mounds and then perform chemical tests on these samples to determine the presence of gold and other minerals that could be commercially mined. If they find gold in the termite mound, the prospectors know they should sink a mine shaft below the termite nest.

Those prospectors believe that there is gold in the Kalahari, and they are willing to seek diligently for it. Can you imagine their joy when they find gold traces in a termite mound? They will be like the man that Jesus told about who found a great treasure in a field and sold all that he had in order to buy that field so that the treasure would be his. Of course, the treasure we seek is Jesus.

STARFISH HELL

But the day of the Lord will come as a thief in the night; in the which the heavens shall pass away with a great noise, and the elements shall melt with fervent heat, the earth also and the works that are therein shall be burned up. 2 Peter 3:10.

During the winter of 1977-1978, along the Pacific Coast of California and Mexico, a type of common starfish called the sea star began to die by the billions. By the end of the summer of 1978 what had been an abundant many-pointed starfish was virtually gone, and no one knew why at first.

Up until that time the four-inch sea star had delighted the searchers for sea creatures everywhere. It was so plentiful that its population averaged one per square yard.

Dr. Donald Thomson, a marine biologist at the University of Arizona, decided to see whether he could find out what was responsible for the massive die-off. He discovered that the cause was heat. During the winter of 1977-1978 unusual winds from the south blew steadily along the Pacific Coast where the starfish lived, bringing warmer water farther north than they were known to have come in recent history. The temperature of the tidal waters increased by two to four degrees. Although this was not much of a rise in temperature, these few degrees were lethal to the starfish, whose systems were delicately adapted to the usual temperatures, which heat up in the summertime and cool down again in winter. By also being subjected to the heat in winter, the sea stars were weakened, developed skin sores, and died of bacterial infections that they could not resist.

But a few survived, and when the next winter arrived without the warm southern winds and water, a new, healthy crop of sea stars began to multiply again.

At the end of this world the sin and wickedness that is rampant on the earth will be destroyed by a heat that it can no longer resist. The cup of iniquity will be full, but a few, those of us who trust in Jesus, like gold tried in the fire, will be saved to live forever in a world made new.

343

EVERYBODY'S DIFFERENT

Whosoever believeth on him shall not be ashamed. For there is no difference between the Jew and the Greek: for the same Lord over all is rich unto all that call upon him. Romans 10:11, 12.

It is obvious that a bird is different from a turtle and that a butterfly is different from a fish. It is also obvious that there are differences between kinds of animals—a mouse is different from an elephant, and a bluejay is different from an eagle—just as it is apparent that differences exist between people.

There are differences not only between members of the same race but also between members of the same family (although sometimes it is hard to tell identical twins apart). There are always differences that make every individual unique. There is no one in the world just like you.

An ornithologist studied the black markings on the faces and heads of bluejays in Massachusetts to see whether there were differences. You would think that all bluejays look aliked, but that isn't so. After studing many bluejays, the scientist discovered that every one of those bluejays was so different that it could be picked out of a crowd of bluejays!

Sometimes we let differences between individuals become a basis for condemning others—differences in skin color, height, and size of nose are examples. In our text today God has made it very clear that these differences don't matter at all when He is supplying the needs of those who call upon Him. No matter what we look like, God loves us exactly the same. But He also knows that everybody's different. Jesus made that point when He said "the very hairs of your head are all numbered" (Matt. 10:30).

Remember that the features that make you different are the very things that make you special. Just imagine how dull and confusing the world would be if everybody looked exactly alike.

"CALLING ALL BUGS"

For nation shall rise against nation, and kingdom against kingdom: and there shall be famines, and pestilences, and earthquakes, in divers places. Matthew 24:7.

Throughout the world, the various superpowers, and some that aren't so super, have radio systems to detect what is going on in the military plans of other countries. It is possible for the leader of one country to call up the leaders of as many countries as he wishes, to invite them to join in a war. The ability of world leaders to have such communication is so simple today that we take it for granted. The only thing keeping the world from being at war is the power of God; He is first waiting for us to hear His Spirit and respond to Him one way or the other.

You know that insects have antennae on their heads. You also know that these antennae are used to receive information. Until recently it was supposed that the information came in the form of scents; when a scent molecule was released by one insect and picked up on the "feelers" of another insect, it was understood to mean something. Well, now there is evidence of a new and much more sophisticated theory—what if the antennae that insects have are really just like our radio antennas, and suppose that what they are picking up is the electromagnetic radiation of the scent molecule instead of the scent itself?

If this is true, then it will soon be possible to control insect movements by learning to transmit the right signals to the entire population of, let's say, potato bugs. Having this ability would be fine, except that an enemy power could transmit another message that would cause the bugs to eat our food. A whole new form of warfare could be born if the theory is proved correct!

Remember, the Creator who made the insects also made you and me, and He is calling us. Is your antenna tuned in to Jesus? Are you getting the message? The end is near, as the insects would tell us, if they could.

KING ON THE MOUNTAIN

But the Lord is the true God, he is the living God, and an everlasting king. Jeremiah 10:10.

When I was a boy we loved to play a game called king on the mountain. It usually started when a bulldozer would push up a pile of dirt in our neighborhood. It was a challenge to stay on top of that mound of dirt the longest, constantly pushing the others back as they tried to take over the hill. Usually no one was able to withstand the onrushers for long, and the "king" on that mountain would change many times.

There is an animal that plays king on the mountain for real. Dall sheep, one of the types of mountain sheep, live high on the mountain slopes of Alaska and northwestern Canada. Living on grass, flowers, and shoots growing on rocky crags and in mountain meadows, the Dall sheep graze peacefully most of the year. They have very sharp eyes, which assist them in avoiding timber wolves and hunters. They may live as long as fourteen years, and the rams weigh up to two hundred pounds and stand about forty inches high at the shoulder. The rams have the well-known, large, curled horns that give them such a magnificent appearance.

Young rams practice playing king on the mountain by doing exactly what we used to do. One will dash to the top of a boulder and try to bump the others off. But there comes a day, when the ram is grown up, that the mating season arrives. The rams hold butting battles to determine who is king. The rams run full speed at each other, and the crash of the impact of their horns can be heard more than a mile away. Again and again they "ram" into each other until one gives up, leaving the other one king on the mountain. But his kingship is constantly challenged in additional battles, and he has no peace as he continues to defend his title. Becoming king is one thing; staying king is very hard work.

We have a King whom we can always trust to *stay* King, and He will always take care of His kingdom in peace. Speaking of His kingdom, God says, "They shall not hurt nor destroy in all my holy mountain" (Isa. 11:9).

carmen

"THE QUETZAL IS GONE"

Behold your house is left unto you desolate: and verily I say unto you, Ye shall not see me, until the time come when ye shall say, Blessed is he that cometh in the name of the Lord. Luke 13:35.

The quetzal is the magnificently beautiful bird that was named for the Aztec god of peace, Quetzalcoatl. It is the national bird of Guatemala. But, alas! There are no more quetzals in Guatemala. The quetzal is gone!

There is not a more beautiful bird in all the world, and seeing one in the wild has been a long-cherished dream of mine. I cannot see paintings, drawings, or photographs of the quetzal without thinking that it must have descended directly, without change, from the Garden of Eden. With its resplendent tail, the quetzal is four feet long. Most of that length is that long, loosely floating tail, which trails shimmering and undulating like a ribbon of emerald light, as the bird flies through the cloud forest.

One of my friends tells of coming down the side of a mountain in southern Mexico. As he emerged from the cloud that enshrouded the mountain above, his eyes were immediately focused on the heavenly sight of a male resplendent quetzal performing its mating flight above the trees below. Back and forth, up and down, in and out of the wisps of fog, like a dancing sunbeam dressed in green, the bird flew, while my friend watched spellbound.

But in Guatemala the quetzal is gone. The people of that country have cleared all the forests where the bird lived. There is no place in the land for the bird that so beautifully portrayed the spirit of peace. And the areas of Mexico, Honduras, Nicaragua, Costa Rica, and Panama where the bird still survives are also being cleared as rapidly as the people can cut and burn the forest.

The quetzal didn't want to leave. It had no place to stay, and therefore had no choice. When we leave no place for Jesus in our lives, we are left as desolate as the land without the cloud forest—and without the quetzal.

THE SEA WASP

O death, where is thy sting? O grave, where is thy victory? 1 Corinthians 15:55.

There are about three thousand different kinds of jellyfish in the world. They are found in every ocean on earth, and a few even occur in freshwater. Many of the world's jellyfish are dangerous to swimmers, but none is so potent as the sea wasp, of the waters around Australia and Southeast Asia.

Hanging down from the underside of jellyfish are slender threadlike or fingerlike projections called tentacles. On these tentacles jellyfish have tiny cells that contain even tinier little darts connected by hollow threads to poison glands. When a fish or other form of life comes close to one of these tentacles, these little darts are fired like harpoons that explode and drive the poison-filled darts into the skin of the potential dinner. If you are stung by a jellyfish, you will remember the experience for a long time. The tiny stinging cells are still potent even after the jellyfish is dead, or after the tentacles have broken off from the jellyfish's body. Most of them, though painful, aren't too dangerous, but the sea wasp is an exception; its darts are filled with *deadly* poison.

Swimmers in the waters where the sea wasp occurs have to be very careful. The sea wasp is only about four inches in diameter, and there are records of human death occurring within three minutes of its sting. There is no antidote for the sea wasp's sting.

In our text for today the apostle Paul asks about another kind of deadly sting—the sting of sin. First he asks whether or not there is any safety from this sting and the resulting death, since "the wages of sin is death" (Rom. 6:23). Then he answers the question for us:

"The sting of death is sin. . . . But thanks be to God, which giveth us the victory through our Lord Jesus Christ" (verses 56, 57). Jesus has promised that where the sting of sin and death is concerned, He will always "make a way to escape" (1 Cor. 10:13). Isn't He wonderful?

THE BEEHIVE

And they rest not day and night, saying, Holy, holy, holy, Lord God almighty, which was, and is, and is to come. Revelation 4:8.

John just couldn't find the words to describe what he saw, so he did the best he could and described it in this way. Apparently heaven is the dwelling place of many beings that never cease their praise and service to God. They never rest, as you and I do, for they never get tired or bored. Maybe a good example of this way of life is a hive of bees.

As soon as the worker bees hatch out and dry their wings, they start to work. Each has her job. I say "her" because all the workers in a beehive are females. And each worker has a task in the hive. Some are nurses, some are janitors, some are air-conditioners, and some gather nectar to make honey. Once they start working, they don't get any time off for a vacation or even a weekend of relaxation. When they can't work outside, they work inside the hive, helping to tidy up the place and tending to the many other chores. Bees are incessant working machines that wouldn't know what to do with time off; they have only one purpose for living—to serve the queen. It seems that they literally work themselves to death, because the worker bees never stop working (except at night) from the time they hatch until they die.

How would you like it if you had one chore to do and you were to do nothing else but, let's say, wash dishes from morning till night for your entire life? Aren't you glad that you aren't a bee?

But in one sense we too have a charge, to be continuous in our work for the King and in our worship of Him. The Bible tells us to "rejoice evermore. Pray without ceasing" (1 Thess. 5:16, 17). By letting the Holy Spirit dwell in our hearts, we can be constantly open to God's influence and can respond in praise at any time, with our hearts totally dedicated to serving Jesus, the King of kings and Lord of lords.

GREAT WHALES

And God created great whales, and every living creature that moveth, which the waters brought forth abundantly, after their kind. Genesis 1:21.

Jesus must have had a a great time planning and creating this world with all its wonders. I don't know exactly how He created things, but the Bible says that "he spake and it was done" (Ps. 33:9). For example, I wonder just how Jesus made whales. Do you suppose that Adam might have had a pet whale? The blue whale, the world's largest whale, can weigh more than 150 tons—that's more than 300,000 pounds. What a pet that would have been!

Whales have been in the news quite a bit lately because they are being hunted so much that some kinds are in danger of extinction. It must make Jesus very sad to see His largest creatures being hunted and killed so relentlessly.

Scientists who study whales tell us that whale mothers exhibit almost human tenderness in caring for their young. The mother whale stays very close to her baby at all times, often touching and caressing it with her flippers, which she uses much as we use our arms.

Baby whales are called calves, and since whales are mammals, the babies drink milk produced by the mother, which is, as you might have guessed, called a cow. At birth the blue whale calf is *only* twenty-four feet long; it can roll its tongue into a tube like a straw and drink milk from the mother, or the mother will squirt milk directly into the calf's open mouth. But whichever way the baby blue whale gets its milk, you won't believe how much it drinks—one hundred gallons a day!

Whales sing. I have a phonograph record that is nothing but whale songs. They seem to have a language all their own. I wonder whether Adam understood the whale's language.

The great whales of the world are among the most wondrous of all animals. By studying their habits we learn even more about the power and love of our Creator. Maybe in the earth made new you will be able to talk to a whale.

PROTEIN LANGUAGE

manifold are thy works! in wisdom hast thou made the earth is full of thy riches. Psalm 104:24.

You know that we are made up of skin and bones and muscles, and you know that we have glands, veins, arteries, lungs, a heart, a stomach, and a whole bunch of other things. All of these body parts are made up of cells. Cells, in turn, are made up of microscopic parts of many different kinds. Our bodies are so complicated that no one knows even half of what goes on in them. One of the most interesting subjects is the way we manufacture proteins.

It is important to get plenty of protein to eat, but the protein that you eat provides only the material for the production of proteins in your body. Proteins are made up of amino acids. You could think of the proteins as words and the amino acids as the letters. Just as there are twenty-six letters that make all the words in the English language, there are twenty or more amino acids that make up all the proteins found in nature. There are special ways in which the cells manufacture these proteins. Simply put, in order to build a protein, a part of the cell sends out a coded messenger called RNA (ribonucleic acid). Each RNA messenger contacts a protein-production factory called a ribosome. The ribosome receives the message and sets about to make the protein that has been ordered. Since proteins are made of amino acids, the ribosome checks the coded message brought by the RNA messenger and sends out for each needed amino acid by name. Remember, there are only twenty different kinds. As these are put together in the specified form, the protein is built and is then ready to go to work in taking care of you.

Proteins do such things as transmit nerve signals, clot your blood when you cut your finger, and protect your system through immunity to disease. What a wonderful Creator we have, who can build us so well!

351

EDIBLE INSECTS?

Even these of them ye may eat; the locust after his kind, and the bald locust after his kind, and the beetle after his kind, and the grasshopper after his kind. Leviticus 11:22.

It may surprise you to know that the Lord gave the children of Israel permission to eat certain insects. The word "beetle" in the above text is probably a mistranslation of the Hebrew word for "cricket." Three groups of insects were considered "clean": locusts, crickets, and grasshoppers. It is interesting to note that the preceding text (verse 21) further identifies the edible insects as the "flying creeping things" that "have legs above their feet, to leap withal upon the earth." All of the three types of insects mentioned are flying hoppers and are very closely related. As are the clean beasts and birds mentioned in the same chapter, these insects are plant-eaters. Thus, they would be much less likely to carry disease. Now, do you want to go out and have some crickets and grasshoppers for lunch? We must recognize this text is not recommending such things. It was simply a rule for people who were used to eating *all* kinds of insects.

Even today, insects make up a significant portion of the diets of the people in the underdeveloped nations. The Bushmen of Africa eat cockroaches. Hot, deep-fried ants are sold by vendors in the streets of Bogota, Colombia. In Bali, lightly toasted butterflies and moths are common fare. In Thailand, praying mantises are mashed into a paste and served as a spread for bread.

However, grasshoppers and locusts are the staple insect food in many parts of the world, especially in Africa and Asia, where the locusts are boiled, fried, roasted, baked, and stewed for food. They are also dried, smoked, and stored for later use. But that still doesn't make me want to try eating insects. God takes people where they are and helps them to grow to where they should be. His original diet of fruits, grains, and nuts is still the best.

A PLAGUE OF CLAWED FROGS

Thus saith the Lord, Let my people go, that they may serve me. And if thou refuse to let them go, behold, I will smite all thy borders with frogs. Exodus 8:1, 2.

Some time ago, probably in the 1940s in southern California, some African clawed frogs escaped from a research laboratory. Nothing was said about the escape, and nothing came of it for nearly thirty years. But in 1969 a California game warden found one of these frogs in a drainage ditch. Soon it was discovered that there were thousands of them; they had been quietly multiplying over the years. Now it is estimated that there are more than a million of them, and the number is growing. The frog is a problem because it eats virtually every living thing that it can swallow.

The game warden who found the first one reports that there are small ponds where the frogs are the only visible animal life left. The frogs can exist quite happily in 120° F. heat and in temperatures as low as 45° F. If you try to poison the water to kill them, they simply bury themselves in the mud until the effect of the poison is gone. And because they have a protective covering of mucus, they can survive even in a pond that is made up mostly of oil. When all natural food is gone, they begin to eat one another until only the strongest are left. These strong survivors then move to another pond, which may be as much as five miles away.

The African clawed frog has no natural enemies in its new California habitat. Scientists have found only one thing that will eat them—piranha fish. No one wants to stock the ponds of California with *that* aquatic demon.

When things in this world get out of order, there are other things that happen as the result. The same truth holds in our spiritual life. Some small, insignificant habit may not seem to be worth worrying about, so we may just let it go instead of taking care of it when it is small. But eventually it may become uncontrollable, and only the power of Jesus can take care of it. It took the power of God to get rid of the frogs in Egypt.

NATURE'S PLOW

Sow to yourselves in righteousness, reap in mercy; break up your fallow ground: for it is time to seek the Lord, till he come and rain righteousness upon you. Hosea 10:12.

A single acre of fertile soil may contain 3 million earthworms. These small creatures have been called the most important animals on earth because their natural habits can turn unproductive ground into fertile soil.

Earthworms live for only two or three years, but their many eggs hatch in little more than a month, providing thousands of additional tiny "plows," which in turn produce millions of earthworms. And so it goes, unless the ground is poisoned by chemicals that kill the earthworms.

Earthworms are quite literally small fertilizer factories, in addition to being plows. In one year in an area the size of a football field, they can produce up to fifty-thousand pounds of castings that are rich in nutrients.

Earthworms also provide an extensive irrigation system for the roots of plants. Their tunnels extend downward for as much as ten feet below the surface, and when it rains these tunnels fill with water, creating an extensive network of underground water tanks. Roots also need air, and when earthworms have passed through the soil, they leave tiny air spaces trapped between the bits of soil that have been chewed up and deposited throughout the ground where they live.

Earthworms have spots on their bodies that are sensitive to all light except red light. If you shine a red light on an earthworm at night, you can watch it; but normal light will cause the earthworm to back into its burrow.

It is impossible to say just how valuable the earthworms are in making good soil. The Bible has much to say about sowing seed in good soil. Jesus said that the seed represents the Word of God. He plants His seed in our hearts, which represent the soil. The same Jesus who provides nature's marvelous earthworm—a veritable factory producing good soil—will also provide for good soil in my heart; He will break up my hard heart, and He will rain righteousness upon me, because He has promised it.

SUNGLASSES

But unto you that fear my name shall the Sun of righteousness arise with healing in his wings. Malachi 4:2.

The rays of the sun contain not only visible light but also ultraviolet light and other invisible rays, and some of these rays can be quite damaging to our eyes.

Such conditions as snow and white desert sands are particularly dangerous because they reflect more of the sun's rays directly into our eyes. Special eye protectors are used on the polar ice fields, where the summer sun's rays beat down for almost twenty-four hours every day, bouncing off the snow, as well as coming directly from the sun.

We have all known what relief it is to put on a pair of sunglasses on a bright sunlit day. But some scientists have been studying the effects of wearing sunglasses and have learned that their use prevents us from exercising the natural protective measures of squinting and shading our eyes. Thus, our eyes are more often exposed to the sun's more dangerous rays when we are wearing sunglasses.

While the visible light rays are cut out by the glasses, making us feel the same effect as when we shade our eyes, in actuality most sunglasses do *not* filter out the ultraviolet rays, but instead leave our eyes open wide and exposed more directly to them. The result, over time, is a weakening of sight when we were actually thinking to protect our eyes.

Jesus is the Sun of Righteousness, according to the words of the prophet Malachi. When He shines in our lives, we are often painfully aware of things that should not be there. We see our faults clearly when compared to His perfect life. We can put on darker and darker spiritual sunglasses, but the Sun's rays will continue to shine. When we try to shut out the brightness of Jesus' glory in our lives, we also become spiritually blinded in time.

Let's ask Jesus to open our eyes so that we may see Him clearly and follow Him. And when He shows us things in our lives that shouldn't be there, let's not put on sunglasses to hide from His light.

THE WHOLE CURE OR NOTHING

Then goeth he, and taketh with himself seven other spirits more wicked than himself, and they enter in and dwell there: and the last state of that man is worse than the first. Even so shall it be also unto this wicked generation. Matthew 12:45.

Jesus was referring to the Pharisees and their followers, of course, when He told of the man who was delivered of an unclean spirit but failed to replace that spirit with the right Spirit; therefore the evil spirit and seven of his evil friends, more wicked than himself, were able to move in again.

When you get a "bug" and are sick, you sometimes go to the doctor. The doctor may recognize a serious infection, probably caused by some type of bacteria, and prescribe an antibiotic. You will be told to take the medicine until it is gone, not just until you feel better. The antibiotic begins killing the germs in your body, and as the bacteria are being killed, you begin to feel better. The mistake many people make is to think that because they feel so much better, the infection is all gone. Nothing could be further from the truth; the germs have merely reduced in numbers to a point where they can't make you feel bad, but they are still there, ready to begin reproducing again. If you keep taking the medicine, as you were told to do, the bacteria will usually be completely eliminated, and that illness will not be caused again by the same germs.

One of the things that happen when you don't take all of the medicine is that the remaining bacteria can begin to develop an immunity to the antibiotic. Then the next time you take the medicine, the germs can "laugh at you" and pay no attention to the stuff.

You know, dealing with sin is exactly like treating a bacterial infection—if we don't continue to take the medicine, it becomes harder and harder to resist the disease that will eventually kill us. Do you know what the medicine for sin is?

THE 9.6 MYSTERY

While the earth remaineth, seedtime and harvest, and cold and heat, and summer and winter, and day and night shall not cease. Genesis 8:22.

In 1942 the U.S. Army Air Forces selected Ascension Island, off the west coast of Africa, as a strategic refueling station for the B-25 bombers flying World War II missions. It was known that the island was the nesting ground for tens of thousands of sooty terns, and flying birds represent a hazard to planes taking off and landing. But it was naturally assumed that the birds would be there only once a year—at breeding time. The danger seemed minimal.

So the first nesting season was noted, and the planes took care to avoid the birds at that time. When the terns left, the pilots thought that there would be a year of relief from the potential hazards of flying birds. But this was not the case. About three months before they were expected, the birds were back, and the Army was disturbed. Officials contacted an ornithologist with the American Museum in New York and learned, to their amazement, that the sooty terns, on Ascension at least, breed every 9.6 months rather than annually, as do most birds. When asked why sooty terns have a shorter breeding cycle there, the ornithologist indicated that no one knows, and we still don't know some forty years later.

Records going back to 1735 show that the Canadian lynx populations reach a peak every 9.6 years. Atlantic salmon fishermen have their best salmon catches every 9.6 years. Chinch bugs in Illinois show 9.6-year cycles, as does the amount of wheat harvested in the United States and the number of cases of heart disease in New England.

What is the secret of 9.6? We are constantly aware of seasonal cycles and daily cycles, but there are apparently other equally important cycles that the Creator has in His calendar of events. God used these cycles as a promise to Noah (and to you and me) that His words are sure.

357

LAZY ANTS

The sluggard will not plow by reason of the cold; therefore shall he beg in harvest, and have nothing. Proverbs 20:4.

It may be hard to believe, but there *are* some lazy ants in the world. The Bible uses the normal industry of ants to tell the sluggard how he should act when, in Proverbs 6:6, it says "Go to the ant, thou sluggard; consider her ways, and be wise." But there are other types of ants that are certainly not examples that we would want to copy.

Take the teleuto (pronounced tell-OO-toe) ants, for instance. This form of ant may be the most extreme example in the insect world of a social parasite. Teleuto ants live in the Swiss Alps, and they have degenerated to a point where they not only don't do any work but hardly even move. For some reason, the teleuto ants are cared for by a large host ant. In other ant settings the host ant might be called a slave, since it does all the work for the colony; but in this case it hardly seems right to call the helpless, delicate, and tiny little teleuto ant the master of slaves, although it may be. Teleuto ants are found only inside the nest of the host ants, and they spend much of their time riding around on the backs of their hosts. They have even developed concave (curved inward) undersides, which help them cling to their hosts!

When scientists first discovered these lazy ants, they theorized that originally the teleutos were slavers and were strong and healthy; however, over time, by being cared for constantly by their slaves, they lost their strength, their size, and eventually even their importance in the colony. So the scientists decided that this strange ant had come to the end of its development as a species and gave it the scientific name *Teleutomyrmex,* which means "final ant."

In the Bible we are clearly told, "Whatsoever thy hand findeth to do, do it with thy might." There is physical, spiritual, and emotional strength in that rule.

100 BILLION PEOPLE

After this I beheld, and, lo, a great multitude, which no man could number, of all nations, and kindreds, and people, and tongues, stood before the throne, and before the Lamb, clothed with white robes, and palms in their hands. Revelation 7:9.

How many people do you suppose will be in that number? Bible commentaries and theologians aren't sure what the text means when it says a "multitude, . . . which no man could number," but we can be sure there will be a lot of extremely happy people—all the people who have ever lived who fully accepted Jesus as their Saviour from sin.

Before long there will be 5 billion people in the world, and we are told that it won't be very many more years before that number will double, and then double again. If Jesus doesn't come soon, there could be untold billions of people here on earth. How many people do you suppose can live on this planet? No one knows for sure, but it has been estimated that there is enough air, water, and land for 100 billion people. You can be sure, however, that long before that number is reached, there will be many more wars, and crime will increase to a point that we can't imagine. Just the increase in population has brought about the increase in woes that Jesus described as signs of His coming.

But with every baby born in the world there is a new little soul that Jesus loves. When His Spirit is poured out without measure, as it will be very soon, who knows how many of those living in the world will give their hearts to Jesus and be ready to join Him in that multitude without number?

Can you imagine what it will be like to stand in that throng and feel the swell of emotion when the millions of people who have been saved express their joy and praise to Jesus, the Lamb of God and the King of kings? Even in our wildest imagination we cannot fathom what that experience will be like. This one thing I do know, however: It will be worth everything that we give up on this earth to be there.

"ALL FLESH IS GRASS"

The voice said, Cry. And he said, What shall I cry? All flesh is grass, and all the goodliness thereof is as the flower of the field: the grass withereth, the flower fadeth: because the spirit of the Lord bloweth upon it: surely the people is grass. Isaiah 40:6, 7.

In a very real sense, "all flesh *is* grass." That is, every living creature from the lowliest microbe to man has a basic ingredient that comes only from plants. That ingredient is carbon. Carbon is the basic ingredient of every living cell of every living thing on earth. And there is only one original source of carbon— plants. Every living animal on earth, even if the animal feeds only on the flesh of other animals, is dependent on the carbon from plants.

Only plants have the ability to take carbon and make it digestible by animals. And the plants perform this function through the process of photosynthesis, in which they take carbon dioxide from the air, water from the soil, and, with light from the sun, combine these two substances to form sugar, which is the basic fuel and building material of all living things. The fact that only plants can produce sugar means that every creature has to be able to trace its food back to plants. The lion eats the zebra, which eats grass. The hawk eats a snake, which eats a mouse, which eats grass. No matter what animal you pick, you can trace its source of energy back to plants. Plants are the basic food of all animals. It has been that way since the Creation.

The mystery, however, is how the plants can take carbon dioxide and water, two substances that have absolutely no food value whatsoever, and make sugar, the ultimate source of energy. The secret, of course, is in the green chlorophyll of the plant, which by some yet-to-be-discovered means captures energy from the sun and packages it in the form of sugar molecules. These sugar molecles, like timed-release capsules, are able to provide just the right amount of energy for your body and for mine.

360

ARmen

SCARED TO DEATH

Men's hearts failing them for fear, and for looking after those things which are coming on the earth: for the powers of heaven shall be shaken. Luke 21:26.

Have you ever been scared to death? Obviously not, or you wouldn't still be here, but you may have been scared to a point where you thought that you were going to die. A Christian need not ever feel such fear, because the Bible promises that you will have perfect peace if you trust in the Lord (Isa. 26:3).

It has been known for a long time that animals can die when put under severe stress. Fear is stress. Being scared to death would be to suffer such a great amount of stress from a frightening experience that your heart would be damaged. When you are under stress, your body begins to take precautions to handle the stress. There are some types of stress that are normal and healthy, as when you look up and see something falling toward you. In such a situation, your body goes into high gear and prepares you to move more quickly than you might otherwise be able to move. What is happening is that the knowledge of some immediate danger causes your brain to send a messenger to your adrenal glands, which in a split second release a powerful chemical called adrenalin. When the adrenalin hits your system, you actually have more strength than normal. You can move faster, your senses are sharpened, and you are better able to do what needs to be done to get out of danger in a hurry.

If for some reason you aren't able to do what you need to do to get out of danger, your adrenal glands just keep on producing adrenalin, which is so powerful that it destroys the heart muscle and causes death. Such deaths have been documented many times in people and animals.

At the end of time, when people see the world coming to an end and don't know what to do to save themselves, they will be literally scared to death. It is happening today, friends. We need to share with them the love of Jesus and let them know the peace that comes with Him.

THE FIFTH QUARK

When Jesus therefore perceived that they would come and take him by force, to make him a king, he departed again into a mountain himself alone. John 6:15.

There is great news in the world of physics. A new quark has been discovered. This atomic particle, which is the fifth type of quark known, has been called the upsilon particle. It is described as having a mass three times greater than any of the other quarks, which makes it huge by quark standards. Remember, however, that no one has ever seen a quark. They are too small to show up even under the most powerful electron microscope.

The problem in trying to study quarks is that they hang together pretty tightly. In fact, the force that holds the proton together in the nucleus of every atom is so great that man has not been able to find a force great enough to blast it apart to release the quarks so that they can be studied by themselves. It was when man split the atom that we began to understand the electrons, but that force is nothing compared to the force holding quarks together.

The theory is that there are mysterious forces holding the protons together. These forces have been called gluons. It is assumed that there is no stronger "glue" in the universe and that the particles that are thus held together represent the absolutely basic building blocks of matter. Well, this is what they thought about electrons in the atom, also—and now look where we are. The electrons, protons, and neutrons of the 1930s have expanded into the muons, neutrinos, pions, kaons, lambda particles, quarks, and so on.

For a Christian, I think all of this atomic talk is of great significance. The Creator of the force that man only dreams of understanding walked here among men, trying to help us understand the even greater forces of His character. Can you imagine what power Jesus had at His command? Yet He set all that aside to lead gently a stubborn people who believed that they could take *Him* by force.

THE JUNK-FOOD GRIZZLIES

Wherefore do ye spend money for that which is not bread? and your labour for that which satisfieth not? hearken diligently unto me, and eat ye that which is good, and let your soul delight itself in fatness. Isaiah 55:2.

What a wonderful text for healthful eating! Modern man is rapidly becoming an undernourished being in the presence of an abundance of good food. Why? Because we have become addicted to that which is not bread. Junk food does not satisfy, but it tastes good in the mouth, so we eat and eat and eat and wonder why we are still hungry or why we feel so terrible.

When the United States Government established the National Park System, beginning with Yellowstone National Park, the protected park bears became addicted to garbage. Since the bears in such parks as Yellowstone and Glacier National Parks found a ready supply of food so easily obtained at the dumps, they no longer had to get food the hard way. They became tramps, hanging around the piles of smelly garbage thrown out at the restaurants and campgrounds. The garbage dumps became a favorite gathering place for not only the bears but also for the people who came to see these wild creatures behaving in such a depraved manner. It is sad when such a magnificent creature as the grizzly bear is reduced to pawing through clanking cans and ripping open plastic wrappers in search of moldy and spoiled leftovers. The bears rarely wandered far from the garbage pit. They were considered big, lovable park bums. No one thought about the potential for danger until 1967, when a young lady, camping just a few hundred yards from a dump where the grizzlies fed, was dragged away in her sleeping bag and killed.

Many of the crazy actions of people in our world today have been linked to the crazy food that we consume by the ton—mostly sugar and chemicals, which are not part of the diet that God provided for us to keep us healthy.

EGGS BREATHE!

Let every thing that hath breath praise the Lord. Praise ye the Lord. Psalm 150:6.

This is the very last verse in the book of Psalms, and what a fitting way to end some of the most beautiful texts in the Bible. The psalmist, in summing it all up, feels that every living thing throughout all creation should praise the Lord. Whether you realize it or not, all creatures—great and microscopic—breathe. Breathing is essential to life.

Did you know that eggs breathe? A book in my library has a picture of the surface of an egg as viewed through an electron microscope, which magnifies the surface features by 3,800 times. There, on the surface of the egg, are pores—holes through the shell. They look like gaping caves when magnified 3,800 times, but they are actually so small that only air molecules can get through them. Oxygen is taken in by the egg, and carbon dioxide is expelled through these tiny pores. Eggs breathe! In every egg from the giant egg of the ostrich with a shell that is two millimeters thick down to the tiny hummingbird's egg, which has a shell that is only four one-hundredths of a millimeter thick, there are breathing pores that assure enough oxygen for the baby chick growing inside.

A baby bird takes its first breath before it hatches. You have probably noticed when you peel a hard-boiled egg that there is an air space inside the shell at the large end of the egg. As the egg breathes, this space is kept filled with pure, fresh air. When it is time for the chick to hatch, the baby bird first pecks through the soft membrane between it and the air space. When the chick pecks through that membrane, it is able to take its first breath, and soon it has the strength to peck its way out of the egg.

A baby bird's struggle to emerge is accompanied by small peeping notes, first inside the egg, and finally, as it emerges. I like to think that the chick in the egg is praising the Lord with its first breath.

jose

100,000 CROWS

Enter ye in at the strait gate: for wide is the gate, and broad is the way, that leadeth to destruction, and many there be which go in thereat. Matthew 7:13.

If you happened to be living in Holdrege, Nebraska, during the winter of 1981-1982, you know about the invasion of crows that took place there. There were seventeen times as many crows there that winter as there were people—and that is a lot of crows, when you consider that more than five thousand people live in Holdrege. Why were they there? No one knows. They just happened to select that town and decided it would be a great place to spend the winter. When asked why she thought they were there, one woman who lives in Holdrege said, "I suppose because it's such a nice town."

There were so many crows that when they went to roost at night in the large trees, their weight would break limbs two inches in diameter. During the day they would forage in the town and in the fields outside the town. At times so many of them would gather on one garbage can that they would tip it over with their weight.

The city authorities, in desperation, resorted to the drastic measure of shooting the crows. At night when the crows were settled, the city employees would arrive with guns, searchlights, and wooden clappers. The loud noise was to drive the crows away from the residential areas before shooting them. Thousands were killed. They collected the dead crows in pickup trucks every morning after the nightly killing. Do you think the crows went somewhere else? Absolutely not. They liked it there. It didn't matter that thousands of their friends were dying all around them. They were used to that place and didn't want to leave—so they stayed. No matter what the city tried to do to eliminate the birds; they would not leave.

You might say those crows were stupid to stay in a place where they were sure to be killed. But I wonder whether people aren't just as stupid when they persist in living the sinful lives that they know will end only in death.

365

MISTLETOE

Nevertheless they departed not from the sins of the house of Jeroboam . . . and there remained the grove also in Samaria. 2 Kings 13:6.

It was the custom of idol worshipers to set up their idols in a grove of trees and other plants, for it was believed that the trees had special spiritual powers. One of the special plants that some of the ancient pagans worshiped was mistletoe.

Mistletoe produces green leaves even in the middle of winter, when the tree on which it lives looks lifeless, so people believed that the mistletoe had magical powers. The Druids, who were pagan priests in France, Britain, and Ireland about two thousand years ago, believed even mistletoe to be some sort of spirit, since it appeared to live without roots. (Actually it does have roots, but they are so small that the ancient people apparently did not notice them.)

Then there were other people who thought that mistletoe had powers to heal the sick and dying. These people would pick branches of the plant and bring them into their houses to make sure that their homes were free from the evil influences of witchcraft.

The early Scandinavians would meet their enemies only under branches of mistletoe, and from that tradition comes the custom of kissing under the mistletoe at Christmas time.

Actually, mistletoe is a type of organism, called a parasite, that obtains all its substance from another organism. Sticky mistletoe seeds stick to a limb of a tree. Then hairlike roots enter the bark of the tree and begin to draw food from the juices that the tree brings up for itself. About the only value that the mistletoe has is that its white berries are food for the birds. But don't ever eat one—they are very poisonous to people.

Even though we don't believe in the idols of the groves, it is still possible for us to have sins in our lives, even when Jesus has promised to deliver us from evil and to cleanse us from all unrighteousness.

HELLION

And it shall be, that thou shalt drink from the brook; and I have commanded the ravens to feed thee there. . . . And the ravens brought him bread and flesh in the morning, and bread and flesh in the evening; and he drank from the brook. 1 Kings 17:4-6.

You've heard of seeing-eye dogs, and you may have even heard of dogs for the deaf. But have you ever heard of the helpmate monkeys? Well, meet Hellion.

Robert Foster had just graduated from high school. He was 18 years old, and he had just gotten a good job when he was involved in an auto accident that left him paralyzed from the shoulders down. He had been a very independent person before the accident, and he didn't want to be a helpless man.

One day he was watching a TV show featuring a scientist who was training monkeys to help handicapped people. He contacted Dr. Willard, of Tufts University, in Massachusetts. Robert learned that only capuchin monkeys (pronounced ka-POO-chin) were used because they are very intelligent, affectionate, and loyal. (These are the monkeys that organ grinders use.) They are only eighteen inches tall and weigh from five to eight pounds. Because they can live for thirty years, they are good prospects for helpers of the disabled.

This is where Hellion comes into the picture. Hellion is Robert's "helpmate." Hellion picks up things, brushes Robert's hair, turns the lights off and on, operates his stereo, and even dusts and vacuums! (She has her own special vacuum cleaner with a short handle). She gets Robert's food from the refrigerator, sets it before him, and feeds it to him with a spoon. With Hellion's help, Robert has become the independent person that he wants to be. And naturally Robert and Hellion have grown quite fond of each other. He says that she is like a pet, but so much more. She is indeed a helpmate.

Just as God used the ravens to feed Elijah, His creatures are being used today to bring help and comfort to those in need.

A WHITE-BREASTED NUTHATCH

I am come that they might have life, and that they might have it more abundantly. John 10:10.

One December afternoon a biology professor was watching a pair of white-breasted nuthatches at the bird feeder outside his large picture window in Michigan. As birds often do, one of the pair (the male) left the feeder and flew directly against the window. The bird struck the glass and dropped to the snow below. His mate immediately flew from the feeder to the spot where he had fallen.

The female gently prodded the stricken bird around the head and neck as if trying to revive him. She tried to push and then pull the fallen bird, but to no avail. At this point the female inserted her bill into the bill of the male, apparently trying to revive him with some form of bill-to-bill resuscitation. At least that is what it looked like to the professor watching, but no one knows for sure. Anyway, she seemed to be doing all in her power to get her mate back into action. Her ministrations continued for four or five minutes and might have gone longer had not a cat been attracted to the scene.

The professor had to intervene to keep the fallen bird from becoming the cat's dinner. It wasn't until he examined the bird, however, that he knew that the nuthatch was dead.

It is generally believed that animals and birds do not do things for their kind out of love as we know it, but no one knows that for sure, either. I just can't help believing that God made the birds and animals with a little bit of his love in their hearts, too. What do you think? The female nuthatch certainly put forth a lot of effort to do what she could to revive her mate.

Sometimes we are tempted to think that God has given up on us. Nothing could be further from the truth. The Jesus who made the nuthatches is not only even more persistent in His love and attention toward us, but is able to revive us when we fall. He can even keep us from falling in the first place if we will just accept His love in our hearts.

QUASARS

The heavens declare the glory of God; and the firament sheweth his handywork. Psalm 19:1.

In 1960 radio astronomers discovered much more than normal amounts of radio signals coming from what they thought were ordinary stars not far away. These signals aren't messages like those we get on the radio; they are electrical impulses like those normally emitted from radioactive materials. Our sun produces relatively small amounts of such radio signals, so the astronomers were quite surprised to find so much radioactivity coming from these small stars.

Attention was quickly focused on these stars, and a most remarkable discovery was made. The stars were not close at all. In fact, they proved to be the most distant heavenly bodies ever discovered. The first one, named 3C273, was judged to be 3 billion light-years away from us. In miles, that would be a 2 with twenty-two zeros after it! That's a long, long way, and some of these stars have since been found to be five times that far away.

These stars have been named quasars. Each one appears to be the center of a distant galaxy, and is so far away and so bright that we can't even see the galaxy surrounding it. No one knows why quasars emit such intense radiation. What is their purpose? How did they come to be? These are just two of the many unanswered questions about quasars.

Astronomers tell us that these quasars appear to be moving through space at a speed that is 90 percent of the speed of light. That is incredibly fast—more than 600 million miles per hour! Where are they going at such speeds? Could they be revolving around the center of the universe, just as our earth revolves around our sun?

And what is the meaning of the intense radiation? Is it possible that there is a fantastic network of intersteller communications created and used by the Creator to sustain the universe? We can only speculate in the absence of direct information, but won't it be wonderful when we can travel through the universe and be fully aware of the fantastic ways that God has of declaring His glory?

369

THE DODO
AND THE CALVARIA TREE

There is a way which seemeth right unto a man, but the end thereof are the ways of death. Proverbs 14:12.

Everyone has heard of the dodo—that bird that became extinct some three hundred years ago on the island of Mauritius in the Indian Ocean. This bird has been used as the symbol of stupidity ever since the last one died, because it was unable to sense danger or even try to survive. The dodo was large and clumsy, but until European settlers came to the island there was nothing for it to fear; the dodo had no reason to develop any sense of danger. Through the years the dodo became so tame that it was easy prey for the settlers. And before long there were none.

Recently, a new fact involving the dodo has come to light. On the island of Mauritius there is a tree known as the calvaria. There are only thirteen of them left, and they are all more than three hundred years old. They produce seeds, but since 1681 no one has been able to get one to sprout. A scientist wondered whether the dodo might have played a part in causing calvaria seeds to sprout, since the last tree sprouted about the time the dodo became extinct.

Dr. Stanley Temple had a theory. He knew that the calvaria seed has an extremely tough shell and that the dodo used to eat the seeds. He wondered whether perhaps the seed might have had to endure all the grinding of the dodo's gizzard, as well as the chemical action of the acids and other fluids in the bird's stomach, before it could sprout. To test his theory, Dr. Temple took ten calvaria seeds and force-fed them to turkeys, whose gizzards are thought to be much like those of the extinct dodo. Wonder of wonders! Three of the ten seeds sprouted. Now it is known that when the last dodo died, the calvaria was also doomed—but it took three hundred years to figure out the connection!

Those early settlers couldn't have imagined that their killing off the dodos would eventually eliminate the important calvaria tree. Our actions often have far-reaching effects, either for good or for ill.

370

jose

VULCANIZED CHRISTIANS

For unto us was the gospel preached, as well as unto them: but the word preached did not profit them, not being mixed with faith in them that heard it. Hebrews 4:2.

Rubber is useless unless it has been vulcanized. To begin with, rubber is much like modeling clay in consistency. You can mold it, stretch it, knead it, or roll it up in a ball with ease. But when you pull it, fresh rubber won't snap back like the rubber bands and other types of rubber that you use. You wouldn't want your car's tires to act like modeling clay, would you?

Rubber can be made either from the gummy sap of the rubber tree or synthetically from petrochemicals. To produce rubber initially, chemists have to have several different substances from a class of chemicals called monomers. Monomers are strange chemicals. They don't mix well with other monomers, but they do link up with them in a way that forms a tangle of strands. These combinations of monomers in strands are called polymers. That is where rubber begins—the mixing of monomers to make polymers. How about that? But we're still at the modeling-clay stage. What makes the rubber act like the substance that we know and depend on? The polymers have to be vulcanized.

Vulcanization is a process that involves several chemicals and heat. What happens is equivalent to tying all the polymer strands together with atomic knots, since it is accomplished by a process of rearranging the atoms and molecules to hold the polymers together. After the rubber has been vulcanized, it can be pulled and it will snap back into shape; it can also be bounced like a rubber ball.

God's church on earth is a lot like the production of rubber. A bunch of individuals, each with his or her own personality, get together as a church. But not until Jesus adds extra ingredients and heats up the program does the church begin to hold its own and bounce. Can you name some of the ingredients that must be added to make God's church?

A BEAST OF THE FOREST

For every beast of the forest is mine. Psalm 50:10.

It has a body like that of a pig, ears like those of a horse, feet like those of a rhinoceros, and a nose like that of an elephant. It swims like a fish, runs faster than a dog, trills like a bird, and weighs up to eight hundred pounds. What do you suppose it is?

This animal lives in South America and in Southeast Asia, but nowhere in between. The ancient natives of Thailand believed that after the Creator finished making all the other animals, He made this one and called it *psom-sett,* which means "the mixture is finished." This animal comes in more than 150 varieties ranging in weight from four hundred to eight hundred pounds when full grown. Have you figured out what it is?

Robert Wilson, a mammalogist who studies the animal described above, raised one of them on his back porch. One day he returned home to find that the animal had opened the back door by turning the knob with his nose, had gone into the kitchen, opened the refrigerator, taken out thirty pounds of bananas, and had neatly pealed and eaten the whole bunch. Then the animal went into the bathroom and dislodged the sink, which broke the water pipe and sent a jet of water over into the bathtub. The beast then jumped into the tub, pulled down all of the towels, and stopped the drain. Mr. Wilson found Mr. Animal lounging in the tub making contented grunting noises. Have you guessed what it is?

When they are full grown these animals are usually brown to black in color, sometimes with large patches of white. But from birth to about eight months of age the babies are said to look like banded watermelons with legs. In their range they live from sea-level tropical forests up to the rain forests, as high as fifteen-thousand feet in elevation, but nearly always in the densest, most impenetrable forests and underbrush. I'd better tell you that the animal is a tapir.

The tapir doesn't look very smart or talented, but it is. Our Creator, who made all the animals in the forest, gave each of them something special to make it interesting; and He made each of us special too.

CHARLES DARWIN AND THE EYE

He that formed the eye, shall he not see? He that chastiseth the heathen, shall not he correct? he that teacheth man knowledge, shall not he know? The Lord knoweth the thoughts of man, that they are vanity. Psalm 94:9-11.

There is probably nothing on earth that defies the evolutionist's logic as much as does the eye. Yes, the eye that you or someone else is using right now to read these words is one of the most effective sermons in favor of Creation by God as it is told in the book of Genesis.

Even Charles Darwin, the most famous pioneer of the theory of evolution, had a great deal of trouble trying to explain how the eye could have evolved. In a letter dated April 3, 1860, Darwin wrote, "To suppose the eye, with all its inimitable contrivances for adjusting the focus to different distances, for admitting different amounts of light, and for the correction of spherical and chromatic aberration, could have been formed by natural selection, seems, I freely confess, absurd in the highest degree."

One of the main problems that evolutionists have with the eye is that at all levels of development in what they call the evolutionary tree are creatures with eyes. There are no intermediate, partially developed eyes to explain how they were evolved. Eyes are there, on hundreds of thousands of different kinds of creatures. Some creatures, such as those living in the depths of the sea or in caves, appear to have lost the use of their eyes, but nowhere do we find creatures that have fully-developed eyes while others of their kind have no form of eyes at all.

In the human eye alone there are more than a million light-sensitive cells making up the retina, which is that portion of your eye that receives the light through your pupil and translates the light into nerve impulses, which the brain again translates into colorful, three-dimensional pictures, which can even be stored for remembering later.

KISKADEES AND CORAL SNAKES

And Jesus answered and said unto him, Get thee behind me, Satan: for it is written, thou shalt worship the Lord thy God, and him only shalt thou serve. Luke 4:8.

The coral snake is the deadliest snake in the United States. Would you recognize one if you saw it? There are other snakes about the same size that are colored in a very similar way and in an almost identical pattern. All of these look-alike snakes have three basic colors—black, yellow, and red—and all of them are ringed in these three colors from their heads to the tips of their tails. But only in the coral snake do the red rings touch the yellow rings. The other snakes have the red rings separated by black rings. We had a saying at camp that helped us remember which snake is which: "Red and yellow—kill a fellow; red and black—friend of Jack." This is a safe rule if you are talking about those found in the continental United States. It seems that at least one kind of bird also recognizes the poison colors.

The kiskadee is a bird about the size of a bluejay, but it belongs to the flycatcher family. Besides insects, it also feeds on small lizards and snakes. Some experiments were performed with hand-reared kiskadees to see whether they recognized coral snakes—because if they didn't, to catch one would be almost certain death.

The young kiskadees were quick to pounce on sticks painted like nonpoisonous snakes, but when sticks painted with the pattern of the coral snake were put into the cages, the birds would not touch them. In fact, when the kiskadees saw these sticks, they flew to the far end of the cage and uttered loud alarm calls. An additional test found that sticks painted with just red and yellow stripes brought the same results. Kiskadees are born with the instinct to avoid the poisonous snake. They apparently know that red and yellow will kill a fellow.

Remember the kiskadee the next time you are tempted. Jesus has promised that if you resist the devil he will flee from you (James 4:7), just as the coral snake slithers quickly away when his true colors are discovered and the alarm is sounded.

SCRIPTURE INDEX

GENESIS

1:2 296
1:2, 3 82
1:4, 5 256
1:21 350
1:24 229
1:25 209
1:26 185
1:30 143
2:7 94
3:1 164
3:3 81
3:4 123
3:14, 15 257
4:9 134
6:6, 7 223
6:17 263
7:22 260
8:22 357
9:13, 14 103
10:32 27
13:12 274
14:3, 12 149
19:14, 15 44
37:3 160

EXODUS

2:3 212
8:1, 2 108
8:1, 2 353
9:9 268
20:13 317
34:7 50

LEVITICUS

4:33 37
11:9 311
11:22 352

NUMBERS

17:8 333
32:23 39

DEUTERONOMY

22:6, 7 200
32:11, 12 181
33:13, 14 184

1 SAMUEL

17:45 11

2 SAMUEL

22:31 234

1 KINGS

17:4, 6 367

2 KINGS

6:17 100
13:6 366

1 CHRONICLES

16:32 84

JOB

8:14 309
9:7 129
11:7 325
12:7 308
14:7 255
22:13, 14 63
22:15, 16 337
34:15 247
38:1 190
38:4, 7 292
38:16 225
38:22 19
41:1, 2 51
41:31 80

PSALMS

3:1, 3, 8 258
8:3, 4 30
17:8, 9 218
18:6 208
19:1 369
19:7 55
23:4 20
23:5 182
24:1 326
27:5 321
29:2 107
34:7 332
36:5 227
36:7 253
40:5 140
40:11 43
45:7, 8 305
50:10 372
51:2 161
51:7 304
59:1 272
63:1 166
72:6 204
73:20 83
75:10 315
76:14 69
78:1 224
84:11 151
89:37 169
90:2 53
91:2 331
91:10 241
91:11 210
94:9-11 373
95:4, 5 271
96:1 79
100:2 120
100:3 250
103:5 186
104:14 286
104:16, 17 92
104:24 351
107:35, 36 139
113:5 13
118:12 336
119:1 207
119:11 243
119:18 242
119:27 61
119:30 114
119:31, 33 58
119: 90, 91 179
119:99 34
119:165 330
121:5, 6 220
124:4-6 295
139:14 318
143:9 335
146:8 45
147:8 206
147:9 35
147:13, 14 322
148:3-5 89
150:6 364

PROVERBS

6:6 264
12:18 261
14:12 370
14:23 91
15:22 126
16:20 339
16:25 251
16:28 173
17:22 279
20:4 358
20:11 18
22:6 170
30:5 306
30:27 68
31:28 142

ECCLESIASTES

3:17 175
8:5 211
9:5 313
11:7 180
12:3 290
12:14 291

ISAIAH

11:6 64
11:9 213
14:12 165
22:23 137
25:9 145
28:15 176
31:5 214
40:6, 7 360
40:8 54
40:22 340
40:26 60
40:28 168
41:6 93
41:6 141
41:10 266
42:10 307
43:2 245
53:5 277
55:2 363
55:9 198

57:20 96
58:8 246
60:4 301
61:3 46
63:2 22
65:21, 22 244

JEREMIAH

5:22 131
10:10 346
13:15 162
13:23 156
17:8 148
29:12, 13 16
31:35 230
33:3 294

EZEKIEL

36:27 65
44:18 314

DANIEL

6:27 177
9:23 153
12:4 112

HOSEA

8:7 187
10:12 354

AMOS

3:3 163
9:3 146

JONAH

2:7 85

MICAH

7:4 75
7:19 289

ZEPHANIAH

1:8 217

HAGGAI

1:6 33

ZECHARIAH

4:6 41

MALACHI

3:11 327
4:2 355

MATTHEW

4:19 98
5:9 228
5:16 21
5:48 87
6:5 144
6:13 133
6:19, 20 115
6:28, 29 125

6:33 338
6:34 113
7:13 365
7:15 130
10:28, 29 29
10:30 32
12:30 252
12:45 356
13:30 132
13:43 9
13:44 48
14:14 78
14:28 216
16:23 254
23:37 24
24:4 195
24:7 345
24:13 105
24:24 135
24:27 328
24:30 155
24:35 189
24:44 147
25:6 12
25:21 312
28:19 236

MARK

1:35 219
6:31 231
8:17, 18 104
10:7 118
11:17 47
13:6 226

LUKE

4:8 374
4:18 15
5:5 285
9:58 171
10:19 300
10:24 25
11:1 203
12:6, 7 302
13:8, 9 174
13:25 197
13:34 159
13:35 347
15:7 262
15:20 233
15:24 265
19:10 90
19:37 86
21:4 70
21:11 49
21:11 71
21:26 361
22:19 26

JOHN

1:1-3 36
1:4 323
1:12 194
3:17 117

3:19 320
4:14 235
4:35, 36 138
6:9 59
6:15 362
6:44 278
8:23 72
10:10 368
11:35 191
12:20, 21 172
12:32 221
14:2, 3 303
14:9 56
14:18 17
14:26 270
15:5 237
16:33 281
19:34 192

ACTS

1:8 67
1:11 259
7:36 239
17:27 10
20:28 127

ROMANS

1:16 128
1:19, 20 324
1:23 122
5:3 40
5:8 167
8:28 202
10:11, 12 344
11:33 267
12:2 341
12:4 183
14:13 316

1 CORINTHIANS

1:27 74
10:11 282
10:12 14
10:13 287
13:11 201
13:12 248
14:40 215
15:55 348
15:57 178

2 CORINTHIANS

4:8 298
4:11 38
5:17 196
10:4 276
11:13-15 249

GALATIANS

1:4, 5 222
4:4 319
5:14, 15 297
5:15 293

EPHESIANS

3:20 273
4:19 199
6:13 310

PHILIPPIANS

2:3 152
2:5 73
2:15 288
3:21 102

1 THESSALONIANS

4:16 150
4:17 299
5:5 124
5:17 280

2 THESSALONIANS

2:11 329

1 TIMOTHY

5:18 158

2 TIMOTHY

3:15 28
4:4 106

TITUS

3:9 154

HEBREWS

4:2 371
6:7 109
8:10 269
11:6 342
12:1 57
13:5 99

JAMES

1:2-4 66
1:17 23
1:19 110
3:8 238
4:7 284
5:5 240

1 PETER

1:15 95
5:8 42
5:8 275

2 PETER

2:9 121
2:20 88

3:6 52
3:8 157
3:10 343

1 JOHN

1:7 62
1:8 76
2:11 334

3 JOHN

8 111

REVELATION

1:8 97
3:11 119
3:18 232
3:20 31
4:3 101
4:8 349
7:9 359
14:3 283
14:6, 7 116
14:10 77
18:4 193
20:12 205
21:5 188
22:17 136